THE IMAGE OF AMERICA
IN CARICATURE & CARTOON

Join, or Die. Benjamin Franklin. 1754. Courtesy Collections of the Library Company of Philadelphia.

THE IMAGE OF AMERICA
IN CARICATURE & CARTOON

Accompanying Exhibition Presented at:
Amon Carter Museum, Fort Worth
Fort Wayne Public Library, Fort Wayne
National Museum of Man, Ottawa
Museum of Art, Rhode Island School of Design, Providence

AMON CARTER MUSEUM OF WESTERN ART, *Fort Worth*,
In cooperation with the Swann Collection of Caricature and Cartoon, *New York City*,
and the Lincoln National Corporation, *Fort Wayne*

AMON CARTER MUSEUM
OF WESTERN ART
BOARD OF TRUSTEES

Mrs. J. Lee Johnson III, Chairman
Mrs. Adelyn D. Breeskin
Mrs. Amon G. Carter, Jr.
Amon G. Carter, Jr.
Mrs. Katrine Deakins
Richard M. Drew
John D. Entenza
Eldridge C. Hanes
Bartlett H. Hayes, Jr.
Sherman E. Lee
C. R. Smith
Mrs. Charles D. Tandy

Mitchell A. Wilder, Director

THE AMON CARTER MUSEUM was established in 1961 under the will of the late Amon G. Carter for the study and documentation of westering North America. The program of the Museum, expressed in publications, exhibitions, and permanent collections, reflects many aspects of American culture, both historic and contemporary.

The Museum has been assisted by the National Endowment for the Arts, a federal agency, and the Lincoln National Corporation in publication of this catalogue and the accompanying exhibition.

©1976. Amon Carter Museum of Western Art. 2nd edition, revised and enlarged.
All rights reserved in all countries. No part of this book may be reproduced or translated in any form, including microfilming, without written permission from the publisher.
International Standard Book Number 0-88360-050-1
Library of Congress Card Catalog Number 76-11930
Lithographed in U.S.A.

Type set by G & S Typesetters, Austin
Printed by Brodnax Printing Company, Dallas
Bound by Universal Bookbindery, San Antonio
Design by William D. Wittliff, Austin

TO ERWIN SWANN

Whose enthusiasm and encouragement kept the idea alive; whose generosity and cooperation made it possible; whose friendship and counsel are now sadly missing as this project, near and dear to his heart, is completed.

It is our hope that *The Image of America* helps fulfill the purpose of the Swann Collection in its sponsorship of scholarly exhibitions and catalogues.

INTRODUCTION

THIS EXHIBITION is eloquent testimony to the continuing vigor of American popular government. The energy, ingenuity, wit, and perceptiveness with which these artists observed the American scene are proof of the traditionally high level of interest Americans take in their political life. The long survival of the art of political cartooning speaks well, too, for the good sense, skeptical outlook, and jovial attitude of the artists' audience. America is a country which has not feared self-criticism. This is a healthy trait that merits celebration and one that should not be overlooked as we reflect on what has made our two centuries of history so successful.

Art critics who study high culture sometimes call a bad painting a "mere cartoon"; they have largely ignored American political cartoons. Historians think of cartoons only when book publishers demand illustrations to enliven their text. The art critic is puzzled by political history, and the historian deals with words and statistics rather than pictures.

Nevertheless, political cartoons remain an extremely popular art form, and to view American history through this medium is to see the American experience as the people saw it—in popular images, widely distributed and within the reach of most pocketbooks. This is an art exhibit appropriate for a democracy.

To view American history through political cartoons is also to see the controversy, criticism, and downright acrimony which at times marked that history. The Lincoln National Corporation is named for the President who steered this country through its greatest period of controversy by far. The Lincoln supports this exhibit because we are confident that America, like Abraham Lincoln's durable reputation, has the strength to benefit from criticism and the vitality to survive controversy.

THOMAS A. WATSON, President
Lincoln National Corporation
Fort Wayne, Indiana

ACKNOWLEDGMENTS

BY REASON of the ephemeral nature of cartoons and because the vast holdings of many institutions have defied cataloguing, the presentation of this exhibition required more than three years of research and organization. The Museum began by mailing a detailed questionnaire to more than 2,000 institutions and individuals throughout the country, then followed as many as possible with correspondence and personal visits. Such a graphic distillation of the more than 200 years of American history would not have been possible without the determined work of many people. Mildred Constantine of New York City worked closely with the Museum throughout the project, advising on picture selection and assisting in research. Amon Carter Museum Trustee John Entenza and former Trustee William H. Goetzmann offered invaluable criticism along the route.

The exhibition has been assembled from the seventy-seven participating institutions with the indispensable aid of curators and librarians across the nation. Notable among them are Wendy Shadwell of The New-York Historical Society, Dr. Alan Fern of the Library of Congress, Alison Dodd of the Swann Collection (which will soon be housed at the Library of Congress), Mrs. Paul Rhymer, former print curator, and Julia Westerberg, curator, of The Chicago Historical Society, Stefanie Munsing of the Library Company of Philadelphia, Dr. William Cagle of The Lilly Library, Indiana University, Kathleen Gee of The Iconography Collection, Humanities Research Center, University of Texas at Austin, and Dr. James Whitehead of the Franklin D. Roosevelt Presidential Library.

Working cartoonists have been most generous in their support. Draper Hill of *The Commercial Appeal* loaned from his personal collection as well as his personal drawings. Bill Mauldin of the Chicago *Sun-Times*, Pat Oliphant of the Washington *Star*, and Brad Holland, Richard Hess, John Cayea, Ralph Steadman, André François, and William Gropper, whose works have appeared in numerous magazines and newspapers, including the New York *Times*, have also loaned their personal drawings.

Dr. Frank T. Reuter of Texas Christian University and Dr. Mark Neely, Jr., of the Lincoln National Life Foundation read the manuscript. Jozanne Rabyor, Kay Krochman, and Karen Dewees of the Museum staff aided in the research and caption writing. Many others aided with the preparation of the exhibition and catalog. Their individual institutions are noted in the credit lines accompanying the illustrations.

A few explanations will aid in interpretation of the catalogued material. If the title of the picture is unknown, we have supplied a title in brackets. If we are uncertain as to artist or title, a question mark appears in parenthesis after the entry. If we do not know the artist, the picture is listed as anonymous. In measuring, height precedes width.

RON TYLER

THE IMAGE OF AMERICA
IN CARICATURE & CARTOON

THE IMAGE OF AMERICA

CARICATURE AND CARTOON were long-practiced and sophisticated methods of expression by the time the Americans rebelled in 1776. Caricature had originated during the Renaissance as the individual gradually gained stature and respect. A distortion of personal features, type, or action, it was a reaction to the orderliness and decorum of the early sixteenth century that derived its name from the Italian verb *caricare* (to change, burden, or overload) and is similar to the word *caraterre* (character). Cartoons, originally defined only as full-size patterns for a painting, tapestry, or mosaic and related to the Italian *cartone* (pasteboard), gradually acquired a new meaning as caricatures were combined to create a new style. Directing his barbs toward groups and types rather than individuals, William Hogarth employed cartoons in what became the classic style in his series entitled "Marriage à la Mode." This is not to say that comic and grotesque drawings of the human figure did not appear until the Renaissance, for such visual exaggeration is probably as old as drawing. Ancient Egyptians and Greeks created mythical figures by combining certain aspects of humans and animals, by distortion, by humorous and allegorical creations. Albrecht Dürer and Leonardo da Vinci exaggerated and experimented with facial characteristics; other artists followed, infusing humor and satire to develop cartoons in the modern sense by the mid-seventeenth century.

Few Americans had produced cartoons by 1776. Some pictures like Benjamin Franklin's *Join or Die* (fig. 1) had appeared in colonial newspapers, badly reproduced because of the inferior nature of printing equipment shipped to America only after British printers had discarded it. (One of the more peculiar circumstances about American printing is that it began so late—Mexican printers had been at work more than a century when the first wood engraving appeared in what became the United States in 1670.) Undoubtedly there were qualified engravers in America, because when the first intaglio-engraved paper money published in the colonies appeared in 1690, it was quickly counterfeited by unknown craftsmen possessing abilities to rival those of the official engravers.

The earliest American cartoons appeared as illustrations in the colonial newspapers—*Join or Die* (fig. 1), *The Federal Edifice* (fig. 15). Only later were prints issued in the British tradition and sold separately in bookstores, or printed at the order of and distributed by political parties. Most of the early American cartoons were copied after British models, such as *The Deplorable State of America, or Sc---h Government* (fig. 2), which was copied by John Singleton Copley and Wilkinson of Philadelphia. The best known engraver of early America, Paul Revere, also copied British prints. His *Cabinet Junto* (fig. 7) was most likely inspired by the London cartoon of a similar title and composition, showing the same figures grouped around a table discussing the end of American liberties. Revere also copied *The Able Doctor, or America Swallowing the Bitter Draught* from *London Magazine* of April, 1774 (fig. 5).

Almost simultaneously with the cartoons certain constant American themes developed. To organize an exhibition of cartoons around American history and culture is almost to presuppose a conflict theme, for cartoons most eloquently portray conflict and confrontation. The colonists objected to English domination—to the Stamp Act, the Intolerable Acts, the economic dependence. American political parties continued the strife almost immediately. Today conflict has permeated the whole of society, as diverse citizens define their relationship to each other and to the government. It is also true that during periods of less conflict and strife, there are fewer and less powerful cartoons, such as during the Era of Good Feelings and during World War II, when the nation was virtually unanimous in support of the war.

Americans have historically feared power, whether from within or without, providing another theme for cartoonists. The basic reason for a weak national government (the Articles of Confederation) with no executive was fear of a powerful centralized government or a dictatorship, and any strong president or nominee risked being portrayed as a dictator: Andrew Jackson as Richard III (fig. 31), Martin Van Buren as his heir (fig. 37), Grant in Andrew Johnson's shadow (fig. 72), and Senator Huey P. Long of Louisiana, who might have been a presidential contender had he not been assassinated, in company with Hitler, Stalin, and Mussolini (fig. 159). Because they feared power from the outside, the founding fathers encouraged no "entangling alliances" with foreign countries, and the Federalists lived in dread of the French threat throughout Jefferson's administration (fig. 21). Later politicians tucked the cloak of isolationism around the United States to ward off the foreign threat. The Monroe Doctrine is the most important isolationist statement (fig. 106), but the isolationist leanings of the 1930s were actually drafted into law in the form of neutrality acts, and Congress almost passed a bill requiring that there be a national referendum before Congress could declare war.

Significant visual themes, soon to become recognized American icons, also emerged in the cartoons. The United States initially was portrayed by European artists as an innocent Indian or as virginal Columbia. It was also shown as an eagle, the official bird, and later, as Uncle Sam, a character probably first used in the early 1830s by H. R. Robinson, the prolific Whig lithographer, in a print showing an almost unrecognizable Uncle Sam. But he quickly developed into the character that we know today (fig. 74 might be a step in the development; fig. 87 is the fully developed character). The eagle recurs to show the state of the nation in the Civil War (fig. 55) and the Vietnam War (fig. 263). Presidential aspirant Martin Van Buren appeared in a cartoon for the 1848 contest on a bison (fig. 39), one of the best-known animals found in America. After the Statue of Liberty was placed in New York harbor it became a well-known symbol. Most frequently this emblem of American welcome to the world has been used to point out shortcomings in American society: Thomas Worth's racial image (fig. 79), Leslie Illingworth's reference to McCarthyism (fig. 192), Mark Podwall's and R. O. Blechman's comments on visual and urban pollution (figs. 261, 262).

Literary and historical figures are often adapted by cartoonists to make a contemporary point. Adalbert Volck employed the Don Quixote and Sancho Panza image to point out the relationship between Lincoln and Butler (fig. 58), Saul Steinberg used it to comment on Uncle Sam's reputation as the world's Santa Claus (fig. 205). Gregory Duncan compared Roosevelt's New Deal policy toward business to the Dutchess of *Alice in Wonderland* trying to cure the baby of the illness that the cook had brought on (fig. 161). Successfully recalling the image of Louis XIV to comment on the royal trappings of the Nixon administration, Edward Sorel published *Milhous I* on the cover of *The Rolling Stone* (fig. 244).

Through caricature and cartoon this exhibition covers more than 200 years of American history, beginning in 1754 with Benjamin Franklin's *Join or Die* and concluding in 1974 with John Cayea's *American Eagle*. These pictures illustrate or interpret literally hundreds of opinions, facts, and events of our history, and are the actual images that persons contemporary with each event or personality might have seen. Because of the nature of cartoon and caricature, they tend toward the critical, but this does not lessen the truth or history they contain. This exhibition is a contemporary record of our society through more than two centuries.

I

1754–1787

A DECEPTIVE CERTAINTY permeates the history of the United States: although the original thirteen colonies made up of "different schemes, notions, customs, and manners" overcame their differences to win independence from the greatest imperial power of the day, seldom is the frailty of the Congress, the Army, and the nation itself recognized today, 200 years after the fact.[1] Founded in the immutable truths of the Enlightenment and led by luminaries like Washington, Jefferson, and Adams, the nation seemed destined for immediate success. Nor is this a phantom of hindsight, for the founders themselves expressed irrepressible confidence in the soundness of their venture. "The foundation of our empire was not laid in the gloomy age of ignorance and superstition," wrote George Washington, "but at an *epocha* when the rights of mankind were better understood and more clearly defined, than at any former period, the researches of the human mind after social happiness have been carried to a greater extent, the treasures of knowledge ... are laid open for our use, and their collected wisdom may be happily applied in the establishment of our forms of government."[2] "The ... accomplishment ... was perhaps a singular example in the history of mankind," concluded John Adams. "Thirteen clocks were made to strike together—a perfection of mechanism which no artist had ever before effected."[3]

Such statements completely obscure the experimental nature of America. Created during an era in which both kings and philosophers wanted a better society but were incapable of bringing it to a Europe weighed down by tradition, fastened in rigid class, and divided by war, America was an experiment in at least two senses. First, it was the pragmatic attempt of thirteen self-contained colonies to create a workable government and "the world does not afford a precedent to go by," commented Elbridge Gerry.[4] Second, it was an experiment implemented according to the principles of the enlightened philosophers of Europe by their American disciples. The ruling monarchs of Europe could not condone such an experiment themselves, for the very nature of the divine right rule prevented kings from resigning their thrones for so little a matter as the happiness of the individual. America was their test case, where reason, nature, order, and humanitarianism would be enthroned and maintained by the popular will. "This country opens to the philosophic view an extensive, rich and unexplored field," Charles Thomson, the Secretary of Congress, wrote Jefferson in 1782.[5]

One could not have predicted the American Revolution without a careful knowledge of these philosophical concepts and of the Americans themselves. To Andrew Burnaby, an Englishman who visited the colonies in 1760, "fire and water are not more heterogeneous than the different colonies in North America. Nothing can exceed the jealousy and emulation, which they possess in regard to each other." But Benjamin Franklin, speaking from his unparalleled knowledge of the colonies, disagreed: "tyranny and oppression," specific violations of the enlightened concepts the colonists held dear, could alter the situation.[6]

As the Revolutionary conflict developed, the usually business-minded Americans carefully prepared their philosophical justification. The hated Stamp Act was termed "taxation without representation," despite the Parliament's contention that it represented all the empire. At Patrick Henry's urging the Virginia Assembly passed a resolution claiming that all laws applying to Englishmen in America had to be "derived from their own consent." Massachusetts was more violent. The proposed distributor of stamps was hanged in effigy from the "Liberty tree," his house ransacked, and he was forced to resign his office. English cartoonists depicted Liberty lamenting, "Tis all over with me" as Britain forced the Stamp Act on her (fig. 2). When the Stamp Act was finally repealed the new Rockingham ministry ordered printed a cartoon entitled *The Repeal*, depicting former Prime Minister Grenville taking his dead brainchild to the "Family Vault," which proved to be one of the most popular cartoons of the Revolutionary period and sold more than 16,000 copies (fig. 3). Both *The Deplorable State of America, or Sc---h Government* and *The Repeal* were copied by American engravers in a slightly altered form.

The traditional ties between mother country and colonies that Benjamin Franklin pointed out in testifying against the Stamp Act before Parliament did not prevent the ultimate breach. Colonists declared the March, 1770, incident in Boston a "massacre." The Tea Act of 1773 led to the famous "Boston Tea Party" in December, again inspiring the cartoonists to comment on the royal treatment of the colonies. In *The Able Doctor* America is restrained by rather lewd characters while Lord North pours "the Bitter Draught" down her throat (fig. 5). Colonists also claimed the Coercive Acts of 1774 which the Boston Port Bill represents were beyond the power of Parliament. This popular cartoon, originally published in London, was copied in both Ireland and America (by Revere). When Commissioner of Customs John Malcomb tried to enforce the new laws, Bostonians tarred and feathered him, an incident that led publisher Carington Bowles to issue his print (fig. 6) of *A New Method of Macarony Making* (Macarony referring to a dandy or fop).

Thomas Paine, a new arrival to the colonies, added enlightened logic and rhetoric to the Revolutionary cause after the British had let American blood at Lexington, Concord, and Bunker Hill. Is it logical for an island to rule a continent? he asked in his none-too-subtly-titled pamphlet *Common Sense*. King George III was a tyrant who did not deserve his position, and the only alternative remaining for Americans with "common sense" was independence. Even George Washington concluded after reading Paine's pamphlet that America was the victim of King George and that "we are determined to shake off all connections with a state so unjust and unnatural."[7]

Parliament helped the nation-makers overcome their hesitation in February, 1775, by declaring them in open rebellion. Delegates to the Second Continental Congress meeting in Philadelphia, now facing execution as rebels, agreed to "mutually pledge to each other our lives, our fortunes and our sacred honor" and began the grand experiment while General George Washington and his tiny Continental Army held 35,000 Redcoats in New York at bay. Although Thomas Paine characterized the following days as "the times that try men's souls," others saw them as the dawn of a new era. The American Revolution was "the beginning of a new social order for the entire world," exulted the Marquis de Lafayette. A change had occurred "in the minds and hearts of the people," John Adams later wrote, "a change in religious sentiments of their duties and obligation," a "radical change in the principles, opinions, sentiments, and affections of the people. . . ."[8]

The Revolution itself was a rather languid affair that began with Lexington and Concord in April, 1775, proceeded through Washington's Valley Forge winter, General Horatio Gates' surprising victory over the Redcoats at Saratoga, and Washington's brilliant capture of Lord Cornwallis at Yorktown (fig. 10). Meanwhile, Gates' victory had encouraged the French to enter the fray in support of the Americans, and John Paul Jones led the rebel privateering effort at sea (fig. 9). Aboard the *Ranger*, he slipped through the British blockade in November, 1777, and captured two prizes in April, 1778.

He then landed at Whitehaven, England, spiked the cannons of the fort, and set fire to another ship. The American sailors were particularly vexing to British trade, and were rendered even more troublesome when Holland permitted them to refit in Dutch harbors.

The British probably could have quelled the resistance but for the lackadaisical attitude and bungling conduct of their commanders in America. Feeling that they could defeat the Americans by holding the provincial cities of New York, Philadelphia, and Boston, the British generals did not pursue Washington's army at times when they could have routed him. The vulnerability of America is seen in the cartoons that picture the colonies as the weak and feminine Columbia or a naïve Indian. The British colossus is seen as a feeble old man (fig. 8) or a huge dog held at bay by the European allies while America escapes (fig. 9). The image of America suddenly changed with the surprising victory at Yorktown. Then the huge American rattlesnake was shown engulfing the small British armies (fig. 11). "The Serpent in the Congress reigns, as well as in the French," commented the cartoonist.

Although the Americans were creating a new government, "as in the beginning of the world," said Paine, they "had no occasion to roam for information into the obscure fields of antiquity, nor hazard ourselves upon conjecture." Insight from Jefferson, Franklin, and other Congressional thinkers allowed them to see "government begin, as if we had lived in the beginning of time." Jefferson took the concept of a *tabula rasa* (blank tablet), property rights, the right to happiness, and personal freedom from the English philosopher John Locke. He wrote in the Declaration of Independence that "all men are created equal," meaning that everyone (specifically Englishmen and Americans) stands equal before the law and that "talent and virtue" should be the criteria of superiority rather than class and wealth. Thus natural order would prevail. It was a radical philosophical change, but, as Jefferson pointed out, "the creation of a proper political system was the whole object of the revolution, for should a bad government be instituted for us in the future, it would have been as well to have accepted at first the bad one offered to us from beyond the water."[9]

America was indeed a *tabula rasa* for immigrants who fled the rigid social structure, the overcrowding, and the disease of Europe to begin life over as a member of a classless frontier society where there was more land than could be occupied. "A European, when he first arrives, seems limited in his intentions, as well as in his views," wrote Hector St. John de Crèvecoeur in his *Letters From an American Farmer*, "but he very suddenly alters his scale. . . . He no sooner breathes our air than he forms new schemes, and embarks in designs he never would have thought of in his own country. . . . He begins to feel the effects of a sort of resurrection; hitherto he had not lived, but simply vegetated; he now feels himself a man, because he is treated as such. . . . The American is a new man, who acts upon new principles; he must therefore entertain new ideas, and form new opinions."[10] The Revolution itself helped the new man along in his development, because Americans then abolished primogeniture and entail, separated church and state, and expanded educational opportunities. Many loyalists returned to England, thereby removing a conservative and wealthy element and modifying the social structure even more.

European philosophers had anticipated this "new man" just as they had earlier looked for the noble savage, but they were hesitant to accept him as proof of the successful American experiment until time had proven his durability. There were drawbacks, as contemporaries claimed. America was said to be full of swamps and impenetrable forests, "with humid and noxious vapors" in the atmosphere that were "unable to purify themselves or to profit by the influence of the sun, which darts in vain his most enlivening rays upon this frigid mass." Such an environment would naturally affect even the healthiest man, boasted De Paw: "the least vigorous European is more than a match for the strongest American." Nor had the political system helped: "You have kept all the bad English laws, and all of England's bad customs," Du Pont de Nemours wrote Jefferson. "One of the worst is the establishment of popular elections."[11] Others felt that America possessed more land than could be controlled. How could a decentralized government administer such a vast territory? How would it defend the frontier? What about communication? Transportation? No less a figure than Samuel Johnson predicted that "a nation scattered in the boundless regions of America resembles rays diverging from a focus. All the rays remain but the heat is gone."[12]

Americans readily admitted that the vastness would have to be overcome. As early as 1754 Benjamin Franklin had called the colonies together at Albany and warned that they would have to unify for the common defense or be gradually beaten by the French and the Indians. Nathaniel Hawthorne wrote despairingly to his friend Longfellow years later that "we have so much country that we really have no country at all." Even Patrick Henry feared that governing the whole continent was "a work too great for human wisdom."[13] In unity, however, they saw the solution. Franklin's *Join or Die* snake cartoon (fig. 1) remains one of the lasting images in American history. Christopher Gadsden agreed with Franklin's urging the Stamp Act Congress toward unity in 1765, saying that "there ought to be no New England man, no New Yorker, known on the Continent; but all Americans."[14]

In reality the large land mass worked to America's advantage, so much so that President Jefferson felt compelled to add to it at the first opportunity over his own and other doubts about his constitutional authority to do so. Distant boundaries kept possible enemies farther away. Unoccupied lands meant space for what would become the greatest movement of peoples in the history of the world. Immigrants carved out ethnic communities in the cities; they built utopian villages like Bishop Hill and New Harmony in the wilderness. They helped carry the American flag from the Appalachian Mountains to the Pacific Coast in less than fifty years, and they helped the United States become the leading industrial power in the world by 1885 and the greatest power in the world by 1946.

Jefferson defended the new United States against the charge of Abbé Raynal, who wondered why America had not produced a "single good poet, or able mathematician, or a man of genius in any one of the arts or the sciences." Washington and Franklin should be geniuses enough to satisfy the Abbé, Jefferson argued, but America's real contribution was on a higher level: America had "given hopeful proofs of genius of the nobler kinds, which arouse the best feelings of man, which call him to action, which substantiate his freedom, and conduct him to happiness."[15] John Adams in noting the youth of the country answered the question more directly: "I must study politics and war that my sons may have liberty to study mathematics . . . philosophy . . . and agriculture . . . in order to give their children . . . painting, poetry, music."[16]

In asking such a question Raynal ignored the great, democratic contribution America had made to learning. American literature, unlike European writings, was not produced for the intelligentsia. It was directed, instead, toward the common man, the new man, who could read because of the American belief in mass education. Europeans disregarded this literature—*Poor Richard's Almanac*, Parson Weems' fable—as unworthy of consideration, but it revealed the mind of the American. Much of American society was classed with this "subliterature" and ignored by European visitors and haughty native writers. This new man unfolded his secrets not in the halls of learning or the salons, but in rude, embarrassing, sometimes crudely done, vulgar expressions accurately representing his part of American society and culture. Even when the cartoons in this exhibition are considered, they are not often seen as serious attempts at art, but rather as political and social satire. This is hardly unusual, considering that caricatures were originally a "counter-art" intended to be outside the normal modes of aesthetic expression, but with the same qualities that characterized the new man—extroversion, utopianism, naïveté. It was virtually impossible for this art to be sophisticated. In this the Americans were again only copying the English tastes, for they were forthright in their expressions as well. *The General P--s, or Peace* (fig. 14) is an excellent example of the vulgar expressions of the day, while *The Federal Edifice* (fig. 15) conveys the message intended, but is not as well drawn as the British cartooning of the day.

Even after the Articles of Confederation had been proved unsound and replaced by the Constitution, after the United States had solved its colonial problem by the unique method of taking new territory into the nation as states, and after the solution of the undeclared naval war with France, skeptical Europeans were not ready to admit the twenty-five year old experiment a success. Americans were less hesitant. Full of confidence generated in the conquest of the noblest of all enemies, nature, they reflected upon their past. "Never did a government commence under auspices so favorable, not ever was success so complete," wrote James Monroe in his first inaugural address. "They *realized* the theories of the wisest writers," said John Adams.[17]

"A thousand years hence, perhaps in less, America may be what Europe is now," predicted Thomas Paine. "The innocence of her character . . . may sound like a romance, and her inimitable virtue as if it had never been. . . . The ruin of that liberty which thousands bled for or struggled to obtain may just furnish materials for a village tale. . . . When the empire of America shall fall, the subject for contemplative sorrow will be infinitely greater than crumbling brass and marble can inspire. It will not then be said, here stood a temple of vast antiquity, here rose a Babel of invisible height, or there a palace of sumptuous extravagance, but here, ah painful thought, the noblest work of human wisdom, the grand scheme of human glory, the fair cause of freedom, rose and fell."[18]

II

1788–1851

THE EVENT that proved to a distrustful Europe the success of the United States was the War of 1812. Knowledgeable observers had predicted disaster for the country even after ratification of the new Constitution. "The future grandeur of America and its being a rising empire . . . is one of the idlest and most visionary notions that ever was conceived, even by writers of romance," claimed the economist and cleric Dean Josiah Tucker. Alexis de Tocqueville, the Frenchman who traveled across the United States interviewing President and slave alike thirty years later agreed: "I shall refuse to believe in the duration of a government which is called upon to hold together forty different peoples, disseminated over a territory equal to one half of Europe."[1]

Perhaps American cartoonists subconsciously reserved judgment, for they had not yet developed a composite character to represent the new country as John Bull embodied Britain. European artists had presented the United States as the virginal Columbia or as an American Indian lurking in the background as Europe occupies center stage. But American artists stuck to well-known figures such as Washington and Jefferson, or copied from the Europeans. American cartoonists also pictured their exaggerated characters grappling not with specific issues but with the fate of the country itself, perhaps an unconscious reference to the precarious existence of the country, for the political partisans of 1796 and 1800 actually felt that the fate of the country hinged on their victory. The ever-present theme of conflict is easily seen as President Washington at the reins of a Federal cabriolet tries to stop an invasion of French Republican "cannibals" (fig. 16). Jefferson and his Gallic friends are trying to halt Washington, while the Federalist artist has predicted on the left side of the print the fate of the country if the cannibals are allowed to land. One of the most divisive conflicts of the day was what attitude America would take toward the raging French Revolution. Realizing the weakness of the new country, Washington opted for neutrality. But Jefferson, who had spent years in Paris as the American envoy and had grown to love the French and their culture, favored closer ties with the emerging Republic. Thus a Federalist cartoon for the 1800 presidential election shows candidate Jefferson bowed before the altar of French despotism where the works of Paine, Rousseau, and Voltaire are already burning (fig. 21). The American Eagle has just snatched the Constitution from a similar fate, which might be interpreted as the essence of American survival.

Another conflict that led to innumerable cartoons was the emergence of political parties. Political strife was particularly bitter during the Jeffersonian years in office. The embargo, which prevented Americans from trading freely with merchants from other nations, severely hampered the nation's prosperity without achieving its diplomatic goals (fig. 22). Many federalists also resented Jefferon's so-called favoritism toward France, a favoritism which was punished several times as Jefferson extended the hand of friendship to Napoleon, who tried to use the United States in his almost global conflict with Britain.

The War of 1812 was, however, one of the turning points of American history. The war had proceeded badly. The Americans were bedeviled at sea (fig. 23), frustrated in their attempt to invade Canada, and even suffered the invasion and burning of Washington, D. C. (fig. 27). The only bright spot was General Andrew Jackson's defeat of crack British troops at the Battle of New Orleans—after the peace treaty had been signed at Ghent. But the war accomplished two things: Americans matured politically when they overcame sectionalism sufficiently to prosecute the war, and by negotiating as equals at Ghent they shed the cloak of British diplomacy that had obscured their independence since 1776. It also "renewed and reinstated" the feeling of the Revolution, said Albert Gallatin, a member of the peace commission. "The people have now more general objects of attachment with which their pride and political opinions are connected. They are more American; they feel and act more like a nation."[2]

Despite the indignities of the war, Americans, remembering the New Orleans victory over troops fresh from the Napoleonic campaign and the favorable portions of the settlement at Ghent, gained confidence. But they were still an inscrutable people. Both Charles Dickens and Mrs. Anthony Trollope reached erroneous conclusions—that they were "not a humorous people, and their temperament always impressed me as being of a dull and gloomy character"—but when Mrs. Trollope discovered the political and comic character Jack Downing, invented by Seba Smith and used in both writings and cartoons, she recognized another facet of the American character and admitted that she had been wrong. With this developing sense of nation a new kind of humor, not as biting or as sophisticated (if that term can be used) as that of the contemporary British cartoons, appeared in American cartoons and subliterature. The leading political artist of the day was David Claypool Johnston, of Boston, dubbed the "American Cruikshank" by contemporary critics. Johnston's humor developed, perhaps, more rapidly than his victims' sportsmanship, for in one well-publicized encounter he was physically attacked by a rival journalist who wanted to stop distribution of a particularly offensive cartoon. The attack backfired when Johnston threw the attacker out of his office and issued a print depicting the event.

The humor that appeared in the subliterature was less political than vulgar. Often centered around mythical characters like Jack Downing and Mike Fink, with fictional or semi-fictional stories about historical heroes like Davy Crockett, the sub-literature was as grossly exaggerated as the most far-fetched caricatures. The woodcuts that appeared in *Davy Crockett's Almanac* marked a change in that they were intended to personify the personality of Crockett rather than an incident, really the first time that American cartoonists had become interested in personality per se. Crockett supposedly killed four wolves by the time he was four, hugged a bear to death, and killed a rattlesnake with his teeth. He actually did become the "coonskin congressman" from Tennessee and fight in the Battle of the Alamo, so his readers might have had some difficulty separating fact from fiction. These unsophisticated stories were humorous primarily because of their heroic, mythic qualities as well as for the crude woodcuts (fig. 36). The fact that they also included some truth or were based on real characters gave them their credibility.

Now confident of their abilities and with the British no longer in possession of the Old Northwest forts, Americans began the unimpeded conquest of the continent. Louisiana Territory stretched almost as far as the imagination with a western boundary yet to be determined. Few details were known about it except for the monumental Lewis and Clark report, but enthusiasm was so great that settlers preceded even the explorers, fear of the unknown subservient to the desire for a new land (fig. 19). Not even Colonel Stephen H. Long's pessimistic 1819 report of a Great American Desert slowed the pioneers. "What of the 'Great American Desert,' which occupied so much space on the map a generation ago?" Josiah Strong, a popular Congregationalist minister, later asked rhetorically. "It is *nomadic* and elusive; it recedes before advancing civilization like the Indian and buffalo . . . . [It] seems to have become a fugitive and vagabond on the face of the earth. It was located for a time by the map-makers in Utah, but being persecuted there, it fled to Arizona and Nevada."[3]

Social equality provided the dynamics the country needed to settle an almost limitless amount of land. Benjamin Franklin had first noticed the trait when he returned from Europe. Few Americans are "so miserable as the poor of Europe" or as rich as the European upper class, he had said, but consist of "a general happy mediocrity." Speaking from his experience, Tocqueville was firmer: American men were "on a greater equality in point of fortune and intellect . . . more equal in their strength, than in any other country in the world," he concluded.[4] The same independence that Baron von Steuben noticed during the Revolutionary War—he had to explain the "why" to a soldier before he would carry out an order—now led them to migrate westward. Andrew Jackson, the victor at New Orleans, was their hero, and it was Jackson who forced the Easterners to realize that the western lands were an increasingly important part of the country, and that the western man was the new American image.

"Far from desponding of the great political experiment in the lands of the American people," President Madison yielded the presidency to James Monroe, who witnessed the enthronement of the common man.[5] It did not come at once, because of the safeguards the founding fathers had written into the Constitution. Although Andrew Jackson led the 1824 election in popular votes, no one had a majority in the Electoral College, and the House of Representatives chose John Quincy Adams, son of the second President, to be the sixth President. "The Era of Good Feelings," the accolade accorded the years from 1815 to 1824, came to a hectic close marked by the assumption of power by a new social class and by the renewal of bitter political cartoons (fig. 30).

Some of the most sardonic political cartoons and caricatures of our history punctuate the decade following 1827, the years roughly corresponding to Andrew Jackson's terms in office. Issue-related cartoons intended to influence the election of 1828 began to appear in 1827. That summer Jackson had renewed the charges of a "corrupt bargain," in which Henry Clay supposedly supported Adams in the 1824 House election in return for a Cabinet appointment. Johnston, the Boston caricaturist, patterned an acrimonious caricature of Jackson as a military despot after a similar picture of Napoleon, recalling Jackson's brutal treatment of Indians in Spanish Florida in 1819 and his victory over the British at New Orleans (fig. 31). "I cannot believe that killing 2500 Englishmen at New Orleans qualifies [him] for the various difficult and complicated duties of the Chief Magistracy," scowled Clay.[6] Clay soon became an influential member of the new Whig Party, which took its name from the loyal opposition in the English Parliament that had as its unifying factor dislike of arbitrary power. But even Clay would not have pictured Jackson with a face composed of bodies of dead Indians, an epaulet made of six hanging men, a collar made of two pieces of artillery, a military tent for a hat, and a cannon belching smoke as a pompon, as did Johnston.

Two reasons probably explain the explosion of cartoons during the Jacksonian era. One was the widespread use of lithography, a method of printing perfected in Germany in the 1790s but not allowed to spread to other countries until the turmoil of the Napoleonic wars had ceased and international commerce was restored. True, a New York craftsman had experimented with imported stones and ink in 1808, but the European process proved far superior to the crude work he produced. The first now-known American lithograph was finally produced in Philadelphia in 1819, and the simple process spread as rapidly as the fine stones could be imported from Bavaria. The first lithographic cartoon in America showed Jackson (on the alligator) and Adams (on the tortoise) contesting the 1828 election (fig. 32). Craftsmen who had spent long hours etching a metal plate welcomed the simpler method, which could produce as detailed a picture in finer tones more quickly. The second reason was the controversy surrounding Jackson and his policies. Artists had developed the capability of producing fine cartoons during the Era of Good Feelings, when they were without inspiration for their acerbity, but "Old Hickory" provided controversial politics as well as a scandalous social climate for sedate Washington.

Some of the finer prints were hand-colored, making them more attractive to a public that already sought the lurid details of a political squabble or an international encounter. The cartoons were distributed through bookstores or by peddlers who picked up their prints each day and left a deposit. They walked the streets or set up small stands hawking them to the public, then paid for the prints they had sold, returned the others, and reclaimed the day's deposit. Compared to modern standards distribution was limited, but firms like Nathaniel Currier (later with James Ives) managed to sell thousands of prints. Existing records indicate that a popular picture was often reprinted months later to meet the continuing demand. Some cartoons might have been issued during more than one campaign, because some of the same issues and candidates were current throughout the Jackson years.

Jackson's portrait as Richard III is clearly one of Johnston's best, incorporating the events of Jackson's career with an artistic technique not fully developed until the twentieth century, and made more trenchant by the quotation from *Richard III*: "Methought the souls of all that I had murder'd came to my tent." Lithographs also made possible new and bolder designs by better artists. The pseudonym "Hassan Straightshanks" conceals the identity of one of the ablest cartoonists of the nineteenth century, particularly in terms of concept and design. His interpretation of Jacksonian government as a refuse wagon pulled by an ass (with Jackson's head) and led by Martin Van Buren is typical of the era. But the wagon driver is not. A combination of kitchen implements—a pot, tongs, a bellows, coffee pots, among others, the driver is unusual in nineteenth century lithography (fig. 33). Perhaps it is a complex reference to Jackson's Kitchen Cabinet, an unofficial group of advisors who counseled the President instead of his official Cabinet.

One of the most popular subjects for early cartoonists was the Bank of the United States, established by Alexander Hamilton in 1791 (rechartered in 1816 for twenty years) to regulate the nation's economy much as the Federal Reserve System does today. The Bank proved unpopular with regional financiers because it limited circulation of notes from smaller state banks. Farmers traditionally resented the small group of moneyed men whom they thought regulated their prices, and New York City bankers were jealous of the economic power centered in Philadelphia. Jackson hoped to make political gain of these sectional concerns and therefore opposed the bank's 1836 charter renewal. In an effort to secure the bank's recharter, Bank President Nicholas Biddle attempted to bring political pressure on Jackson in 1832, an election year. But Biddle had miscalculated Jackson's resolve and popular support. Congress passed the renewal, but Jackson successfully vetoed it (fig. 34). Meanwhile, cartoonists had a field day portraying President Jackson and the "Many-headed Monster," *The Modern Balaam and his Ass* (fig. 35), and other humorous or cynical interpretations of the gargantuan struggle that left the United States without any clear financial policy or direction, and led directly to the Panic of 1837.

Although Jackson did not run for reelection in 1836, he continued to dominate the Democratic Party and American politics until his death in 1845 and his protégé, Martin Van Buren, followed him into office. The tremendous popular support accumulated by War of 1812 hero General William H. Harrison pulled Van Buren from his "executive throne" in 1840, as pictured by lithographer Henry R. Robinson (fig. 37). Another Jackson candidate won office in 1844 on a platform of annexation of Texas and Oregon. Called "Little Hickory" because of his allegiance to Jackson, James K. Polk was the first "dark horse" candidate to be elected President.

The most important campaign issue was expansion, with annexation of Texas accompanied by the threat of war with Mexico and annexation of Oregon Territory with its possibility of conflict with Great Britain. Printer James Baillie produced a cartoon showing Dame Texas in all her hideousness, waiting to see which Democratic presidential aspirant, Van Buren or Polk, would welcome her (fig. 38). She need not have worried, for the incumbent President, John Tyler, also campaigned on an independent ticket for "Tyler and Texas." Whig candidate Henry Clay was less enthusiastic.

The bitterness involved in the Texas issue was not clear until Generals Zachary Taylor and Winfield Scott invaded and conquered Mexico, and the Southwest had been added to the national domain at the expense of enduring Mexican suspicion. A sectional effort at best, the Mexican war created division and even resistance in some quarters, while establishing one of the firmest traditions in American political history: military heroes make good presidential candidates (fig. 40). George Washington, Andrew Jackson, and William H. Harrison had preceded Taylor in the office. Democratic cartoonists created one of the most memorable pictures of the nineteenth century when they depicted General Taylor atop a pyramid of skulls, "the one qualification for a Whig President."

One bright spot in the conflict was the acquisition of California, one of the most fortunate incidents in our history, for gold was discovered in enormous quantities just a few months after the war ended. With the press full of fantastic rumors of wealth and citizens heading for California by the thousands, lithographers produced outrageous prints that depicted the mania that had commandeered the country in 1849 (fig. 41). California was America's (fig. 42). No other country could participate in the bonanza, but even Europe noticed the discovery of gold, as Honoré Daumier, the great French caricaturist, issued a cartoon showing two Frenchmen absorbed in talk of the gold rush (fig. 43).

Shortly after effects of California's wealth

reached the East Coast, Senator Henry Clay spoke on the floor of Congress in defense of a bill destined to be known as the Compromise of 1850, one of the most heralded but most disastrous agreements in our country's history. With increased population and wealth, California had requested statehood. Would it enter slave or free? The question was fraught with potential political consequences since the South had managed to hold a balance between slave states and free states in the Senate. Should California be admitted as a free state, the balance would swing in favor of the North, probably forever. Hoping to settle the differences between North and South enough to allow California to enter, Senator Clay offered his Great Compromise. In return for the admission of California, New Mexico territory would be organized without mention of slavery, and a Fugitive Slave Act would be passed requiring Northerners to help capture runaway slaves. The bill passed, momentarily halting the country's rush to self-destruct.

But slavery was an issue that would not compromise. Sidney Smith, of the *Edinburgh Review* spoke with perhaps more insight than most Americans when he predicted that "it is scarcely possible to conceive that such an empire should very long remain undivided or that dwellers on the Columbia should have common interest with the navigators of the Hudson and the Delaware."[7] Clay's effort did little to avert the onrushing disaster and many Europeans wondered if they might have prematurely declared the experiment a success.

III

1852–1875

THE ONE GREAT and abiding issue that would not recede, would not be side-stepped, would not resolve itself, and that made the Civil War inevitable, was slavery (fig. 46). Historians for decades have argued that the differences between North and South were many and complex, that they had developed over centuries of separate existence, that they and not slavery combined to guide the squabbling sections down the narrowing path to fratricidal conflict. But the inescapable fact, proclaimed at the time by abolitionists and moral men across the nation, was that slavery would not endure in spite of its profitability and rapid expansion.[1] These "Free-Soilers" promised to lead the death-defying crusade until the words that Thomas Jefferson had enshrined in the Declaration of Independence three quarters of a century before applied to men of all color—that all men are created equal before the law.

Once slavery is seen in its proper context, the issues leading to the Civil War simplify considerably. New York Senator William H. Seward insisted that the conflict was "irrepressible" as long as "a slaveholding nation" existed in the South.[2] Some early writers agreed but were overcome by stacks of economic and philosophical data gathered by later historians that pointed to irreconcilable regional differences as the cause of the war. Writing after the war, historian James Ford Rhodes noted the "risk in referring any historic event to a single cause," but concluded that "it may safely be asserted that there was a single cause [for the Civil War], slavery."[3] Rhodes' "single cause" was discredited years later by the work of revisionist authors like Charles and Mary Beard, who explained the conflict as economic in origin. The truth is, however, that slavery was the only irreconcilable difference between North and South, and it alone fastened conflict on the country.

There were, of course, significant regional differences between North and South. The South was an agrarian community, the North an industrial one; the North knitted together by miles of railroad, the South a scattering of farms and plantations. One was a society of class, the other a society of merchants and industrialists; one spawned shipbuilders and sailors, the other horsemen and leaders. The North harked to the puritanical voice of Henry Ward Beecher, the South to Methodism and Episcopalianism. But as concrete as these facts are they could hardly have caused the war, or the two sections would still be locked in mortal combat, for the South remains a basically agrarian region, the North an industrial one. The South maintained its class structure through the war, the North became even more democratized. And, although there was great psychological difference between slavery and freedom, the condition of the Negro changed little after the war, some blacks even commenting that they had lived better under slavery. Economic and civil rights for the black man did not come simply with the military victory of North over South, or even after rancorous Reconstruction that probably created more hatred than the war.

The cartoons of the 1850s and 1860s clearly emphasize the importance of slavery (fig. 46). Artists dwelt on racism, crusading characters, and war-delaying political compromises that pleased neither side. Were these cartoonists all abolitionists? Were they more sensitive to moral truth than most of their contemporaries? Or did slavery and abolition simply lend themselves to easier depiction in caricature and cartoon?

Perhaps many of the cartoonists were abolitionists; at least they were Northerners. Most of the lithographers worked in Northern cities like New York, Boston, and Philadelphia. But important regional centers had developed by 1860 and fine etchings and lithographs were produced in Cincinnati, Richmond, and Baltimore, and by no means were all the cartoonists pro-Negro. Although most of the artists were born in the North, several—Thomas Nast and Adalbert Volck—were German-born. It is also true that slavery, being a controversial issue with complex implications, obviously was an easier subject to treat than, say, agrarianism vs. industrialism, although later artists sharpened their techniques on the farm vs. the city theme without sacrificing poignancy.

With the Compromise of 1850 still fresh in mind, both the Whigs and the Democrats adopted platforms for the 1852 election supporting its clauses, even the controversial Fugitive Slave Bill (fig. 47). When Illinois Senator Stephen A. Douglas, the "Little Giant," introduced legislation organizing Kansas and Nebraska territories, the immediate question became whether slavery would be permitted in the territories (fig. 49). Douglas hoped to solve the problem (and thrust himself into contention for the 1856 presidency) by allowing the voters in the territory to decide the question for themselves. Known as "popular sovereignty," this doctrine was accepted in 1854 by Congress, but led to violence in "bloody" Kansas (fig. 48). Advocates of both sides streamed into the territory, anxious to have a majority so they could dictate the terms of the new state constitution. Neither side worried when violence furthered their cause; abolitionists felt morally justified, slaveholders needed another state for balance in the Senate. Propagandists spread literature and prints across the nation, including one by J. L. Magee showing the Democrats "Forcing Slavery Down the Throat of a Freesoiler" (fig. 48). So worried about the slavery issue in Kansas were the Democrats that Franklin Pierce and Douglas, who had committed themselves irrevocably on the issue, lost the nomination to James Buchanan (who had been out of the country as American minister in England) and John C. Breckenridge.

Slavery also dominated Douglas' race for reelection to the Senate when Abraham Lincoln, a little-known former member of Congress who regarded slavery as "a moral, a social, and a political wrong," challenged him.[4] Douglas responded with his "Freeport Doctrine," arguing (contrary to the Dred Scott decision) that a state or territory could legally exclude slavery, a position that cost him Southern support and ultimately perhaps the presidency (fig. 52).

But even Lincoln, the "Great Emancipator," was not as radical as the abolitionists (fig. 50). While contending that slavery was morally wrong, he admitted in his debates with Douglas that "I have no purpose to introduce political and social equality between the white and black races."[5] His 1860 platform was a carefully drawn document reaffirming the principles of the Declaration of Independence, the Wilmot Proviso (stating that slavery would be prohibited from the territories), and the right of each state to control its domestic institutions, rather than a strident manifesto calling for abolition. A moderate on the issue of slavery, he swept the North, winning a clear majority in the electoral college (without a single Southern vote), substantial enough to have defeated his three opponents even if they had unified against him.

True to their word Southern states began seceding (fig. 54). Without waiting for the newly-elected President to speak, South Carolina passed an ordinance on December 20, 1860, declaring that "the union now subsisting between South Carolina and the other States, under the name of the 'United States of America,' is hereby dissolved." Some, even Southerners, thought South Carolina's action precipitate: an Arkansas editor castigated South Carolina for having "whirled herself" out of the Union "without even passing the compliments of the season" with her sister slaveholding States.[6] But the six other lower South states immediately followed course, with four of the upper South states joining later (fig. 55).

European observers who had watched the United States for the past half-century felt certain that the great democracy had finally ended. They had often pointed out that the raw materials of the South fed the industrial might of the North and predicted that neither could survive without the other. Britain, the mother country—sympathetic as any offended mother might be—hesitated, not knowing whether to support the South, with whom she agreed socially, or the North, with whom she agreed morally. The South won a diplomatic victory when Britain declared neutrality in regard to the Northern blockade of Southern ports, thereby recognizing the South as a belligerent power, but all observers could agree with the cartoonist Woolf that the national bird had been "murdered" (fig. 55). The French comment might have been more appropriately the European opinion: "I do not understand anything about it all" (fig. 56).

The war began slowly, with the South hoping to strike a blow that would convince Northerners of its ability and will, then reach a quick settlement that would recognize its independence. Lincoln initially rested his case on the sanctity of the Union, a course with impressive historical support among the founding fathers as well as great popular appeal, but Northerners inspired by Harriet Beecher Stowe's *Uncle Tom's Cabin* were not as willing to fight for an idea as they were a cause. Lincoln's modest goal of luring the South back into the Union by remaining silent on the question of slavery and loyal to the principles of the Constitution had failed. After several bloody matches at Bull Run, Shiloh, Antietam, and Fredericksburg, the President finally concluded that the major issue of the war could not be avoided. He issued the Emancipation Proclamation on January 1, 1863 (fig. 57). While true that the document applied only to those slaves in states that had seceded (and not those in border states like Maryland that remained in the Union), it is not true, as is often stated, that it therefore did not free a single slave. The rationale that all masters in Confederate states disregarded Lincoln's proclamation is not based on documentation. Loyal Unionists living in the South, such as Sam Houston, who gave up the Texas governorship rather than swear allegiance to the Confederacy, freed their slaves as soon as they learned of the Proclamation.[7] Lincoln, the final architect of abolition, was now even more hated by Southerners. David H. Strother of Richmond, an illustrator for the short-lived magazine called *Southern Punch*, probably represented the majority Southern view of Lincoln when he drew him as a monkey presenting the Emancipation Proclamation to the overjoyed but obviously naïve Negro.

Strother was joined in his intense dislike of Lincoln by another Southern artist, Baltimore dentist Adalbert Volck, who pictured the President and General Benjamin F. Butler, a particularly despised Northern officer whom many Southerners had depended on to join their cause (fig. 58). For no reason other than that Lincoln and Butler were equally disliked, Volck pictured them together as Don Quixote and Sancho Panza. Thomas Nast, a pro-Union cartoonist for *Harper's Weekly*, also included Lincoln and Butler in a cartoon. Nast depicted Butler as if he were a valued Northern leader whom Lincoln planned to cut into several pieces so he could send him to different places simultaneously (fig. 59). Butler's presence in the cartoons of the era is a graphic lesson in how history virtually forgets a personality that occupied only a supporting role throughout his career (fig. 66). Although Butler had presidential aspirations following the Civil War and actually ran on the Greenback Party ticket in 1884, the most influential position he held was member of Congress, and his reputation rested primarily on his dictatorial rule of New Orleans during the early years of the war.

The final victory of the overwhelming Union forces by no means settled the issues that had precipitated the war. More than 600,000 men lay dead, slavery had been eliminated; nevertheless, Negroes did not automatically receive equal treatment or even equality under the law. And any national hope of seeking solutions under Lincoln's leadership was obliterated by the assassin's bullet in 1865 (fig. 62). Andrew Johnson of Tennessee took office to face one of the most troubling problems of the Republic, the readmission of the Confederate states to the Union. What would be the terms? Would the Southerners be granted full citizenship? Were they to be punished? Although the nation faced difficult problems, it had survived its greatest crisis. Skeptical Europeans who had predicted the decline of "the last best hope of earth," as Lincoln had put it, were wrong. And they were once again reminded of their dislike for the hybrid that had developed in North America and of how it might now flex its new-found muscles internationally (fig. 74).

Lincoln's plan to normalize the country was lenient. Arguing that the Confederate states had never left the Union, he offered amnesty to all Southerners who would swear allegiance to the government and planned to recognize state governments when ten percent of the 1860 electorate had taken the oath. Certain radical Republicans in Congress, however, viewed the South as a defeated enemy and demanded punishment. The Wade-Davis Bill, submitted to Congress before the war ended, would have restructured Lincoln's plan by requiring that a majority of the electorate in each state take the oath before the state would be readmitted. Lincoln pocket-vetoed the bill, and Johnson made it clear upon his assumption of power that he favored Lincoln's terms.

The Radicals immediately realized that if their plan were to be instituted it would be in spite of Johnson. Under the leadership of Thaddeus Stevens of Pennsylvania, the Radicals outlined a reconstruction program designed to chastise the South and, if necessary, rid themselves of an uncooperative President. Stevens claimed that the Southern states were "conquered provinces." Senator Charles Sumner of Massachusetts considered them to have committed "suicide." In either case the states would have given up their membership in the Union, and to be readmitted they would come under the authority of Congress, just as the territories do. Then Congress drafted the thirteenth and fourteenth amendments abolishing slavery and granting all citizens due process of law before any of their rights could be abridged, two moderate measures that Lincoln himself had favored.

Johnson's cause was not helped when New Orleans erupted in a racial riot in July, 1866 (fig. 64). Thousands of freedmen expecting radically different treatment headed for the Crescent City, only to find that little had changed, that the government was in the hands of the Democratic party in accordance with Lincoln's and Johnson's plans. The

Radicals tried to take over the government by reconvening the "loyalist" convention of 1864, but they were attacked by police and a white mob. Thirty-seven Negroes and three white sympathizers were killed. The riot stirred great indignation in the North, and Congress blamed Johnson. When the 1866 congressional elections placed more Radicals in office, they moved to tighten their grip on Johnson and the government. Virtually removing the President's power over the army by the Command of the Army Act requiring him to issue orders through the General of the Army, U. S. Grant, the Radicals then passed the Tenure of Office Act, stating that officials appointed by and with the advice of the Senate could be removed only by the same procedure, thus fixing Johnson with a host of officials hostile to his goals.

Congress proceeded to outline the manner in which former Confederate states could return to the Union (fig. 65). The First Reconstruction Act passed over President Johnson's veto in 1867 divided the South into five military districts and established martial law. For civil authority to return, the states would have to present a new constitution for Congressional approval, adopt universal manhood suffrage, and ratify the fourteenth amendment. If Southerners refused to act, Congress required the military commanders in each district to initiate the measures.

Johnson, doubting the constitutionality of the Tenure of Office Act, determined to test it by dismissing Secretary of War Edwin Stanton. The House of Representatives then impeached Johnson, charging that he had violated the Tenure of Office Act, the Command of the Army Act, and had disgraced and ridiculed the Congress (fig. 66). In a six-week trial before the Senate, Johnson was acquitted, but he could no longer block Radical legislation. They finally defeated him as war-hero Grant swept into office in 1868 (fig. 67).

Congressional Reconstruction of the South has been one of the most controversial issues of our nation's past. The traditional view holds that by disenfranchising all the Southerners who had supported the Confederacy Congress allowed outsiders and turncoats ("carpetbaggers" and "scalawags") to take legal advantage of honest former Confederates who wanted nothing more than to return peacefully to the Union. The official law enforcement agencies were often corrupt and military commanders concerned themselves as much with illegal activity by the Southerners (in the Ku Klux Klan and similar organizations) as by the intruders. "Our principal danger was from lawless bands of marauders . . .," said one observer. "Our country was full of highwaymen . . . the off-scourings of the two armies and of the suddenly freed negro population." As late as 1879 a journalist reported that the migrants from the Old South to Texas had "no progress in them, no love for adventure, no ambition." And a Northern visitor to New Orleans in 1873 was shocked when he saw "these faces, these faces. One sees them everywhere; on the street, at the theater, in the salon, in the cars; and pauses for a moment struck with the expression of entire despair." Mobile was "dilapidated and hopeless." Norfolk was "asleep by her magnificent harbor." Savannah was "at a standstill."[8]

The contrary view contends that Reconstruction had its faults, as would any military occupation, but that the end—in this case equal rights for blacks—justified the means since Southerners would not voluntarily cooperate. Some revisionist writers even suggest that the basic problem with Reconstruction was that it did not go far enough, that the Southern states were readmitted to the Union before transformation was complete. This point of view further alleges that proper reconstruction would have rendered most of the civil rights problems of the 1960s avoidable.

Even adequate reconstruction would have left the prejudices of the Northern states intact, prejudices which only fully emerged in the 1970s. Historical hindsight has permitted us to criticize both views, and to observe that perhaps the Northern states were no more ready for total equality than were the Southern states. When those rights did materialize more than 100 years after the bitter war, however, the legal foundation was the constitutional amendments written and passed after the Civil War.

As soon as the Confederate states were readmitted to the Union with full political rights, the military districts were abolished and home rule returned. With the presidential election of 1876 politics returned to a "business as usual" status, and the Democratic Party again contended for national offices. It was by coincidence that the most dangerous threat to the experiment begun in 1776 was finally over on the 100th birthday of the experiment, overcome by a tenacious President who refused to acquiesce when almost half the country attempted to secede.

IV

1876–1900

ONCE SURVIVAL of the grand experiment had been clearly established, the years from 1876 until 1900 seem marked by a resolution to solve the country's fundamental problems. The memories of this era, however, appear to be of the worst failures of society. These were years when reformers and problem-solvers crusaded for black rights, for prohibition, for governmental and political reforms, for humanitarian reforms, and for business regulation. But most of all, these were years of industrialization and urbanization, years during which the foundations of modern American society were laid.

Americans abroad in 1876 were seldom so sophisticated or talented as the first ambassadors who visited France and England, but all had to be taken more seriously for they represented an increasingly powerful force in world affairs. From the brilliance of Jefferson and the creativity and wit of Franklin the American image had evolved into the democracy of Jackson and the stoic martyrdom of Lincoln. The post-Civil War American spirit, however, was personified in a G. Bridgman caricature—the businessman (fig. 74). Dressed in the best Yankee tradition, the new "national type" swashbuckled onto the world's economic stage with a bag of "greenbacks" under his arm, a Cuban cigar clenched in his teeth, and a ravenous home market to supply. By 1885 the United States had become the leading industrial nation in the world.

Undreamed of technological advances made possible the new age of industrialism. Farm boys from the Midwest and recently arrived immigrants alike were whisked to their urban destinations by the railroad, which soon linked coast to coast via five transcontinental lines. Inland waterways served as arteries for steamboat traffic, and new pipelines brought oil to the developing markets. Businessmen soon made important contacts via the telegraph and newly-developed telephone as each phase of industry leapt forward to keep up with the pacesetters.

Quick-minded, shrewd businessmen, inspired as much by the quest for power and money as by the possession of them, found numberless opportunities in the developing economy. They designed new methods of distribution, discovered new resources or new ways of using old ones, and invented solutions to problems that only they could foresee. Thomas A. Edison pointed out the difference between invention (purposeful creation) and discovery (more or less an accident), then chose to enter the "invention business": America did not have time to wait for discovery. John D. Rockefeller, according to one of his contemporaries, not only had foresight, he "could see around the corner"[1] (fig. 140). Prompted by a government that espoused capitalism itself and allowed the entrepreneur to keep the profits, they built undreamed of fortunes. Rockefeller refined the increasing oil flow until he controlled ninety percent of the country's refineries. He was the first man to accumulate more than a billion dollars' worth of personal wealth. Andrew Carnegie, a Scottish immigrant working on the railroad, wisely predicted the many possibilities for steel and earned millions more dollars than he could spend when he sold his Carnegie Steel Company to the company that eventually became United States Steel. Charles Goodnight, thinking of himself as a "solitary adventurer . . . in a great land as fresh and new as a spring morning," turned worthless longhorn beef into millions of dollars by driving the animals overland to starved markets. These entrepreneurs knew that "there's gold from the grass roots down," as a guide in the Dakota gold country of the 1870s said, but they quickly learned that "there's more gold from the grass roots up."[2]

America's industrial titans shared another mania—philanthropy. At age sixty, the religious Rockefeller began to disperse his fortune, believing that God had intended it for the good of mankind. Establishing the world-famous Rockefeller Foundation, he gave away more than $530 millions before his death. Carnegie shared his philosophy as well as his wealth with the world. Believing that "the problem of our age is the proper administration of wealth," he donated church organs, library buildings, and money for an endowment for peace. Of his estimated fortune of $400 millions, more than $350 millions went to public benefactions. "The man who dies rich dies disgraced," he announced.

Neither Rockefeller nor Carnegie earned their money with a new discovery or invention. Their contribution was organization—organization in an oil industry consisting of hundreds of small refineries, producers, and consumers with no industry-wide cooperation; in a steel industry unaware of the potential for new bridges, steamships, and a thousand other necessities. America provided few manufactured goods that were not already available in other countries. The great genius of America—and the great democratizing agent—was distribution which made manufactured goods available to all Americans at a low price. The emerging urban centers demanded—and consumed—goods at an impressive rate. "Palaces of consumption," chain stores, mail order houses, and department stores like R. H. Macy's and Lord & Taylor in New York City, John Wanamaker's in Philadelphia, and Field, Leiter & Company (later Marshall Field & Company) in Chicago, met the demand with clothing, drugs, hardware, jewels, hats, furniture, and shoes (fig. 75). These huge emporiums drove many small businessmen into bankruptcy or into another line of work by centralizing distribution of related items, lowering overhead, and selling at a fixed, lower-than-usual price that put an end to price haggling. The American public got more and better goods than the citizens of any other industrialized country in the world.

Few countries could have supplied the workers to support this expansive economy, but America was the recipient of hundreds of thousands of immigrants who, still speaking their own tongues, moved directly into the work force (fig. 76). Immigration reached a nineteenth century peak in 1882 when almost 800,000 foreigners arrived, then leveled off to approximately 400,000 per year; 1,285,000 arrived in 1907. In all some 20 millions came to the United States from 1865 to 1914, most settling in eastern cities and living in their own ethnic communities isolated from the English language until their children enrolled in public school.

Industrialization and urbanization was possible because of another American miracle: farm productivity. Although young people left farm communities in growing numbers, production did not suffer. Improvements in the plow facilitated planting, while McCormick's reaper speeded up the harvest. Other mechanical devices aided virtually every facet of farming. By 1900 there were more acres under cultivation and more animals grazing the land than ever before in the history of the country; the United States led the world in agricultural production while employing the smallest percentage of its population on the farm.

As the number of immigrants grew and American labor began its fledgling efforts at organization, an understandable animosity developed between the two. Anxious to improve conditions in what they publicized as a "slave market," workers resented foreigners who migrated to this country and took jobs at a lower wage. Thousands of Chinese workers, brought in to work on the railroad and in the gold mines in California, stirred resentment among white workers there, while the East Coast, used to immigrants from northern Europe, pictured itself as inundated by a stream of South and East European immigrants, the "new" immigration. These people spoke different languages, were Catholic, and had darker skins, factors that placed them under immediate suspicion when contrasted with the "old" immigration that had been going on for decades (fig. 77). The "sandlot riots" in San Francisco in July, 1877, resulted in a new treaty with China that permitted the United States to "regulate, limit or suspend" Chinese immigration, but not to prohibit it, and anti-foreign pressure produced the Contract Labor Act of 1885 which forbade the importation of laborers already contracted for a job (fig. 78).

Few people realized or cared about the conditions the immigrants found when they arrived, but the experience was traumatic from the moment of departure on over-crowded ships to arrival at Ellis Island, "the isle of tears," to settlement in a fast-growing urban slum. Thomas Worth, a cartoonist for Currier & Ives, mixed racism with his comment on immigration as he pictured a "frightening" Statue of Liberty waiting to abuse the immigrants who came under her care (fig. 79). New York Port quickly became famous for corruption, both in the treatment of immigrants and for the criminal way in which the jobs were parceled out to political hacks. More than one politician made his reputation while lining his pockets at the expense of the poor immigrants, and at least one national figure, Roscoe Conkling, ended his career in a huff because New York Port patronage had gone to a political rival.

As the Industrial Revolution came of age, pools, trusts, and holding companies concentrated unprecedented economic power in the hands of a few, raising fundamental questions about the role of government in a capitalistic society. Business operated according to unwritten codes, asking for a *laissez faire* policy yet soliciting support such as land grants for railroads as encouragement to lay more track. One economic expert saw the "progress of the country" as being "independent of legislation." Nor would any good businessman want regulation in the manner of William M. ("Boss") Tweed, the head of Tammany Hall (fig. 80). To get a New York City contract a supplier had to agree to a "kickback" return of a certain percentage of the total contract to Tweed and his henchmen. The city paid more than $11 millions for a courthouse worth not more than $3 millions and more than $2 millions for stationery alone during Tweed's reign. "'Things regulate themselves,'" claimed Harvard Professor Francis Bowen in explaining the philosophy of *laissez faire*, which "means, of course, that God regulates them by his general laws."[3] Business operated so independently of government that H. H. Rogers, one of Rockefeller's associates, told a New York State legislative committee in 1879 that there was a "question" in his mind as to "whether it is a proper thing for me, even if there is not harm done by it, to divulge my business secrets."[4]

Despite the dogged opposition of businessmen, Congress passed several landmark laws to correct the most serious abuses. The Interstate Commerce Act of 1887 and the Sherman Antitrust Act of 1890 established the precedent of government regulation of business and laid the foundation for future legislation, while correcting unfair practices such as the long and short "haul," (railroads charging more for a short trip than a long one because of lack of competition) and "restraint of trade" by trusts controlling one or more industries.

The theories of Charles Darwin (first published in his book, *The Origin of Species*, in 1859) apparently offered an alternative to the Biblical version of the creation—evolution. Darwin upset Christian fundamentalists by implying that humans lived by the same principles, a theory which they saw as animalistic and degrading to a creature made in God's image (fig. 82). Most preachers condemned this attack on their theology, but Henry Ward Beecher, brother of Harriet Beecher Stowe and preacher for a 2,500 member congregation in Brooklyn, espoused it, claiming that evolution and Christianity were truths that could exist side by side. He hoped to win respect for an enlightened Christianity that would admit the findings of science, but he unfortunately discredited his cause when a member of his congregation sued him for adultery (fig. 82).

1876 was America's centennial year, a time of back-slapping and reaffirmation of the country's traditional values. It was also a time during which values that many Americans held dear were under attack (fig. 83). "Demon Rum," a personal blight to many, was assaulted by the Woman's Christian Temperance Union, the Anti-Saloon League, and religious groups. It was also a political issue that helped doom Senator James G. Blaine's presidential hopes when he neglected to disagree with a preacher who denounced "rum, Romanism, and rebellion" in his presence. An enterprising reporter promptly publicized the remark for all immigrants and Southerners (many of whom loved rum and were Catholics and former Rebels) to see.

A more tangible attack on traditional values was the small but vocal crusade for woman's rights that began after the war, continued into the 1872 presidential contest when Victoria Woodhull announced her candidacy, and found its greatest expression in the cities, where women assumed new roles as clerks, secretaries, and shopkeepers (fig. 72). A host of myths had to be debunked before women would be admitted to schools, jobs, and certain societies, but there was no denying Southern women who had managed plantations and farms while their husbands were away at war, or Northern women who organized charities, including the forerunner of the Red Cross, during the Civil War (fig. 70). Conservatives feared that "enforced familiarity" in the classroom would lead to losing "the delicate bloom of womanhood," resulting in "race suicide" when the process reached its natural end. Mark Twain, on the other hand, welcomed the "new woman" (fig. 84). "I dearly want the women to be raised to the political altitude of the negro, the imported savage, and the pardoned thief, and allowed to vote," he wrote in 1873, "it will be the last time . . . to give over trying to save the country by human means."[5] The "weaker vessel" was finally admitted to colleges and universities after the Civil War, most institutions following suit by the 1870s, but equality under the law, guaranteed by the fourteenth amendment, was not seriously offered until a century later.

"The Gilded Age," to use Mark Twain's famous phrase, reached its apex during the "gay nineties," a heady era that followed a resurgence of the economy and the election of a Republican president in 1896. America became embarrassingly aware of itself and the criticisms of sophisticated Europeans. Walt Whitman bemoaned the fact that "America has yet morally and artistically originated nothing," and the Irish poet Mary Colum called it "intellectually America's most colonial period." American humor was to real literature what Negro minstrel shows were to drama, said the *Nation*, the intellectual conscience of the country in 1883. American letters could not yet claim another Jefferson, but Henry James and Twain created some of the greatest prose of any American, and artists like William M. Harnett, Thomas Eakins, and Winslow Homer produced superb canvases.

The 1890s fed instead on the practical genius of America. Louis D. Brandeis pointed out that American creativeness was directed more toward a "scientific management" of business, and Americans took pride in the inventions of Thomas A. Edison (first practical incandescent light, first phonograph, first motion picture projector).[6] Presidential hopeful William Jennings Bryan returned from a trip to Europe to declare himself "more widely informed, but more intensely American," and a young Henry Cabot Lodge predicted that "Americans may reasonably look forward to a time when they will have produced a civilization grander than any the world has known."[7]

As opposite as they might seem, industrial advances also aided the artist. With the aid of huge steam presses, publishers like Louis Prang of Boston were able to adapt the lithographic method to mechanical printing and produce multi-colored reproductions of original paintings as well as famous "old masters," which he called "chromos." The technique was quickly employed by several cartoon magazines like *Judge* and *Puck*, patterned after the English humor magazine *Punch*. With a circulation of around 90,000 by the mid-1890s, *Puck* made colored chromolithographic cartoons easily available and immensely popular (figs. 75, 76, 81, 82). Because most chromos were copies of original art and because of the wide-spread intellectual disillusionment with the Gilded Age, this era is often dubbed the "chromo civilization." But recent re-evaluation of the artistic and intellectual attainment of these years and of the chromo has turned the epithet into a compliment.

The Spanish-American War that ended a century of unparalleled progress marked America's entrance into world affairs as a respected participant (fig. 88). A people who had just rooted inhuman slavery from its own bosom at a tremendous expense now looked at other nations' problems with a puritanical eye and zealous heart. Americans only mourned the subjugation of the home of ancient liberties, Greece, by Turkey, but took a more active interest in Spain's domination of Cuba, located just ninety miles off the coast of Florida and close enough to affect (fig. 87). Outright meddling in the Spanish colonial affairs plus militant "yellow journalism" in New York City produced a demand for war on behalf of the Cuban colonials that President William McKinley was not prepared to resist. Although the weak Spanish government agreed to the humanitarian demands that the Americans made, the United States proceeded with a war that lasted only a few months and resulted in the enlargement of America's colonial empire (fig. 89).

America entered the twentieth century ebullient and hopeful of even greater things. The tragic assassination of McKinley left the government in the hands of "that damn cowboy," Theodore Roosevelt, whose enthusiasm encouraged the national euphoria and provided the nation a sense of philosophical progress that it had felt before only when it flexed its industrial and military muscles. The image of America included Progress, which most Americans thought an exclusive gift of democracy.

V

1901–1929

THEODORE ROOSEVELT is a familiar figure—the flashing teeth, the steel-rimmed glasses, the close-cropped hair and busy mustache, the striving, the sportsmanship (fig. 90). Roosevelt was so well-liked, so controversial that he often appears in caricature today. He was caricatured then too: a barrel-chested, falsetto-voiced demigod could not help but make an impression. And when he came with other features so easily recognizable and drawn, he, like Abraham Lincoln and Franklin D. Roosevelt, was a natural, a stereotype, a cartoonist's favorite. He is the remarkable combination of Harvard and the Old West, the military and shrewd politics. He has come to stand for personal energy, vigor, and jingoism. It was Theodore Roosevelt who ushered the United States into the twentieth century.

This inexhaustible man provided excellent leadership for a government languishing under vapid

Republicanism (fig. 91). Torpid William McKinley hardly exuded his own personality; he lent none to the government. Turn-of-the-century reformers struggled with monopolies and trusts of unprecedented size and power (figs. 97, 102). Muckrakers—a term Roosevelt coined—found rapidly developing slums and starving children in the midst of the greatest urban centers. Antiquated laws simply did not provide the legal means necessary to eradicate these problems. This new "Progressive" movement needed a leader, someone to direct its energies, to make it palatable to the established authorities on Wall Street, on Capitol Hill. Roosevelt was that man. "We know that self-government is difficult," he conceded in his 1905 inaugural address, "but we have faith that we shall not prove false to the memories of the men of the mighty past."[1]

Many Americans look back on these magniloquent years and suggest that they were a period of national mindlessness during which the people abandoned their basic values in the face of world pressure. Roosevelt's maverick campaign in 1912 was only one of the unlikely happenings during the almost three decades from 1901 to 1929. Soon American doughboys would march across Europe to snatch victory from the hands of the Kaiser in what had seemed a purely European war. Jazz and prohibition swept the cities, the Republican Party certified its moral bankruptcy in the Teapot Dome oil scandal, materialism was evidently the national philosophy (fig. 128). Calvin Coolidge took office as President and high priest of consumption declaring that "The business of the United States is business."[2] "It was an easy, quick, adventurous age, good to be young in," said Malcolm Cowley, writer and critic, "and yet on coming out of it one felt a sense of relief, as on coming out of a room too full of talk and people into the sunlight of the winter streets."[3] Yet these years are not disharmonious with the rest of our history. The nation reveled in its reckless and self-confident character. Too peripheral to be noticed before, Americans had now earned the right to be heard. America was just being itself.

Cartoonists provided images for the awakening. Coming on the heels of such a lackluster President as McKinley, Roosevelt captured the hero-fancy of Americans. Frank Nankivell showed him as pirate (fig. 90). Otho Cushing pictured him as Ulysses in *The Teddessy*, withstanding the lure of sirens Carnegie, Rockefeller, and J. P. Morgan from his reform position (fig. 92) tied to the mast. Perhaps the most poignant cartoon of Teddy's determination is John Clubb's depiction of him on Sagamore Hill, his home, ready to fly off to war in 1916 (fig. 111). (Roosevelt called on President Woodrow Wilson when the United States entered World War I and offered his services; Wilson declined.) J. S. Pughe (fig. 94), T. E. Powers (fig. 106), and C. K. Berryman (fig. 107) offered a lanky, beared Uncle Sam who stumbled like the adolescent that he was, but spoke with increased authority. The nation could relax with Sam and Teddy at the helm.

Offering the country a "Square Deal," Roosevelt carefully outlined antitrust legislation, government reforms, pure food and drug legislation, and conservation measures (fig. 96). Abroad he flexed the country's new-found muscles, counseling his adversaries that the maturing world power wielded a big stick in spite of its soft voice (fig. 94). He initiated construction on the badly-needed Panama Canal, added the Roosevelt Corollary to the Monroe Doctrine (admitting that the United States probably would have to become the international policeman for Latin America), and maintained the balance of power between the Asian powers of Russia and Japan, winning a Nobel Prize by mediating the dispute.

Roosevelt's aggressiveness is reflected in foreign policy. An ardent supporter of Admiral Alfred T. Mahan, he oversaw the building of a Navy and a show of force in the Pacific as Japan spread its empire. Roosevelt authorized the "Great White Fleet" to make a courtesy call on Japan, even though Congress had not appropriated money for the trip (fig. 94). Reasoning that the demonstration was necessary and that Congress would not allow the fleet to remain on the far side of the Pacific, he ordered the voyage, then left it to Congress to get the fleet back home. The "American scarecrow" might have appeared clumsy to the adroit Japanese, but the point was made: American force—the big stick—was present in the Pacific. Roosevelt invoked the Monroe Doctrine to keep Germany from interfering in Latin America, and his friend Henry Cabot Lodge initiated congressional action to keep Japan from speculating in land on the west coast of Mexico (fig. 106).

Stepping aside to allow his hand-picked successor William Howard Taft (fig. 98) to take office in 1908, Roosevelt turned to personal matters: he went big game hunting and bestowed his trophies on the Smithsonian Institution; he visited scenic spots in the West, thereby calling attention to our national resources; and he otherwise played the senior statesman. But four years on the sidelines left him restless and unsure of Taft. Roosevelt had satisfied himself by regulating monopolies with the countervailing power of government, but Taft had taken more direct action. His attorney general had initiated more antitrust suits during four years than Roosevelt's had in almost two full terms. Displaying the energy and enthusiasm that had become his trademark, Roosevelt again sought the presidency, this time on the Bull Moose (Progressive) Party ticket in 1912. He announced to a curious convention of Eastern industrialists, Western liberals, and old-time Roosevelt followers that "we stand at Armageddon and battle for the Lord."[4]

The progressive cause gained momentum as Woodrow Wilson, the Princeton academician, was nominated by the Democrats (fig. 104). He promised the country the "New Freedom," putting monopoly control at the head of his domestic program. Unlike Roosevelt, Wilson wanted to control trusts by actually breaking them up. With the Republican vote split between Taft, the official party nominee, and Roosevelt, Wilson won easily.

The eyes of the world, meanwhile, were on Europe. "What shall we say of the Great War of Europe, ever threatening, ever impending, and which never came?" asked the director of the World Peace Foundation in 1913. "Humanly speaking, it is impossible." A leader in the American peace movement agreed that this would be the "age of treaties rather than the age of wars, the century of reason rather than the century of force," and a Maine editor claimed that "never since Christ was born in the Manger was the outlook for the universal brotherhood of man brighter than it is today."[5]

World War I began inconspicuously enough in the summer of 1914 with the assassination of the heir to the Austro-Hungarian throne. Traditional hostilities plus a series of entangling alliances had Europe at war by August 4. How could this happen in such an enlightened era, Secretary of Agriculture David Houston asked himself. "I had a feeling that the end of things had come. I stopped in my tracks, dazed and horror-stricken." Then bitterness: "We never appreciated so keenly as now the foresight exercised by our forefathers in emigrating from Europe," declared a Midwestern editor.[6] Following traditional isolationist policy, the United States declared itself neutral and hoped to avoid the conflict that a depraved Europe seemed determined to wage.

But the war was an unprecedented and bloody affair. Sixty thousand British troops perished on the Somme in one single day, over a million men on both sides died in the first five months of battle—and no one gained the advantage. German U-boats sank neutral ships, forcing Wilson to issue progressively adamant diplomatic notes and pacifist Secretary of State William Jennings Bryan to resign rather than send them (fig. 108). To Chicago cartoonist Luther Bradley, Wilson had discovered Roosevelt's big stick (fig. 109), while Louis Raemaekers personified the coming global confrontation in his caricature of Wilson and the Kaiser, the Kaiser astounded at the American's firmness: "Do You Mean to Make a Real War?" (fig. 110).

Many cartoonists supported the intervention; several members of the liberal *The Masses* staff even resigned rather than have the editor put antiwar captions under their drawings. But the artists also called attention to the calculated dementia of war. Robert Minor noted the belittling of the individual's intelligence (fig. 113), Dalrymple the injustice of men dying while others prosper (fig. 114), Boardman Robinson the threat of the October Revolution in Russia (fig. 115). Cartoonists objected to the two-faced attitudes of the United States in jailing men like Eugene V. Debs, a five-time presidential candidate on the Socialist Party ticket, for violation of the Espionage Act, while committing atrocities in the name of liberty in American-owned or dominated territories. Art Young and several other members of *The Masses* staff were even tried for obstructing the draft because of the subject matter in some of their cartoons.

The United States entered the fray in time to insure victory for the Allied powers, but not before sixty percent of the more than fifty-eight millions who participated in it were killed, wounded, captured, or reported missing. Such devastating statistics shocked Americans. Roosevelt's saber-rattling could lead to undreamed-of horror. Wilson's war to make the world "safe for democracy" cost too great a price (fig. 112). Progress that brought the automobile, electricity, mass-production, and the airplane also brought poison gas, machine-guns, tanks, and mobile artillery. "The plunge of civilization into this abyss of blood and horror . . . gives away the whole long age during which we have supposed the world to be, with whatever abatement, gradually bettering," wrote Henry James, a cynical and detached observer. "What the treacherous years were really making for and *meaning* is too tragic for any words." World War I, concluded James, is the "unspeakable giveaway of the whole fool's paradise of our past."[7]

The Unknown Soldier, an anonymous doughboy who was intended to personify the many who died serving the country, seemed instead to emphasize the impersonal quality of a conflict conducted on such a machine-like basis. The nature of patriotism had changed. "I can't explain it," claimed one of John Dos Passos' fictional soldiers, "but I'll never put a uniform on again." The whole world had changed for painter Maynard Dixon too: "people, morals, patriotism—all had a different meaning to me ever since."[8] Americans noted with increasing wonderment the statement attributed to Lloyd George at the Versailles peace conference: "Is it Upper or Lower Silesia that we are giving away?"[9] The Washington disarmament conference of 1921 began with great enthusiasm but finally fell victim to the suspicion and doubt of the age and achieved little in the way of lasting disarmament (fig. 118).

America was ready for peace, but not for world responsibility. The intellectuals turned nihilist, while the country at large drifted toward isolationism. The Senate rejected the League of Nations; mail from the organization's Geneva headquarters lay unopened on a State Department desk for months. Idaho Senator William Borah declared that even "if the Savior of man would revisit the earth and declare for a League of Nations, I would be opposed to it."[10] President Warren Harding's solution was "not heroics but healing; not nostrums but normalcy; not revolution but restoration"[11] (figs. 116, 117). The flapper ruled the day, and politicians were incapable of inspiring greater world consciousness in the nation even if they had favored it. Ever since its birth, the United States had possessed a fear of outsiders, whether represented as immigrants or in foreign affairs. The 1920s were no exception.

Seized with a fit of conscience at the end of the Spanish-American War because of the consequent colonialism, Americans had adopted far-reaching reforms, politically, economically, and socially during the ensuing three decades (fig. 119). With colonies or territories scattered throughout both the Atlantic and the Pacific, the United States suddenly succumbed to the charge of imperialism. Most

Americans shunned the accusation, believing America to be the only powerful anti-imperialistic country in the world. But the workings of overwrought consciences had their effect. Muckrakers investigated corrupt machine politicians in the cities (fig. 103), urban slums kept by wealthy landlords in violation of city ordinances, and food manufacturing and packaging. The cartoonists popularized the findings, with Winsor McKay illustrating the technological revolution of the cities (fig. 125), and A. Redfield picturing William Randolph Hearst shouting the doomsday headlines from the back of his snorting nag in the Paul Revere manner (fig. 100).

Americans sought in religion an underpinning for traditional values. Amid the trials of urban living, pastors tried to adapt the latest scientific findings to Biblical principle, tried to show their parishioners that science and religion were in harmony. Charles Sheldon, author of the best-selling *In His Steps*, urged his readers to ask themselves what Christ would have done when confronted with a certain problem. This simplistic message was reiterated thousands of times across the country as evangelists like Billy Sunday held crusades and camp meetings and set up Bible institutes on the college and university campuses (fig. 133). It suffered a publicity setback when William Jennings Bryan and Clarence Darrow debated the theory of evolution in the Tennessee Scopes Monkey Trial (figs. 131, 132), but renewed when advocates of Andrew Carnegie's "Gospel of Wealth" connected spirituality with correct business practice. The dean of the University of Chicago Divinity School explained to an inquiring reporter that one could make more money if he prayed about his business. A stockbroker pointed out that the book of Exodus contained tips on risk and liability, and a Chicago man revealed that his business philosophy came from Ezekiel. "It is better to trust in the Rock of Ages than to know the age of rocks," counseled William Jennings Bryan.[12]

Reformers turned their attention to their natural surroundings as a new wave of social scientists pointed out the importance of environment. Charles A. Beard reinterpreted American history according to the principles of economic determinism, shocking traditionalists with plausible generalizations that the founding fathers behaved according to their economic class. Economists and sociologists published equally unsettling findings about the relationship between poverty, slums, and crime. "I have an important piece of news for you," a clubwoman told her members in 1904. "Dante is dead. He has been dead for several centuries, and I think it is time that we dropped the study of his inferno and turned attention to our own."[13]

No conservatives ran in the presidential election of 1912. Everyone called himself one kind of Progressive or another, emphasizing reform. The sixteenth amendment to the Constitution permitting Congress to levy direct, graduated taxes—an income tax—had been submitted to the states in 1909 and was approved in February, 1913. The seventeenth amendment calling for the direct election of United States Senators was submitted to the states in May and ratified in two weeks. Perhaps the nineteenth amendment granting full citizenship to all citizens regardless of sex was the most overdue. The woman's rights movement in the United States had been active since the mid-nineteenth century, and had proceeded with various frustrations ever since (fig. 126). ("Call on God," was the now-famous dictum of a philanthropic Mrs. August Belmont to a despairing suffragette, "She will help you.") Successful efforts in other western countries helped the American movement until, in August, 1920, the amendment was ratified.

Religion and reform combined to produce a particular aberration of this abnormal era. Carrie Nation had not chopped up saloons nor pastors called on their congregations to "take the pledge" for naught. After a long fight the Women's Christian Temperance Union, the Anti-Saloon League, and even the Ku Klux Klan succeeded in getting the eighteenth amendment (the prohibition amendment) adopted in 1917 (fig. 127). The new prohibition commissioner promised a revolution overnight: liquor would neither be manufactured "nor sold, nor given away, nor hauled in anything on the surface of the earth or under the earth or in the air," he boasted. But his was an impossible task. Not long after the law went into effect a former Assistant Attorney General in charge of prohibition prosecutions admitted that whiskey could be bought "at almost any hour of the day or night, either in rural districts, the smaller towns, or the cities"[14] (fig. 129). Prohibition is one of the clear examples of the dictatorship of the majority, as well as proof that the minority cannot be successfully controlled in a democratic country.

This widespread religious zeal and the isolationist attitude of the twenties combined to resist immigration. Immigration reached its peak in the years before World War I, and totaled more than 5,000,000 from 1911 to 1920 (fig. 101). With the Bolshevik Revolution in Russia, "internationalism" took on a new anti-American meaning, and foreigners were immediately suspect (fig. 130). Attorney General A. Mitchell Palmer arrested more than 4,000 persons suspected of being Communists. Two anarchists arrested for murder in Massachusetts became a *cause célèbre*. Nicola Sacco and Bartolomeo Vanzetti were finally convicted on flimsy evidence (fig. 193). Liberals and radicals around the world carried on a spectacular propaganda campaign in their behalf, but the conviction was upheld. "I am suffering because I am a radical," said Vanzetti in his last statement, "I am suffering because I am Italian. . . ."[15] They were executed in 1927. The "Red Scare" reached its climax when a terrorist bomb exploded on Wall Street in New York City, killing thirty-eight people.

Dozens of suspected Communists were deported (fig. 130). Others were harassed and arrested without proven charges. The California State Legislature passed an Aliens Land Act which effectively barred Japanese from becoming citizens, the American Federation of Labor supported literacy tests to restrict the number of immigrants, and the anti-Semitic Ku Klux Klan membership reached more than 2,500,000 by 1923 (fig. 134). By 1924 Congress had settled on an immigration formula that was assured to maintain the "racial preponderance [of] the basic strain of our people," and the number of newcomers at Ellis Island declined.[16]

It is unfortunate that the political and social reforms did not extend to the business sector (fig. 97). Businessmen did not want a demonstrably inept government tampering with their money (fig. 102), as government handling of the railroads during the war illustrated (fig. 116). During the war home factories took over markets that foreign companies had supplied, and Americans themselves bought more; they were becoming a consumer society. Henry Ford's first "flivver" rolled off the assembly line in 1909, the fifteen millionth in 1927. President Harding seemed to set the economic pace after the war, stating that "What we want in American is less government in business and more business in government." The bromide seemed true, as government turned to the business community for leadership during war, and business experienced a tremendous boom after the war closed. DuPont and Dow chemicals took over supply of products that were no longer available from German-held North Africa. The economic expansion soon affected other industries as the building boom of the 1920s gave New York City a new skyline (fig. 149). Spurred by the current interpretation of Christian ideals, business seemed en route to perpetual boom. "The man who builds a factory builds a temple," theorized President Calvin Coolidge, "the man who works there worships there." Even Jesus reminded his earthly parents that he had to "be about my father's business" when they suggested that he pay more attention to their instructions. "Brains are wealth and wealth is the chief end of man," said Coolidge, capturing the philosophical creed of the twenties[17] (fig. 117).

The ultimate solution to all the nation's problems was for everyone to own stock in it, said Franklin

D. Roosevelt (fig. 144). "If every family owned even a $100 bond of the United States or a legitimate corporation, there would be no talk of bolshevism, and we would incidentally solve all national problems in a more democratic way." Indeed, the system seemed to be working. The Teapot Dome oil scandal only slowed the growth until it had been removed from the public conscience. In 1928 the United States invested as much in education as the rest of the world combined. The American labor movement (fig. 124) was notably calm compared to other industrial nations, and the muckrakers seemed to have found interests elsewhere. Even Lincoln Steffens, long a critic of capitalism, admitted that "Big Business in America is producing what the Socialists held up as their goal; food, shelter and clothing for all," and economist Stuart Chase suggested that "we lay a wreath on the Uplift Movement in America."[18]

Steffens continued to predict that the full glory of the new order would be exhibited during President Herbert Hoover's administration, and many other knowledgeable men agreed (fig. 143). Average wages were up, business increased each year, and many assumed that this would be the perpetual state of the economy. "Stock prices have reached what looks like a permanently high plateau," concluded Professor Irving Fisher of Yale.

But all was not well, either with the economy or the society. Organized crime was soon recognized as a real problem in the cities (figs. 129, 150); political corruption was so widespread that many citizens lost confidence in the government's ability to remedy the situation (fig. 103). Nor was the booming business community well. Although average wages were up, forty-two percent of all families still earned less than $1,500 per year in 1929. Business profits were up, but they went mostly to the big corporations, who had loaned some thirteen billions of dollars abroad so that foreigners might buy American products. Small businesses were going bankrupt at a startling rate. America had reached the point of manufacturing more than the people could buy, but few realized it because municipal and state governments borrowed more than three billions of dollars to continue the purchases. When the borrowing halted, when products went begging for want of buyers, the stock market crashed. "Black Thursday" was October 24, 1929 (fig. 145). "Wall Street lays an egg," announced the chic show business paper, *Variety*.[19] Two weeks after that fateful day the average price on all stocks was down forty percent. United States Steel dropped from 262 to 22 in three years following Black Thursday. The boom was over. The national euphoria ended.

VI

1930–1945

"THIS NATION asks for action, and action now," declared the new President. "We must act, and act quickly . . . . We must move as a trained and loyal army willing to sacrifice for the good of a common discipline . . . ." The depression-chastened audience gathered on the windy and misty March day cheered hopefully as President Franklin D. Roosevelt took the leadership of a great but troubled nation. "In this dedication of a Nation we humbly ask the blessing of God. May He protect each and every one of us. May He guide me in the days to come."[1]

Former President Herbert Hoover had come into office in 1929 full of confidence that his would be an administration of national prosperity: two chickens in every pot, a car in every garage. He was victimized by the Crash of 1929, crushed by the ensuing Great Depression, and ushered unceremoniously out of office by the voters in 1932. "We are at the end of our rope," he had said at midnight of his last day in office. "There is nothing more we can do."[2]

Franklin Roosevelt had little more idea than

Hoover about what could be done to end the depression that had settled over the country. The statistics were grim. Twenty-five percent of the work force—twelve to fifteen million people—was unemployed (fig. 146). Thousands of stores and factories stood vacant, darkened, decaying. Countless vagabond children roamed the streets and highways, begging for food; twenty percent of New York City's school children suffered from malnutrition (fig. 148). Meanwhile, the suppliers had such surpluses of grain and dairy products that there was no market for the new produce. Farmers had turned to violence: milk trucks in several midwestern states had been stopped, the milk poured into the ditch in a desperate effort to create a new market for their produce. People no longer trusted the mouthings of government officials, nor respected even President Hoover's fruitless efforts to end chaos in the economic community. Testifying before a Congressional committee, the head of the American Federation of Labor predicted that "if the lawfully constituted leadership does not soon substitute action for words, a new leadership, perhaps unlawfully constituted, will arise and act."[3]

Hoping to develop a firm plan, Roosevelt solicited ideas from government and business leaders. A prominent attorney spoke for them all: "I have nothing to offer, either of fact or theory. There is no panacea."[4] The only thing Roosevelt's advisors did agree on was that delay meant further disaster. The budget was in shambles, banks were closing their doors. Without a well-planned approach, Roosevelt simply began (fig. 147). He declared a bank holiday and closed the banks for four days. Then he called Congress into special session, marking the beginning of the "hundred days," during which an almost record amount of legislation was passed. The Emergency Banking Act placed banks under Treasury Department licenses and took the United States off the gold standard. The Unemployment Relief Act created the Civilian Conservation Corps (CCC), the first of the many New Deal "alphabet agencies." The Agricultural Adjustment Act (AAA) was intended to aid farmers, and the Tennessee Valley Authority (TVA) was established to construct dams and power plants in the Tennessee River Valley (fig. 198). Roosevelt also went on the radio with the first of his "fireside chats." Speaking in plain language that the common people could understand, he explained the banking crisis, then admonished, "Let us unite in banishing fear . . . . It is your problem no less than it is mine. Together we cannot fail."[5]

Roosevelt's personal touch turned the tide. He had spoken to every citizen who sat with his family in the living room. He had brought tears of emotion and pride to their eyes, had touched them as had no leader since his distant cousin Theodore Roosevelt. The President had not changed many of the circumstances, for the Depression required fundamental adjustments in the system, but he had involved the common man. Americans cared again, they felt confident again. We "got a man in there who is wise to Congress, wise to our so-called big men," said Will Rogers on behalf of the nation. "The whole country is with him, just so he does something. If he burned down the capitol we would cheer and say 'well, we at least got a fire started anyhow.'"[6]

Cartoonists did not miss the point. From powerful messages of social discontent and the impoverished worker, William Gropper changed his imagery to an abundantly endowed Roosevelt (as Mae West) inviting the Wall Street bankers to "come up and see me sometime" (fig. 152). James Thurber humorously depicted the state of business, and many laughed at their predicament for the first time (fig. 157). The message is still bad, but the drawing is amusing. The mood of the country and the cartoonists had changed.

Roosevelt's efforts toward recovery were only partially successful, but the new federal programs had surmounted the national emergency. Unemployment was still high, farmers still ridded themselves of surplus crops for a government stipend, and the National Recovery Administration (NRA) had proved itself incapable of bringing order out of the chaos of business before the Supreme Court declared it unconstitutional. The "pump-priming" monies spent on public programs were not enough to have any long-range effect on the economy (fig. 156). The situation undoubtedly reminded many people of the well-known Rube Goldberg's cartoons (fig. 173)—in an effort to provide work, raise prices, and feed starving people, the government instituted a program whereby crops were destroyed, unemployed workers were put on the public payroll, and government spending increased. "Do it the hard way," Goldberg advised, as many conservatives thought his convoluted cartoons better designed than Roosevelt's economic measures.

Yet the New Deal had made substantial contributions to the welfare of the country. The Tennessee Valley Authority constituted a successful new approach to flood control and power production (fig. 198). Legislation now guaranteed labor's right to collective bargaining, a minimum wage, and an insurance and retirement program (fig. 154). The cultural life of the country received a boost when the Works Progress Administration undertook the Federal Writers, Arts, and Theater projects (fig. 166). Talented writers, painters, and dancers, now able to exercise their talents in return for a living wage, looked to America as inspiration for creative works and established world-wide reputations reversing the trend that had depicted America as an industrial giant and a mental pygmy (fig. 167).

The AAA and the NRA had served well, but they had not broken the back of the Depression, and the Supreme Court had declared them unconstitutional. Meanwhile, criticism mounted (fig. 163). Father Charles Coughlin, the outspoken radio priest from Detroit, demanded in his weekly broadcasts that the government inflate the currency to put more money in circulation. Dr. Francis Townsend and Senator Huey P. Long (the "Kingfish," as he called himself after the famous character on the *Amos 'n' Andy* radio show) proposed various sorts of "share-the-wealth" programs (fig. 159), and Minnesota Governor Floyd Olson urged nationalization of key industries. The seven and one-half million people still out of work listened for the President's response.

Roosevelt took issues away from his opponents by moving farther to the left himself (fig. 160). He had rejected nationalization of the banks in 1933, but now he classed "business and financial monopoly, speculation, reckless banking, class antagonism, sectionalism, [and] war profiteering" as "old enemies of peace." "They had begun to consider the government of the United States as a mere appendage to their own affairs," he declared. "They are unanimous in their hatred for me—and I welcome their hatred."[7] Roosevelt's overwhelming reelection in 1936, then, was not the result of citizens returning votes for the few welfare dollars they had received, but rather was the reaction to a renewed belief that government might now provide the security and stability that had appeared so precarious only four years before (fig. 162). "Henceforth Democracy has its chief!" said *Paris-Soir*.[8]

Although the level of production had almost returned to the 1929 totals by 1937, Roosevelt realized that he had to take further steps to provide jobs for the millions still unemployed. He also realized, as a result of Supreme Court decisions in the NRA and AAA cases, that much of his program might be in danger of being declared unconstitutional. Taking steps to insure the safety of future legislation and to gain a measure of revenge on the old conservatives on the Court, Roosevelt unveiled his "court packing" plan that would permit the justices to retire at age seventy, but would add a new member (up to a maximum of fifteen) to the Court for every justice who did not retire at age seventy. The plan was widely regarded as a bluff and cartoonist C. K. Berryman expressed much of America's cynicism at the plan for an enlarged Supreme Court (fig. 163). But Roosevelt was serious and abandoned his idea only after conservative Judge Willis Van Devanter, who had been on the bench since 1911, announced his retirement. Other resignations followed, and Roosevelt was able to appoint four New Deal justices from 1937 to 1939.

Despite the continuing crisis at home, Roosevelt's time was gradually consumed by foreign affairs. Joseph Stalin was firmly entrenched in a Russia that President Roosevelt had formally recognized in 1933. Adolf Hitler (fig. 158) had systematically squelched democracy in Germany, and Italian dictator Benito Mussolini had invaded and occupied Ethopia in 1935 (fig. 159). The complexion of democratic Europe had changed radically. Aware of the growing militarism on the continent, Congress passed a series of "neutrality" acts permitting embargo of arms, prohibiting loans to belligerents, and (remembering the *Lusitania*) forbidding American citizens from traveling on ships of belligerents. "In times of so-called peace," said Roosevelt in 1937, "ships are being attacked and sunk by submarines without cause or notice. Nations are fomenting and taking sides . . . . Let no one imagine that America will escape . . . ."[9]

America did not take such warnings seriously. Men were still struggling to feed their families while European militarism was half a world away. "We shun political commitments which might entangle us in foreign wars," said the President. "We avoid connection with the political activities of the League of Nations . . . . We are not isolationists except insofar as we seek to isolate ourselves completely from war."[10] In this the nation supported Roosevelt; public opinon would not have permitted him to become involved. Isolationist sentiment was so strong that when a Japanese airplane intentionally sank a United States gunboat in Chinese waters in 1937, Congress almost passed the Ludlow Amendment that would have required a public referendum before Congress could declare war.

The inevitable conflict began when Germany blitzed hapless Poland on September 1, 1939. As Britain and France declared war on Germany, the United States announced its neutrality. But it was a pro-Allied neutrality based on Roosevelt's sure knowledge that if Germany controlled the eastern Atlantic and Japan the western Pacific, the United States would be isolated in world trade, subject to German and Japanese terms, and victim to their propaganda and sabotage at home. "We must be the great arsenal of democracy," Roosevelt told a 1940 audience as America armed itself (fig. 176). Goods were shipped to Britain on American vessels. Roosevelt allowed the Navy to help British ships locate the dreaded German submarines and cooperated with Britain in a freeze of Japanese assets in American- and British-held territory. Hitler "has every excuse in the world to declare war on us now, if he were of a mind to," the Chief of United States Naval Operations penciled in his diary.[11]

After the fall of France most Americans agreed that the United States could not allow Germany to win all of Europe, but were not yet willing to enter the war. Roosevelt and his advisors decided that if Japan attacked the East Indies the United States would enter the war, even if public opinion did not support the decision. America thus moved toward war in the same wavering, uncertain fashion as in 1917.

Realizing that war with the United States was a certainty, Japanese planners decided to strike first, believing that a crippling blow would further demoralize the United States and perhaps keep it out of the war altogether. The December 7, 1941, air raid on Pearl Harbor could hardly have been more successful: eight battleships were destroyed or damaged, three light cruisers, four other vessels, and 188 airplanes were rendered inoperative. More than 3,000 casualties were reported. But the Japanese had misjudged the American mentality (fig. 179). Facing a nation that only the day before had been isolationist, fragmented politically, and economically destitute, President Roosevelt predicted that this day "will live in infamy." "Hostilities exist," he told the now-united nation. "There is no blinking at the fact that our people, our territory and our interests are in grave danger. With confidence in our armed forces—with the unbounded determination of our people—we will gain the inevitable triumph—so help us God."[12]

All American industrial might was suddenly directed toward war. Never before had the United States so devoted all its productive capacity toward one goal. With fourteen million of its most able citizens serving in the armed forces, American factories still debouched more than ninety billions of dollars worth of war materials and supplies each year. The United States built the strongest army, navy, and air force the world has known, meanwhile increasing the standard of living and the level of consumption at home—an unprecedented feat (fig. 181). It is an accepted economic fact that production and employment are highest during wartime, but no nation had ever been able to produce as much.

American performance and ingenuity in the field matched the production at home. American commanders showed remarkable ability, their tactics consisting primarily of accumulating so many weapons and supplies for an offensive that the human risk was minimal (fig. 182). War had become basically an engineering problem. Over 400,000 Americans died during the war—a tragic figure—but more had perished during the Civil War almost 100 years before.

The most dramatic scientific breakthrough of the war was the successful construction of the atomic bomb. German scientists at work on nuclear fission for several years had proved that atoms of uranium when bombarded with neutrons "split" into atoms of other elements—a revolutionary discovery since it was widely assumed that elements were truly the lowest common denominator of matter and that an atom was its smallest part. If neutrons produced by splitting the uranium atom could be controlled and made to split still more atoms, a chain reaction would be set off, producing, according to Albert Einstein's famous formula ($E=mc^2$), an unprecedented amount of energy. (The energy released from the mass would be multiplied by the speed of light squared!)

The large number of German scientists who had fled or had been deported because they were "non-Aryan" pooled their discoveries with the superior laboratories and equipment of the Americans (fig. 178). Their new studies virtually convinced them that they could produce a bomb of untold power, and that the Germans were at least two years ahead of them in research. After Albert Einstein explained to President Roosevelt the possibilities and the potential assumed to be already in the hands of the Germans in 1939, the President established a committee on uranium.

After Pearl Harbor the government poured millions of dollars more into atomic research without being sure of the best method of splitting the atom (there were five known) or even if a bomb definitely could be produced. But in December, 1942, the Italian political refugee Enrico Fermi, working in a transformed squash court under the stands of Stagg Field at the University of Chicago, proved the neutrons could be controlled and a chain reaction sustained. It was a daring experiment in the midst of an urban center unaware of the potential danger, but from that point on scientists were confident that they could produce a bomb (fig. 186).

As the war in Europe drew to a close and the scientists realized that Germany was not going to develop the bomb, many of them became concerned about how it would be used. "This may sound fantastic," refugee scientist James Franck said in a statement to the President's committee, "but in nuclear weapons we have something entirely new in order of magnitude of destructive power, and if we want to capitalize fully on the advantage their possession gives us, we must use new and imaginative methods."[13] Franck and his colleagues wanted a demonstration of the bomb before representatives of the newly-organized United Nations; if the Japanese did not surrender then, perhaps it could be used against them. A majority of the atomic scientists opposed its surprise use.

With President Roosevelt's death in April, 1945, Harry S Truman inherited the awesome decision. Perhaps the most compelling reason to use the bomb against Japan was not to shorten the war and save American lives, as some have insisted, but rather to demonstrate to the Soviet Union that America was in possession of a dramatically new weapon capable of unprecedented destruction. Secretary of State James Byrnes favored this view and worried only how to justify such an expenditure before Congress. Truman gave the order to proceed, although as Alice Kimball Smith, a personal friend of many of the scientists, later observed, "To have called a halt, contrary to the advice of his most trusted associates, would have required an almost inconceivable exercise of individual initiative."[14] The power of a new age was unleashed on the Japanese cities of Hiroshima and Nagasaki in August, 1945 (fig. 184). Many of the German scientists had worked on the bomb until Hitler's defeat, then worried about the broader implications of their discovery. It was the Japanese fate, said one, to have to take Hitler's medicine (fig. 185).

The United States undoubtedly needed such an advantage because diplomatic blunders had cost the Allies strategic territory. One of the greatest tragedies, although it is far from certain that anything short of full-scale intervention would have turned the tide, was the handling of the Chinese situation (fig. 175). Because China was a potentially strong ally against Japan (fig. 180), American military advisors first wanted to take over Chiang Kai-shek's Nationalist army. When he refused, they urged him to form a coalition government with Mao Tse-Tung and the Communists. Chiang rejected the suggestion and the Americans withdrew, leaving him to eventual defeat and banishment to the offshore island of Formosa. The Communists, who had strong Soviet ties, occupied the Mainland. There was much recrimination and analysis after the Communist victory, but it soon became clear that Mao's forces were much stronger and Chiang's forces much weaker than American military strategists had estimated. No amount of diplomacy could have saved the Mainland for Chiang.

At the end of the war, two strong armies opposed each other in Europe and Asia. Russia had traditionally occupied territory along a line extending from the eastern Baltic Sea to the Black Sea. From time to time it also had controlled the helpless buffer states of Eastern Europe, but Germany had always been the balancing power. Now, the Russians occupied all the buffer states: Czechoslovakia, Yugoslavia, Hungary, part of Austria, and Germany to a line 100 miles west of Berlin. The rest of Europe lay prostrate, the American Army the only force standing between the Red Army and the English Channel. In Asia only American-occupied Japan and the Philippines challenged the expansion of the Chinese and Russians. At a time when monumental decisions were necessary, wrote British Prime Minister Winston Churchill, "The indispensable political direction was lacking.... The United States stood on the scene of victory, master of world fortunes, but without a true and coherent design."[15]

President Truman had presided as the world entered a new age. Now he watched in Fulton, Missouri, as Churchill defined the first epoch of the new age. "A shadow has fallen upon the scenes so lately lighted by the Allied victory," said the recently-retired Prime Minister. "From Stettin in the Baltic to Trieste in the Adriatic, an iron curtain has descended across the Continent. Behind that line lie all the capitals of the ancient states of Central and Eastern Europe. Warsaw, Berlin, Prague, Vienna, Budapest, Belgrade, Bucharest and Sofia, all these famous cities and the populations around them lie in what I must call the Soviet sphere, and all are subject in one form or another, not only to the Soviet influence but to a very high and, in many cases, increasing measure of control from Moscow. ... Whatever conclusions may be drawn from these facts—and facts they are—this is certainly not the Liberated Europe we fought to build up. Nor is it one which contains the essentials of permanent peace."[16] The *Iron Curtain*—the name stuck. The Cold War had begun.

VII

1946–1975

THE COLD WAR and the continual threat of global annihilation were unfamiliar to Americans returning from the war convinced that they had justly defeated the enemy once and for all. They would have agreed with William Jennings Bryan that "destiny . . . is a matter of choice; it is not a thing to be waited for."[1] These Americans had chosen their destiny after being irrevocably provoked by the Japanese and they had won, but for the first time in history the absolute victor had achieved only an uneasy standoff in which the welfare of the country was more precarious than ever, as Daniel Robert Fitzpatrick, cartoonist for the St. Louis *Post-Dispatch*, depicted with his drawing of the awesomeness of atomic power (fig. 186).

Disillusionment and the new awareness had not come immediately; President Roosevelt had been optimistic about the post-war era and told the American people that his friendship with Joseph Stalin of the Soviet Union was built on a firm understanding and common goals. Even before Pearl Harbor a former American ambassador had pointed out that the Russians were fighting for a cause "vital to our security," and in 1943 *Time* magazine named Joseph Stalin, the Soviet dictator, "Man of the Year" as the Russians blunted the German eastward advance and began the long counterattack.[2]

The first disenchantment came when it became apparent that the Soviets would not live up to the terms of the Yalta agreement. Stalin, Roosevelt, and British Prime Minister Winston Churchill had agreed in February, 1945, that Eastern Poland would be awarded to Russia in return for Russia's entry into the Japanese war, but that free elections would be held throughout Poland. Large Polish communities in the United States and the Polish government-in-exile in London required that Roosevelt and Churchill concern themselves with Poland, and Poland, the first country to suffer the Nazi blitz, had become the symbol of liberty and determination throughout the West. "The Poles will have their future in their own hands, with the single limitation that they must honestly follow . . . a policy friendly to Russia," concluded Churchill in one of his more credulous moments. "This is surely reasonable."[3]

But Stalin was not that "reasonable." He did not understand the Americans' concern over Poland, a country not at all strategic to their defense. He had never concealed his goal of self-defensive expansion after the war and surely did not intend to permit free elections. In April a dying Roosevelt wrote Stalin of his "bitter resentment" over the dictator's "discouraging lack of application" of the agreements made at Yalta (fig. 188). In the months following Roosevelt's death, the new American President Harry S Truman (fig. 187) was only slowly disabused of his concept of Russia as the grand ally. Truman desperately chided Foreign Minister Vyacheslav Molotov, demanding that Stalin "carry out that [Yalta] agreement in accordance with his word." Finally realizing that the Russians did not intend to keep their promises, Truman pleaded for understanding: "But you *made* these agreements, didn't you? You *signed* them: Why on earth don't you *keep* them?" Molotov knew the American President had no alternative but to go to war, a decision neither he nor the American people were prepared to make in 1946. "If I had known then what I know now," Truman later remarked, "I would have ordered the troops to the western boundaries of Russia."[4] Even the atomic bomb had not deterred Stalin's effort to fill the power vacuum in Europe, a course so obvious that Alexis de Tocqueville had predicted as early as 1835 that although the United States and Russia were "different and their paths diverse . . . each seems called by some secret design of Providence one day to hold in its hands the destinies of half of the world."[5]

Awareness of the role America would be forced to play in post-war Europe came even more slowly, although before the war ended Stalin had told Harry L. Hopkins, Roosevelt's energetic diplomatic aide, that the United States "was a world power and would have to accept world interests" whether it "wished it or not." Europe was a "rubble-heap" of destroyed factories and farms, disrupted economy, and maimed and wounded people, said Churchill.[6] The once-great colonial powers had descended to second-rate and could no longer dominate or aid the rest of the world, or even protect themselves if the Red Army chose to march to the English Channel. Early in 1947 the British government warned President Truman that because of economic difficulty it could no longer support the Greek government against Communist rebels aided by the Moscow-backed regimes in Yugoslavia, Albania, and Bulgaria.

Truman realized that the Greek government could survive only with outside aid and that American interests were now unwittingly interwoven with European security. But the public would have to be educated. Coming on the heels of complete victory in Europe and the Pacific with abundant assistance from the Soviet Union, tired veterans would not be happy to learn that the one-time ally was now the enemy and that another European war threatened. Most of the Central European countries had already fallen to the Communists and Greece and Turkey appeared to be next, but isolationist Senator Robert Taft of Ohio, a likely candidate for the Republican presidential nomination in the upcoming election, would not be easily swayed. He wanted a return to the pre-war diplomatic simplicity which did not compel the United States to interfere in the affairs of other countries. Secretary of Agriculture Henry Wallace, on the other hand, counted the Soviet Union a genuine friend of America and did not want to damage that relationship.

Yet intervention was necessary to prevent further aggression. "Mr. President," advised Senator Arthur H. Vandenberg of Michigan, a veteran in dealing with the Soviets, "if that's what you want, there's only one way to get it. That is to make a personal appearance before Congress and scare hell out of the country." Meanwhile, the country was getting a good look at the new Soviet policy in action. Early in March the Russians rejected the American plan for sharing its atomic secrets, then demanded that the United States unilaterally destroy all its atomic bombs. Late in April Hungary succumbed to a Communist revolution. "I believe that it must be the policy of the United States to support free peoples who are resisting attempted subjugation by armed minorities or by outside pressure," President Truman told Congress on May 12.[7] Impressed with the ideological justification, Congress voted $400 millions to aid Greece and Turkey in their struggle. The Truman Doctrine, or the policy of containment, has dominated American foreign policy since that day.

In June Secretary of State George C. Marshall followed with a suggestion for restoring any European nation that would develop a plan and assist in its own recovery, even Russia itself. "The initiative . . . must come from Europe," he told a Harvard commencement audience. "The program should be a joint one, agreed to by a number, if not all, of the European nations." Poland and Czechoslovakia quickly accepted Marshall's proposal, but the Soviet Union forced them to withdraw from participation. Sixteen nations sent representatives to Paris to plan for their recovery, and Congress, overcoming initial objections in face of public opinion that now favored resistance to Communism, voted $13 billions for what was now called the Marshall Plan. Still loyal to the Soviet Union, Henry Wallace called it the "Martial Plan." "This is the turning point," said British Foreign Secretary Ernest Bevin, as yet another Communist *coup* pulled Czechoslovakia firmly into the Soviet sphere.[8]

Then American taxpayers received what was probably the rudest shock of all. The Truman Doctrine and the Marshall Plan were not enough; they were only the first steps. A series of crises soon proved that post-war America would have to be ever vigilant, ever mindful of the Communist threat around the world, and ever ready with aid. Hoping to assist European economic recovery, Britain, France, and the United States replaced Russian currency with their own in their three sectors of the occupied city of Berlin, which lay deep in the Russian zone of East Germany. The Soviet response was to shut off all land access to the city on June 19, 1948, threatening the more than two million Berliners with starvation and surrender to the Russians. But President Truman decided, in spite of pessimistic predictions from his Air Force advisors, to supply the city by air. Soon the American and British fliers were delivering 5,000 tons of supplies per day to the beleaguered city.

In addition to the foreign threats, there appeared to be serious security problems at home. In late 1948 Alger Hiss, a bright, young member of the Department of State, was accused of being an ex-Communist and was convicted of perjury in 1950. Between his indictment and conviction, President Truman announced that Russia had exploded its first atomic bomb. Had Hiss and others like him given our secrets to the Russians? The British supplied a partial answer in February, 1950, by announcing that Dr. Klaus Fuchs, an atomic scientist who had worked for both the Americans and the British, had admitted turning over top secret documents to the Russians. Not realizing that there were few atomic secrets to share and that the crucial factor in making a bomb is sophisticated technology and good equipment, Americans were incensed. In the ensuing investigation several Americans who had cooperated with Fuchs were arrested; Julius and Ethel Rosenberg were finally executed for their alleged part in the espionage.

Nor was the Asian front safe. The Chinese Nationalist government, long thought to be a powerful Asian ally of the United States, fled to the island of Formosa in the wake of the Communist takeover of the mainland in December, 1949, and in June, 1950, North Korean Communists crossed the thirty-eighth parallel and invaded South Korea, a government supported by the United States and the newly-founded United Nations.

The nation reeled from this series of confidence-shattering blows. Communist spies within, Communist aggression in Europe and Asia, and a government whose efforts to curb the menace were apparently ineffective. How had the most powerful nation on earth, the sole possessor of the doomsday weapon in 1945, come to this in 1950? Only one man was brash enough to supply simplistic answers. Joseph McCarthy, Republican senator from Wisconsin, made a speech to the Wheeling, West Virginia, Women's Republican Club in February (fig. 192). We were not suffering from weakness, McCarthy told the women. We were suffering from "the traitorous actions of those who have been treated so well by this nation"—men like Alger Hiss in the State Department and scientist Fuchs. Money was pouring into the bottomless pit of Europe, a result of the Marshall Plan; China had been "lost" after assistance totaling more than $3 billions, and now America had entered into an "entangling alliance" (the North Atlantic Treaty Organization, July 21, 1949) for the first time in history. Then, waving a piece of paper in his hand, McCarthy claimed to have the names of dozens of "card-carrying" members of the Communist Party who were at that moment employed by the State Department. "In my opinion the State Department . . . is thoroughly infested with Communists," he charged.[9] Actually he waved a letter from Secretary of State Byrnes to a congressman, making no mention of Communists, but McCarthy had found an insecure America willing to listen to his bombast. Within weeks he was the most talked-of senator in Washington.

For almost four years McCarthy virtually terrorized members of the Senate, Cabinet officers, and bureaucrats throughout the government (fig. 194). When a Senate committee chaired by Millard Tydings of Maryland found McCarthy's charges groundless, McCarthy "invaded" Maryland and helped defeat Tydings, who had seemed assured of reelection until McCarthy's intervention. When President Truman recalled General Douglas McArthur from Korea because of serious indiscretions, McCarthy ardently supported the General, then attacked Secretary of State Marshall for being a part of the Communist conspiracy. In February, 1953, he attacked the United States Information Agency, demanding that books by certain authors not be circulated in their overseas libraries, and some branches of the agency actually conducted book-burnings hoping that the senatorial tyrant would be placated. Then McCarthy turned his venom on the Army, claiming that a certain dentist, already honorably discharged, was a Communist. The Army responded that McCarthy had sought preferential treatment for one of his assistants who had been drafted, and the ensuing hearings were televised. When the nation saw the Senator try to discredit the Army's attorney by charging that a young member of the attorney's firm was a Communist, public opinion swiftly turned against him. The Senate ended his influence a few months later by voting to censure him, only the fourth senator to be censured in 167 years. Nor was the country comforted when the famous FBI counterspy, Herbert Philbrick, revealed at a press conference that the Communists felt that McCarthy had helped them considerably by undermining Americans' confidence in their government.

An advocate of a passive presidency that only carried out Congressional laws, newly-elected Dwight D. Eisenhower hoped to preside over peaceful years during which America restored its calm and confidence (fig. 195). It was his misfortune to be caught in an apparently never-ending arms race. Despite warnings of scientists as to the possible effects, President Truman had ordered in 1950 that work continue on the "so-called hydrogen or super-bomb" (fig. 189). Dr. Albert Einstein had replied that "General annihilation beckons," but the super-bomb had been developed before Eisenhower took office and became the foundation of his foreign policy. When the Russians announced that they, too, possessed the hydrogen bomb less than a year later, Eisenhower remarked that there was now "no real alternative to peace"[10] (fig. 202). Critics immediately questioned Secretary of State John Foster Dulles' policy of "massive retaliation." By sponsoring regional treaty organizations like NATO and by stockpiling nuclear bombs, Dulles hoped to control the small, "brushfire" wars such as the Korean conflict. Dubbed "brinkmanship" by its opponents, Dulles' policy called for massive retaliation against Moscow and Peking if either attempted to spread its influence by violent means. This would be a single and much cheaper deterrent in the long run than a massive defense mechanism spread around the world, he argued, and it would prevent the small conflicts that had proved so costly.

The problem, of course, was that both the United States and Russia had more than enough bombs to destroy the world, and neither would be able to use its atomic weaponry without provoking massive retaliation from the other (fig. 196). No President would start a nuclear war to prevent aggression against a non-strategic country, therefore Eisenhower was left without an alternative on several occasions. When the French were driven out of Vietnam in 1954, Eisenhower not only refused to attack Peking and Moscow, which the policy of massive retaliation would have dictated, he refused to do anything. When Russian tanks rolled into Budapest to quell the October, 1956, revolt, Eisenhower stood by powerless, unwilling to unleash a nuclear attack to free the Hungarian state from the Communist bloc despite pleas from several Hungarian officials for assistance. And when Egypt seized the Suez Canal, provoking an Israeli-British-

French invasion, Eisenhower demanded that they withdraw and leave the canal to the Egyptians. Thus the United States found itself in a costly arms race with the Soviet Union—hydrogen and atomic bombs, missiles, nuclear submarines, aircraft carriers, and long-range bombers—all directed toward a deterrent of doomsday proportions. The brushfire wars that Dulles had hoped to contain continued, forcing the nation to develop that capability too. Americans even became aware of Russia's superior rocket power when the Soviets launched the first unmanned satellite in 1957 (fig. 201).

Even then this fantastic, numbing string of crises did not stop. When Cuban dictator Fulgencio Batista fled leaving the country in the hands of Dr. Fidel Castro in 1959, Eisenhower immediately recognized the new regime, but Castro bitterly denounced the United States, nationalized American businesses, and established close ties with the Russians. A blundering 1962 invasion attempt—the Bay of Pigs (fig. 211)—failed, and Russia began sending medium-range nuclear missiles to the island. "The Americans had surrounded our country with military bases and threatened us with nuclear weapons," Soviet Premier Nikita Khrushchev later wrote in his memoirs, "and now they would learn just what it feels like to have enemy missiles pointing at you; we'd be doing nothing more than giving them a little of their own medicine."[11] President John F. Kennedy mobilized the National Guard and blockaded Cuba (fig. 212). For a few brief moments the world teetered on the "abyss of nuclear destruction and the end of mankind," wrote Attorney General Robert Kennedy.[12] The crisis defused just as quickly. When President Kennedy assured the Soviets that the United States would not invade Cuba, Khrushchev ordered the missiles removed.

Americans who sighed with relief at the termination of the "missile crisis" did not know that even then President Kennedy was considering sending more Americans to assist the South Vietnamese in "their war" (fig. 233). France and Britain had tried to solve the Vietnamese situation with the Geneva Agreement of 1954, which promised free elections in South Vietnam in 1956, but when President Ngo Dinh Diem refused to permit the elections the Communist rebels resumed their activity. By 1961 there were some 3,200 Americans in Vietnam as military advisors. That number increased to 16,000 by the end of 1963 and to more than 184,000 in another year. Meanwhile, President Lyndon B. Johnson had demanded and gotten a "blank check"—the Gulf of Tonkin resolution—from the Congress after North Vietnamese gunboats allegedly attacked American destroyers in international waters. Authorized to "repel any armed attack against the forces of the United States and to prevent further aggression," Johnson upped the commitment (fig. 225). More than 385,000 Americans battled Communist troops throughout South Vietnam by the end of 1965, more than 530,000 by 1969. Of course, Red China and Russia had increased their aid to North Vietnam, and the United States found itself in a full-scale conventional war in Vietnam—the dreaded land war in Asia that previous Presidents had warned against and that Johnson had promised to avoid during his 1964 campaign (fig. 226). Raw nerves were worn further when, at the height of the conflict, North Koreans seized the American spyship, USS *Pueblo*, threatening to renew the Korean conflict.

The Vietnamese intervention did not end until January, 1973, when President Richard Nixon's foreign affairs advisor, Dr. Henry Kissinger, reached agreement with North Vietnam's Le Duc Tho that established a cease-fire in Vietnam and allowed the United States to withdraw its troops (fig. 240). More explosives had been dropped on Vietnam between 1964 and 1968 than on Germany and Japan during all World War II. More than 46,000 Americans had died by 1973, and the war cost some $20 billions per year for the United States alone. Americans, meanwhile, were treated to the spectacles of a massacre of South Vietnamese civilians by American troops at My Lai, "tiger cage" prisons of South Vietnam, and the brutal television documentaries that brought this war closer to the American public than any other war. Kissinger and Le Duc Tho received the Nobel Peace Prize for their efforts, but the war was not finished. It had only stalled.

President Johnson tried to deal with difficult domestic crises simultaneously. In the midst of a massive civil rights movement, riots broke out on an unprecedented scale (fig. 223) in Los Angeles, Newark, Detroit—riots inspired by frustration and aimed toward nothing, riots triggered in one case by a white policeman stopping a black man for a traffic violation, in another case by the shocking assassination of civil rights leader Dr. Martin Luther King (fig. 216). As the nation began to adjust to another crisis, a short supply of oil, the greatest political scandal in the nation's history was unveiled before a disbelieving public (fig. 242).

Watergate, soon to become the code word for any kind of government bungling or corruption, began in 1972 with the "White House plumbers" burglary of the Democratic Party Headquarters in the Watergate apartment complex in Washington, D. C. (fig. 245). By the end of 1974 three cabinet officers, Nixon's two closest advisors, and a number of lesser officials including the acting head of the FBI had been convicted of perjury or obstructing justice or discredited, and Nixon himself had resigned. In an unrelated incident, Vice-President Spiro Agnew (fig. 234), the most outspoken law and order advocate with the possible exception of Alabama Governor George Wallace (fig. 238), pleaded guilty to income tax evasion and accepted a light sentence in exchange for his resignation. The "credibility gap" of the Johnson-Nixon years widened to include government officials on all levels—county, city, state, and federal—as Watergate dumbfounded even the most cynical observer. All government agencies, even prosecution of the Vietnam war, were affected by the backlash of this "third-rate burglary" that escalated into the greatest political scandal this country has known (figs. 245, 246, 247, 248, 249).

The public had not recovered from these unprecedented events when the Watergate-related investigations revealed many other "incidents." The giant International Telephone and Telegraph Company admitted giving Nixon's reelection campaign fund $400,000 in return for less vigorous prosecution in an antitrust case, and Attorney General Richard Kleindienst was convicted of perjury for testifying that Nixon had not pressured him to discontinue his ITT investigation. Several major airline companies confessed that they, too, had illegally contributed to the campaign fund and accepted fines. President Nixon's personal lawyer was convicted of forging the date on the document transferring Nixon's Vice-Presidential papers to the National Archives so Nixon could qualify for a huge tax deduction (Congress having since outlawed such deductions). Nixon then owed more than $500,000 in back taxes and interest (fig. 244).

Gerald Ford of Michigan, the man Nixon had appointed to replace Agnew according to the new twenty-fifth amendment, became President August 9, 1974 (fig. 250). One of his first acts was to grant Nixon a complete pardon, saying that the country had to be unified to face the important matters of the future. As President Ford struggled with an economy suffering from double-digit inflation (figs. 203, 204), rising health care costs, and increasing environmental problems (fig. 259), it became his duty to preside over the first American defeat in war—the fall of South Vietnam. Despite the 1973 agreement in Paris, both sides had violated the cease-fire, and President Nixon would have resumed bombing North Vietnam had he not been so involved in Watergate that he did not want to risk additional criticism. The Communist Viet Cong and North Vietnamese troops gradually tightened the circle around Saigon. When Congress turned down the Ford administration request for $722 millions in early 1975, there seemed no way that the South could hold out. President Ford brought American participation to a halt just days before the final collapse, telling a Tulane University audience that recriminations must cease. The war, he said, is "finished—as far as America is concerned."[13] Only Ford's dramatic rescue of the crewmen of the American merchant ship *Mayaguez*, captured by Cambodian gunboats, salvaged respect for proud Americans unused to losing a war.

The era from World War II until the present has been marked by the perpetual instant, the long-awaited instant that might bring holocaust, the instant captured on film that is preserved forever, the instant (as in the splitting of the atom) that seems to open eternal, infinite possibilities. Such discoveries obviously affect the work of sensitive artists. Fitzpatrick caricatured the threat (fig. 186), while Don Hesse captured the feeling of an endless quest for the ultimate energy (fig. 189); Garrett Price pictured the frustration of many Americans in dealing with modernism (fig. 218), and Benny Goodman (fig. 207) and Louis Armstrong (fig. 219) represent the return of the "good old days." The American spirit was captured by beatniks (fig. 206), hippies, and the apparently overwhelming desire to return to nature in an urban society—organic foods, the youth cult (figs. 229, 257), drug addiction (fig. 256), protection of the environment (figs. 259, 260): all seem to represent fairly simple desires twisted by a modern society.

The painter Jackson Pollock could have spoken for many of his fellow artists in 1950 when he pointed out that, "The modern painter cannot express this age, the airplane, the atom bomb, the radio, in the old forms of the renaissance or any other past culture." The search for new media has given us the photographic composition of Mark Podwall's Statue of Liberty (fig. 261) and Marisol's *LBJ* (fig. 220). The grind of the daily newspaper, meanwhile, has turned up numerous excellent draftsmen who bring the traditional talents of an artist to cartoons: Pat Oliphant (fig. 249), Draper Hill (fig. 245), and Paul Szep (fig. 231) are among the outstanding penmen publishing in daily newspapers, while Leslie Illingworth and David Levine display their unusually good drawing techniques and sharp wit in several newspapers and magazines. Perhaps John Cayea's *Eagle* is the most poignant, the drawing best capable of providing an icon for the 1970s (fig. 263).

Many questions remain unanswered as this great experiment moves toward its 200th birthday—almost imponderable questions that we might have turned away from because we feared the answer. What kind of balance will ultimately be achieved between personal freedom and modern society? Can a truly heterogeneous society, including radicals who would fight violently for their goals, survive under a Constitution intended for a homogeneous nation that originally worshipped the same God, was basically white, and was committed to peaceful settlement of differences? This potential was greatly acerbated with public knowledge that even a brilliant student could produce an atomic bomb.

Although these questions remain unresolved, the peaceful, democratic principles established by the founding fathers still survive. Cayea personifies in his strong drawing the confidence that the entire nation felt as the government peacefully changed hands in 1974. Few citizens even considered the possibility of armed resistance. After a long and eventful life, Thomas Jefferson concluded that "we can no longer say there is nothing new under the sun, for this whole chapter in the history of man is new." The "experiment of changing the constitution by assembling the wise men of the state, instead of assembling armies, will be worth as much to the world as the former examples we have given it." Benjamin Franklin was more modest: "We are making Experiments," he wrote a friend in 1786, but "we are . . . in the right Road of Improvement."[14]

RON TYLER
Curator of History
Amon Carter Museum

NOTES

I

¹Arthur M. Schlesinger, *The Birth of the Nation* (New York: Alfred A. Knopf, 1969), 227.
²Henry Steel Commager, *Jefferson, Nationalism, and the Enlightenment* (New York: George Braziller, 1975), 12–13.
³Ibid., 159.
⁴Daniel J. Boorstin, *The Americans: The National Experience* (New York: Random House, 1965), 391.
⁵Dumas Malone, *Jefferson the Virginian*, Vol. 1 of *Jefferson and His Time* (5 vols.; Boston: Little, Brown and Company, 1948–1974), 388.
⁶Schlesinger, *Birth of the Nation*, 227.
⁷James Thomas Flexner, *Washington, the Indispensable Man* (Boston: Little, Brown and Company, 1974), 74.
⁸Harvey Wish, *Society and Thought in America* (2 vols.; New York: David McKay Company, Inc., 1950), I, 200; Adams to Jefferson, Aug. 24, 1815, in John Adams, *Works*, ed. by Charles Francis Adams (10 vols.; Boston: Little, Brown and Company, 1850–1856), X, 172.
⁹Commager, *Jefferson*, 20.
¹⁰Henry Bamford Parkes, *The American Experience* (New York: Vintage Books, 1959), 39–40.
¹¹Commager, *Jefferson*, 39, 53.
¹²Daniel J. Boorstin, *The Americans: The Colonial Experience* (New York: Random House, 1958), 283.
¹³Commager, *Jefferson*, 176, 179.
¹⁴Oscar Handlin, *The Americans: A New History of the People of the United States* (Boston: Atlantic Monthly Press, Little, Brown and Company, 1963), 150.
¹⁵Commager, *Jefferson*, 44.
¹⁶Adrienne Koch (ed.), *The American Enlightenment* (New York: George Braziller, 1965), 188.
¹⁷Commager, *Jefferson*, 30, 85.
¹⁸Ibid., 153–154.

II

¹Commager, *Jefferson*, 161–162.
²John A. Garraty, *The American Nation: A History of the United States* (New York: Harper & Row and American Heritage Publishing Company, Inc., 1966), 202.
³Boorstin, *The National Experience*, 221.
⁴Parkes, *The American Experience*, 43, 190.
⁵Koch, *The American Enlightenment*, 484.
⁶Richard Hofstadter, William Miller, and Daniel Aaron, *The American Republic* (2 vols.; Englewood Cliffs, New Jersey: Prentice-Hall, Inc., 1959), I, 395.
⁷Commager, *Jefferson*, 161.

III

¹Contrary to traditional writing, slavery was profitable and rapidly expanding—Texas was the fastest growing slave state in the South—at the time of the Civil War. These slightly startling findings are thoroughly documented in Robert William Fogel and Stanley L. Engerman, *Time on the Cross: The Economics of American Negro Slavery* (2 vols.; Boston: Little, Brown and Company, 1974), I, 4–6.
²Kenneth M. Stampp (ed.), *The Causes of the Civil War* (Englewood Cliffs, N. J.: Prentice-Hall, Inc., Spectrum Books, 1959), 132.
³Ibid., 107.
⁴Robert W. Johannsen (ed.), *The Lincoln-Douglas Debates* (New York: Oxford University Press, 1965), 254.
⁵Ibid., 249.
⁶Monroe Lee Billington, *The American South* (New York: Charles Scribner's Sons, 1971), 136.
⁷Mrs. David Winningham, "Sam Houston and Slavery," *Texana*, III (Summer, 1965), 93–104.
⁸Hofstadter, Miller, and Aaron, *American Republic*, II, 7.

IV

¹Alistair Cooke, *Alistair Cooke's America* (New York: Alfred A. Knopf, 1974), 259.
²Daniel J. Boorstin, *The Americans: The Democratic Experience* (New York: Random House, 1973), 3, 5.
³Garraty, *The American Nation*, 475.

⁴Boorstin, *The Democratic Experience*, 418.
⁵Mark Twain, "The Temperance Crusade and Women's Rights," in Charles Neider (ed.), *The Complete Essays of Mark Twain* (Garden City, N. Y.: Doubleday, 1963), 667.
⁶Boorstin, *The Democratic Experience*, 419, 504.
⁷Ibid., 504, 515.

V

¹Hofstadter, Miller, and Aaron, *American Republic*, II, 357.
²Ibid., II, 442.
³William E. Leuchtenburg, *The Perils of Prosperity, 1914–32* (Chicago: University of Chicago Press, 1958), 269.
⁴Hofstadter, Miller, and Aaron, *American Republic*, II, 386.
⁵Leuchtenburg, *Perils of Prosperity*, 12–13.
⁶Ibid., 13–14.
⁷Ibid., 142.
⁸Wesley M. Burnside, *Maynard Dixon: Artist of the West* (Provo, Utah: Brigham Young University Press, 1974), 65.
⁹Leuchtenburg, *Perils of Prosperity*, 104–105.
¹⁰Ibid., 58.
¹¹Hofstadter, Miller, and Aaron, *American Republic*, II, 427.
¹²Leuchtenburg, *Perils of Prosperity*, 219.
¹³Samuel P. Hays, *The Response to Industrialism, 1885–1914* (Chicago: University of Chicago Press, 1957), 73.
¹⁴Leuchtenburg, *Perils of Prosperity*, 214–215.
¹⁵Harold C. Syrett (ed.), *American Historical Documents* (New York: Barnes & Noble, Inc., 1960), 357.
¹⁶Maldwyn Allen Jones, *American Immigration* (Chicago: University of Chicago Press, 1960), 265, 275–276.
¹⁷Leuchtenburg, *Perils of Prosperity*, 188–189; Hofstadter, Miller, and Aaron, *American Republic*, II, 442.
¹⁸Leuchtenburg, *Perils of Prosperity*, 137, 201–202.
¹⁹Cooke, *America*, 327.

VI

¹Syrett (ed.), *American Historical Documents*, 362–365.
²Arthur M. Schlesinger, Jr., *The Crisis of the Old Order, 1919–1933* (Boston: Houghton Mifflin Company, 1957), 1.
³Ibid., 3–4.
⁴Ibid., 5.
⁵Arthur M. Schlesinger, Jr., *The Coming of the New Deal* (Boston: Houghton Mifflin Company, 1958), 13.
⁶Ibid., 13.
⁷Frank Freidel, "The New Deal in Historical Perspective," in Barton J. Bernstein and Allen J. Matusow (eds.), *Twentieth-Century America: Recent Interpretations* (New York: Harcourt, Brace & World, Inc., 1969), 256.
⁸Arthur M. Schlesinger, Jr., *The Politics of Upheaval, 1935–1936* (Boston: Houghton Mifflin Company, 1960), 656.
⁹Syrett (ed.), *American Historical Documents*, 379.
¹⁰Frank Freidel, *America in the Twentieth Century* (2nd ed.; New York: Alfred A. Knopf, 1965), 371.
¹¹Ibid., 384.
¹²Syrett (ed.), *American Historical Documents*, 391–392.
¹³Boorstin, *The Democratic Experience*, 589.
¹⁴Ibid., 590.
¹⁵Winston S. Churchill, *Triumph and Tragedy* (Boston: Houghton Mifflin Company, 1953), 455.
¹⁶Louis J. Halle, *The Cold War as History* (New York: Harper & Row, Publishers, 1967), 103–104.

VII

¹Boorstin, *The Democratic Experience*, 557.
²John A. Garraty, *The American Nation: A History of the United States* (2 vols.; New York: Harper & Row, 1975), II, 775.
³Ibid., II, 778.
⁴Herbert Agar, *The Price of Power: America Since 1945* (Chicago: University of Chicago Press, 1957), 14–15, 17–18, 59.
⁵Alexis de Tocqueville, *Democracy in America*, ed. by J. P. Mayer and Max Lerner, trans. by George Lawrence (New York: Harper & Row, 1966), 379.
⁶Agar, *Price of Power*, 19, 72.
⁷Ibid., 71.
⁸Ibid., 74.
⁹Ibid., 108.
¹⁰Ibid., 52.
¹¹Edward Crankshaw (Intro.), *Khrushchev Remembers*, trans. and ed. by Strobe Talbott (Boston: Little, Brown and Company, 1970), 494.
¹²Robert F. Kennedy, *Thirteen Days: A Memoir of the Cuban Missile Crisis* (New York: W. W. Norton & Company, 1969), 23.
¹³*The New York Times*, April 27, 1975, Sec. 4, p. 1.
¹⁴Koch, *American Enlightenment*, 105, 342.

Fig. 1. *Join or Die*. Benjamin Franklin. May 9, 1754, in the *Pennsylvania Gazette*. Woodcut. 2 × 2 7/8 in. Courtesy Collections of The Library Company of Philadelphia.

As both French and Indian forces on the frontier threatened the colonies, and Britain appeared either incapable of or unwilling to help, Benjamin Franklin urged the delegates to the Albany Convention of 1754 to prepare for their own defense. In addition to some "short hints" for expansion, Franklin offered the delegates *Join or Die* to suggest forcefully that their destiny lay in their own hands. He urged an intercolonial council for defense with taxing powers, an army, fortifications, an expansion plan, and a Crown-appointed presiding officer. The individual colonies rejected his plan, but he believed until his death that its adoption would have prevented the Revolution. Widely thought to be the first cartoon appearing in an American newspaper, *Join or Die* was used again in 1765 (with Georgia added by Paul Revere) as Britain was trying to force the Stamp Act onto the colonists.

Fig. 2. *The Deplorable State of America or Sc---h Government*. Anonymous. 1765. Engraving. 9 5/16 × 15 1/4 in. Courtesy The Lilly Library, Indiana University, Bloomington.

This complicated cartoon depicts America as an Indian being offered the Stamp Act (in the form of Pandora's box) by Britannia. Minerva, the goddess of wisdom, advises America to "take it not," while Liberty is overcome by the serpent with the thistle attached (representing Scottish Lord Bute, former advisor to King George III) and a bystander prays that the Liberty Tree might be allowed to stand. In the left background the enraged American colonists describe the gallows as "Fit entertainment for St[am]p M[e]n." The "Sc---h" in the title suggests that Lord Bute still has influence over George III, although he was forced to resign because he accepted a French bribe.

Fig. 3. *The Repeal. Or the Funeral Procession of Miss Americ-Stamp.* Anonymous. 1766. Etching. 11 3/4 × 18 1/4 in. Courtesy The Museum of Art, Carnegie Institute, Pittsburgh.

Colonial opposition to the Stamp Act was so violent that Parliament finally repealed it in 1766. This British print appeared within two weeks to haunt George Grenville, Chancellor of the Exchequer, who is shown taking his dead "child," the Stamp Act, to the Family Vault, surmounted by skulls dated 1715 and 1745, the dates of two unsuccessful Stewart rebellions and thus the burying place of other lost Whig-supported causes. The officiating priest is "Anti Sejanus" (Against Disunion), probably a reference to a pamphlet supporting the act published by Lord Bute, the mourner in the plaid vest, and the standards behind the priest parody the Stamp designs and show the Rose of England entwined with the Thistle of Scotland, another reference to the Scottish influence on George III.

Fig. 4. *The Colossus*. Anonymous. 1766. Etching. 8 1/2 × 6 5/8 in. Courtesy American Antiquarian Society, Worcester, Mass.

With the repeal of the Stamp Act and the fall of the Grenville government, George III turned in 1766 to William Pitt (the Elder) to form a government. The "Great Commoner" had been known for his pro-American views, but the public widely accepted the rumors that he had agreed to serve as George's Prime Minister in return for a small pension (one of the main crutches shown in the cartoon). This cartoonist pictures Pitt caught in the middle of the debate: conservatives did not trust him because of his colonial views, thus one crutch is shown stirring up sedition in the colonies. Because of rumors that he had "sold out" to the king, and therefore turned against Parliament, he is shown about to crush St. Stephens Chapel, a euphemism for Parliament. The cartoonist also suggests that Pitt's popularity rests only with the "Royal Exchange," that is, with commercial interests, while bubbles of loyalty, honesty, and public spirit break upon it. The accompanying verse (to be said with a mock French accent) accuses Pitt of pro-American feelings only to make himself a nabob (millionaire who enriched himself in colonial dealings) there.

Fig. 5. *The Able Doctor, or America Swallowing the Bitter Draught.* Anonymous. 1774. Engraving. 4 1/16 × 6 7/16 in. (sight). Courtesy The Newberry Library, Chicago.

In 1774 tea became the symbol for all British oppressions against the colonies. Lord North had hoped to rescue the East India Company from its financial difficulties by permitting it to sell directly to the colonies, but he imposed a tax on the tea, which the colonists rejected although they were then able to buy tea cheaper than Englishmen. This pro-American cartoon that first appeared in the *London Magazine* shows Lord North forcing tea down America's throat, while Chief Justice Peter Oliver holds America's hands and his brother, Lieutenant Governor Andrew Oliver, holds her feet. Governor Thomas Hutchinson of Massachusetts and King George III look on approvingly. The grim prediction "Boston cannonaded" in the background never came to pass. This English cartoon was copied in both Ireland and America (by Paul Revere); this is the Irish copy.

Fig. 6. *A New Method of Macarony Making as Practised at Boston in North America.* Carington Bowles. 1774. Engraving and etching. 14 1/2 × 19 1/2 in. Courtesy The Museum of Art, Carnegie Institute, Pittsburgh.

When the Commissioner of Customs, John Malcomb, tried to collect customs duties in Boston, he was subjected to rough treatment, required to drink enormous quantities of tea, and threatened with hanging. The term "macarony" refers to the Italian word for dandy or fop, and Malcomb is being turned into a dandy "American style," that is, tar and feathers.

Fig. 7. *A Certain Cabinet Junto*. Paul Revere. 1775. Engraving. 3 15/16 × 6 1/2 in. Courtesy American Antiquarian Society, Worcester, Mass.

Britain did not abandon the idea of taxing the colonies with the repeal of the Stamp Act, nor the idea of punishing them with the failure of the Coercive Acts. Parliament declared the colonists in rebellion and voted in 1775 to send troops to quell the uprising. Inspired by a 1773 British print, Paul Revere saw the British action as part of a design whereby the colonists would be stripped of their "Civil & Religs liberty" and etched the "Cabinet Junto" for the *Royal American Magazine* in 1775. Liberty watches the proceedings from afar, praying to the Lord that "our hope is in thee."

Fig. 8. *Poor Old England Endeavoring to Reclaim His Wicked American Children*. Anonymous. 1777. Etching. 9 3/4 × 13 3/4 in. Courtesy William L. Clements Library, University of Michigan, Ann Arbor.

A weak and crippled England is having a difficult time holding onto his American colonies in this cartoon, produced after the American successes at Trenton and Princeton. Old England is trying to bring them back under his influence, and the whip is ready to administer punishment should he succeed. Below the caption is a line from Shakespeare's *Henry IV*: "Thereby is England maimed and fain to go with a staff, but that my puissance holds it up," intended to suggest how weak and feeble England has become.

Fig. 9. *Loon Na Werk*. [Reward of Labor.] Anonymous. 1780. Mezzotint. 6 1/2 × 9 in. Courtesy James Ford Bell Library, University of Minnesota, Minneapolis.

This print was published in The Hague or Amsterdam in commemoration of the fact that John Paul Jones (known as John Paul until about 1773) was permitted to leave the Dutch port of Texel with his prizes of war. It shows France, Spain, and America whipping the English dog, while Holland holds the dog's tail with a forked stick. In the background, Jones is beating a crowned lady who is stripped to the waist and tied to a post. One of the most able American captains, Jones had just come from a successful encounter with HMS *Serapis*.

 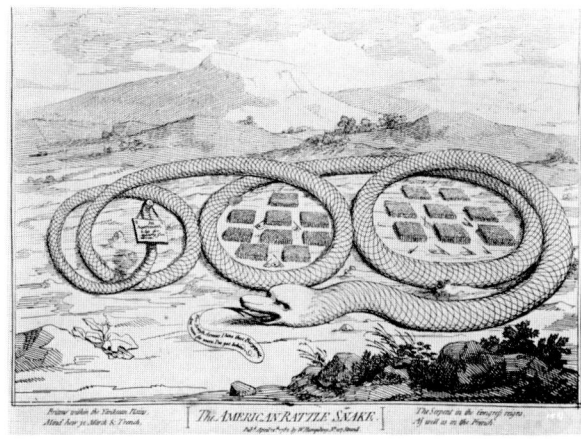

Fig. 10. [John Bull in despair as Cornwallis surrenders Yorktown.] Anonymous. 1781. Engraving. 6 13/16 × 10 1/2 in. Courtesy The Pierpont Morgan Library, New York City.

As Lord Cornwallis surrenders Yorktown to Washington's and Lafayette's combined forces in October, 1781, John Bull, in the foreground despairs over the defeat and over his empty war chest, the gold expended trying to hold onto the American colonies. This Dutch engraver also includes a reference to Europe's view of Britain, as the Frenchman, the Spaniard, and the Dutchman gesture derisively toward Britain's emaciated cow of commerce.

Fig. 11. *The American Rattle Snake*. James Gillray. Apr. 12, 1782. Etching. 9 5/16 × 12 11/16 in. Courtesy the Library of Congress, Washington, D.C.

This cartoon was published on the day the peace negotiations between America and Britain began in Paris. It shows the American rattlesnake coiled around two British armies, Burgoyne at Saratoga and Cornwallis at Yorktown, with yet a third "Apartment to lett."

Fig. 12. *The Tea-Tax-Tempest, or Old Time with His Magick Lanthern.* W. Humphreys. 1783. Colored engraving. 9 15/16 × 13 15/16 in. Courtesy The Lilly Library, Indiana University, Bloomington.

In this elegant and sophisticated cartoon, Humphreys depicts Europe's view of the American Revolution. Using a magic lantern, Time is projecting a scene from the Battle of Saratoga onto the screen. In the center, tea being brewed on a fire of stamped paper has exploded as a French cock fans the fire. In the audience, Europe looks anguishingly toward Asia while Africa seems frightened. According to this print, most of Europe favored the new United States.

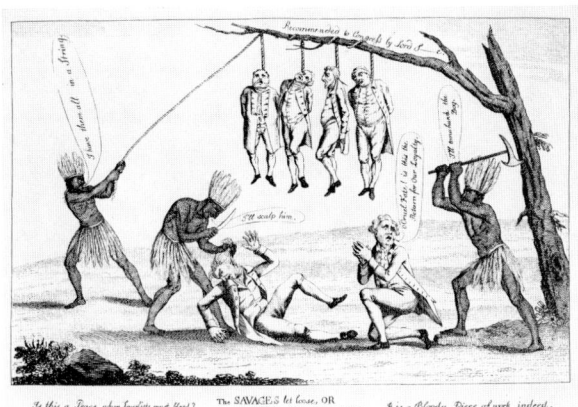

Fig. 13. *The Savages Let Loose, or the Cruel Fate of the Loyalists.* W. Humphreys. 1783. Engraving. 10 15/16 × 14 9/16 in. (sight). Courtesy The Newberry Library, Chicago.

Loyalists fared badly in the American Revolution; many returned to England. All the British negotiators were able to secure on their behalf at the peace conference were two provisions that proved unenforceable: that Congress would "recommend" to the states that property taken during the fighting be returned, and that further confiscation would cease. Lord Shelburne's government fell because of public indignation over what most Britishers felt was abandonment of loyal subjects of the crown.

Fig. 14. *The General P--s, or Peace.* J. Barron. 1783. Hand colored etching. 12 5/16 × 8 5/16 in. Courtesy the Library of Congress.

The Peace of Paris, which ended the American Revolution, was signed on November 3, 1782. It took effect when Britain and France, and Britain and Spain had signed separate agreements on January 20, 1783. James Rivington of New York published a broadside on March 25 proclaiming the treaty and explaining its terms. This English print also announced the "General Peace," as Britain, the Netherlands, the United States, Spain, and France have laid down their drums, swords, and flags. The poet has appended verse to call attention to the unusual event: "The belligerent powers, like good neighbours agree,/ A little time past Sirs, who would have thought this,/ That they'd so soon come to a general P---?"

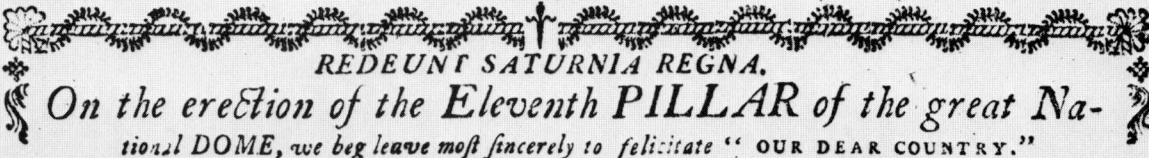

Fig. 15. *The Federal Edifice.* Anonymous. 1788. Engraving. 3 1/2 × 5 1/2 in. Courtesy The New-York Historical Society, New York City.

Having proved the unworkableness of the Articles of Confederation, the United States promulgated the Constitution in 1787. Delaware was the first to approve in December. Only nine states were required before the new document took effect, but for reasons of unity unanimous approval obviously was desired. This print was issued July 26, 1788, to commemorate New York's ratification of the Constitution. Although the two remaining pillars appear to be crumbling, the prophesies printed above each of them proved correct: of North Carolina the printer predicted "Rise it will." By Rhode Island, "The foundation good—it may yet be saved." Rhode Island finally made ratification unanimous in 1790.

Fig. 16. *The Times; a Political Portrait*. Anonymous. c. 1795. Engraving. 12 1/4 × 17 3/4 in. Courtesy The New-York Historical Society, New York City.

Despite the unanimous approval of the Constitution, partisan politics during the formative years of our nation were as bitter as at any other time except the Civil War. Under Washington's able leadership two political factions formed: the Federalists, led by Alexander Hamilton, who believed in a strong central government; and the Democratic-Republicans, led by Jefferson, who favored a weaker central government. In this cartoon, probably one of many that were done about Washington, the President sits high atop the federal cabriolet leading the government, while Jefferson and his two pro-French supporters, Albert Gallatin and Citizen Edmond Genet, try to "stop de wheels of gouvernement." The partisanship demonstrated in this early cartoon is only representative of the fact that the founding fathers earnestly believed that the fate of the nation rested on their being in office at a particular time, to the exclusion of their political opponents.

Fig. 17. *Congressional Pugilists*. Anonymous. 1798 (1864 restrike for *Historical Magazine*). Engraving. 10 3/16 × 12 15/16 in. Courtesy Independence National Historical Park Collection, Philadelphia.

When Congressman Roger Griswold of Connecticut spread an old rumor that Congressman Matthew Lyon of Vermont had been required to wear a wooden sword because of cowardice in the field, Lyon responded by spitting in Griswold's face. A fracas ensued after Congress failed to expel Lyon. The men were separated without dealing any real harm to each other, but they were not satisfied. A few days later they again fought, inspiring this cartoon. They were finally separated, and everyone was quite tired of the affair. Two other cartoons commemorate their altercations.

Fig. 18. *The Gerry-Mander*. Elkanah Tisdale. Mar. 26, 1812, in the Boston *Weekly Messenger*. Woodcut with set type. 19 1/2 × 9 1/4 in. Courtesy The New-York Historical Society, New York City.

When the Democratic majority arbitrarily realigned the voting district in Essex County, Massachusetts, so that the Republican vote in a single town (Marblehead) would outnumber the Federalist vote in eleven other towns, Tisdale designed a new American political monster, the "gerry-mander." The cartoon is made by adding fangs, wings, and claws to a map of the voting district; the name comes from combining Republican Governor Elbridge Gerry's name with part of the word salamander. The district was redrawn the following year.

Fig. 19. *Vente des deserts du Scioto, par des Anglo-americains.* [Sale of the deserts of Scioto, by the Anglo-Americans.] Anonymous. Brumaire an 6eme. [Oct. 23 to Nov. 21, 1799.] Engraving. 11 1/2 × 12 7/8 in. Courtesy The Chicago Historical Society.

As the new United States began to spread into the land of the Old Northwest, land speculators invested in the virgin acres and turned quick dollars by selling to people unfamiliar with what they were buying. The caption of the cartoon explains that "Citizen Mignard signs today for some English companions who are selling imaginary lands in the United States. The better to ensnare dupes, they draw geological maps, converting rocky deserts into fertile plains, show roads cutting through impassable cliffs and offer shares in lands which do not belong to them."

Fig. 20. *Property Protected, a la Francoise*. Ansell (?). 1798. Colored engraving. 10 3/8 × 17 1/16 in. Courtesy The Lilly Library, Indiana University, Bloomington.

When President John Adams sent three American envoys to Paris to assist Charles C. Pinckney in securing an improvement in American-French relations, Talleyrand, the French foreign minister, refused to receive them. Meanwhile, three of his unofficial agents contacted the Americans and suggested that a quarter of a million dollars gratuity for Talleyrand, a loan for France, and an indemnity for criticism that Adams had made against France would correct the problem. The Americans refused the terms, and Adams made the correspondence public, referring to the French officials as X, Y, and Z. This cartoon shows the lovely, young America being plundered by five Frenchmen representing the five Directors of the French government. John Bull (England) watches amused from "Shakespeare's Cliff," while the rest of Europe discusses the situation.

57

THE PROVIDENTIAL DETECTION

OGRABME, or, The American Snapping-turtle.

Fig. 21. *The Providential Detection*. Anonymous. 1800. Etching. 14 3/8 × 13 7/8 in. Courtesy American Antiquarian Society, Worcester, Mass.

While serving as Secretary of State under President Washington, Thomas Jefferson made no secret of his feeling that friendship with France was better for the young nation than alliance with Great Britain (friendship with both being impossible because they were established rivals). When Jefferson campaigned for the presidency in 1800, this Federalist cartoonist pictured his fear that Jefferson would prostrate the country before the French altar. The American Eagle has just taken the Constitution from Jefferson, who would have burned it just as he had certain classic works as well as the Federalist newspaper *Aurora*. In his right hand he holds the incriminating letter to his Italian friend Phillip Mazzei to whom he had written four years earlier that "an Anglican monarchical aristocratical party has sprung up, whose avowed object is to draw over us the substance, as they have already done the forms, of the British government."

Fig. 22. *Ograbme, or, the American Snapping-Turtle*. Alexander Anderson. 1807. Engraving. 7 1/2 × 9 1/2 in. Courtesy The New-York Historical Society, New York City.

During the Napoleonic wars, Britain and France sought to destroy each other's commerce on the high seas. While this was good practice in war, it was hard on neutral countries like the United States. In an effort to get them to stop harassing American shipping, Jefferson urged on Congress the Embargo (spelled backwards is "ograbme") Act in 1807. The embargo stopped virtually all foreign trade. Technically it did not prohibit imports, but few ships would bring goods to the United States if they could not return with a load, which the embargo prevented. Shippers and merchants were not ready to sacrifice so much and began smuggling (in the cartoon the "ograbme" has caught a tobacco smuggler) and otherwise disobeying the embargo. The ban was finally lifted in 1808 after disastrous economic results and virtually no diplomatic impact.

Fig. 23. *The Tory Editor and His Apes Giveing Their Pitiful Advice to the American Sailors*. William Charles. 1813. Colored engraving. 11 1/4 × 15 1/16 in. Courtesy The Lilly Library, Indiana University, Bloomington.

As the Napoleonic wars dragged on, anti-British sentiment in the United States was rekindled because of the British impounding of cargoes and impressment of American sailors. Expansion-minded young Westerners like Henry Clay demanded war, but New England merchants counseled a neutral course. In this pro-war cartoon, strong American sailors are rejecting the advice of the "Tory" editor (with a copy of the Boston *Gazette* under his arm), who apparently has never recovered from the Revolution, as seen in his tired appearance and worn clothes. This cartoon also points out that American sailors were pro-war because they unrealistically envisioned easy victory over the British.

Fig. 24. *The Hornet and the Peacock, or John Bull in Distress.* Amos Doolittle. 1813. Engraving with blue wash. 8 1/2 × 10 3/4 in. Courtesy Kennedy Galleries, Inc., New York City.

Naval rights—free trade and sailors' rights —were the main issues leading to the War of 1812, and even though the main part of the British navy was occupied fighting France, Britain could still put ninety-seven ships on the American side of the Atlantic to hold the sixteen American ships. By avoiding fleet action and concentrating on single ships, nevertheless, the Americans managed several naval victories. One of the most memorable American victories was the *Hornet*'s defeat of the *Peacock*, depicted in this Doolittle cartoon.

Fig. 25. *A View of Winchester in North America Dedicated to Mr. President Mad I Son!!* S. Knight. 1813. Colored engraving. 9 × 13 1/2 in. Courtesy The Lilly Library, Indiana University, Bloomington.

British Colonel Henry Proctor defeated American Brigadier General James Winchester during the first winter of the War of 1812. Hurrying to join General William H. Harrison at the Maumee Rapids, Winchester split his force to rescue some settlers and was unprepared for Proctor's attack. This cartoon depicts the meeting between Proctor and Winchester. Winchester was stripped of his uniform (being worn by one of Proctor's Indian allies), daubed with paint, and presented to the British commander. Winchester's defeat slowed General Harrison's plans to capture the Old Northwest Territory.

Fig. 26. *The Yankey Torpedo.* W. Elmes. 1813. Colored engraving. 10 5/8 × 15 7/8 in. Courtesy The Lilly Library, Indiana University, Bloomington.

The British did not take American threats made during the War of 1812 as seriously as the Americans intended them. On "British Oak" and leaning on a sword of "British Steel," this English sailor challenges the American sea-monster to "kiss my tafferal" (*i.e.*, taffrail, part of a ship's stern). He promises the monster "a taste of the *Shannon*," which defeated the USS *Chesapeake* in Boston Harbor, and a trip to Davy Jones' locker.

Fig. 27. *The Fall of Washington—or Maddy in Full Flight*. Williams. Oct. 4, 1814. Colored engraving. 14 1/2 × 10 in. Courtesy Anne S. K. Brown Military Collection, Brown University Library, Providence.

Hoping to divert attention from their Northern campaign, British forces struck at selected sites along the Eastern Coast in the summer of 1814. Although they were outnumbered, they easily pushed the badly prepared American forces back, leaving Washington, D. C., exposed. President James Madison had retired to Virginia by the time the British arrived. Two hundred Redcoats left "the Capitol wrapped in its winding sheet of fire," after feasting on food that Dolly Madison had prepared for the American troops before she also fled. Rear Admiral Sir George Cockburn and his men took whatever they wanted, then toasted the President with his own wine "for being such a good fellow as to leave us such a capital supper." The entire city might have burned had it not been for a violent thunderstorm that put out the fire.

Fig. 28. *Bruin Become Mediator or Negociation for Peace*. William Charles. c. 1813. Colored engraving. 10 11/16 × 14 3/4 in. Courtesy The Lilly Library, Indiana University, Bloomington.

Although the cartoon pictures John Bull, broken by victories of the American ships *Wasp* and *Hornet* at sea, pleading with the Russian bear to help settle the differences with the United States, the opposite situation was nearer the truth. President Madison had contacted Russian Tsar Alexander I in March, 1813, but the British refused the Tsar's offer of mediation. Negotiation finally began in August, 1814, and the Treaty of Ghent was signed in December. It restored all territory *status quo ante bellum*, granted amnesty for the Indian allies of the British, and provided for commissions to settle the boundary disputes. It did not mention impressment, neutral rights, or Canada and Florida, the main issues that had precipitated the war.

Fig. 29. *A Splendid Procession of Free Masons*. Gebolibus Crackfardi [David Claypool Johnston] (?). 1819. Hand-colored engraving. 6 1/4 × 9 3/4 in. Courtesy Boston Public Library, Print Department.

The Masonic Order was popular early in the nineteenth century, and many influential Americans were members. Those out of power, hearing rumors of the international Masonic movement, immediately suspected a plot by Masons to take over the country. In an exceedingly ugly affair a Mason who was trying to desert the order and publish all its secrets was killed. An Anti-Mason Party was formed in protest and was particularly active in New York State. This cartoon is probably part of the anti-Masonic movement that flourished during the mid-1820s.

Fig. 30. *The Five Aspirants*. Anonymous. 1824. Etching. 8 7/8 × 7 3/4 in. Courtesy Houghton Library, Harvard University, Cambridge, Mass.

The election of 1824 was a rousing affair that marked the end of the politically inactive Era of Good Feelings. Five candidates presented themselves to the electorate—William H. Crawford, John C. Calhoun, Andrew Jackson, John Quincy Adams, and Henry Clay. Here Clay is shown basing his campaign on his support of South American independence and the Treaty of Ghent. Andrew Jackson's reputation rested on his victory over the British at New Orleans and his treatment of the Seminole Indians in Florida. Secretary of the Treasury William H. Crawford, the candidate of the Congressional Caucus, became an issue because the other candidates claimed that he had been nominated by a "secret" caucus instead of the people. John Quincy Adams is shown on the Molasses barrel while John C. Calhoun heads up the ladder toward the chair reserved "for the most worthy."

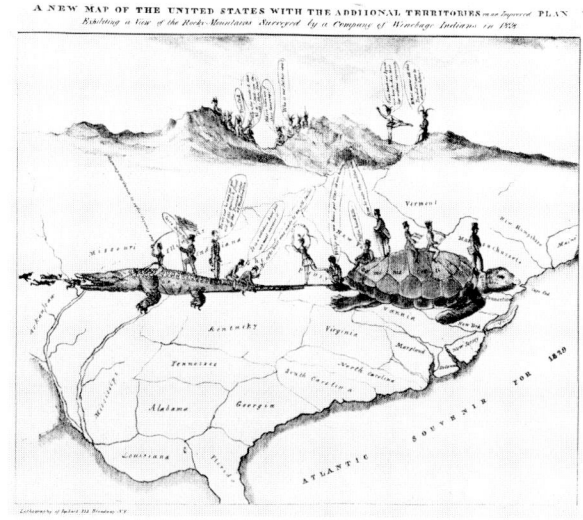

Fig. 31. *Richard I.I.I.* David Claypool Johnston. 1828. Engraving with stipple. 8 1/2 × 5 3/4 in. Courtesy Boston Public Library, Print Department.

Andrew Jackson was the candidate with the most popular votes during the election of 1824, but the House of Representatives elected John Quincy Adams President. Jackson returned for the campaign of 1828, and David Claypool Johnston recalled his military record in presenting this portrait to the public. Johnston has taken the bodies of Indians and other symbols of Jackson's wartime accomplishments as integral parts of the picture.

Fig. 32. *A New Map of the United States with the Additional Territories.* Anthony Imbert. 1828. Lithograph. 11 3/8 × 14 1/4 in. Courtesy Collections of The Library Company of Philadelphia.

When the election of 1824 was thrown into the House of Representatives for a decision, John Quincy Adams won with the support of Henry Clay. Jackson, who had accumulated the most popular votes, claimed that Adams and Clay had formed a "corrupt bargain," and immediately began preparations for the 1828 election. In this cartoon, the first lithographic cartoon produced in the United States, Jackson and his men are shown facing westward on the alligator; Adams and his supporters are on the tortoise facing eastward. Jackson's supporters venture the hope that he can "float up the Potomac as far as Washington," while the Indians behind the mountains in the background relate the developments they noticed during a recent visit into white man's culture.

63

Fig. 33. *"The Government." [!] Take the Responsibility.* Hassan Straightshanks (pseud.). Endicott & Swett, pub. 1834. Lithograph. 8 1/2 × 13 1/8 in. Courtesy the Library of Congress.

Campaigning for the 1832 election was marked by processions of Democrats armed with sections of "Old Hickory" logs and villainous representations of Nicholas Biddle, president of the Bank of the United States. In this cartoon Straightshanks parodies these parades by showing the Jackson government as a garbage wagon pulled by a jackass (with the General's face) led by Martin Van Buren, Jackson's close confidant and chosen successor. The mechanical driver is a hodgepodge of kitchen appurtenances, perhaps symbolic of Jackson's famous Kitchen Cabinet, an informal body of advisors. The rats on the roof are probably a reference to another popular cartoon of the day, "The Rats Leaving a Falling House," which showed Jackson's first cabinet, plagued by resignations and social scandal, deserting the wreckage of Jacksonian government.

GENERAL JACKSON, SLAYING THE MANY HEADED MONSTER.

Published March 1836, by the proprietor, H. R. Robinson, 48 Courtland St. New York

Fig. 34. *General Jackson Slaying the Many-Headed Monster*. H. R. Robinson. 1836. Lithograph. 13 3/4 × 18 1/2 in. Courtesy Smithsonian Institution, Harry T. Peters "America on Stone" Lithography Collection, Washington, D.C.

One of the major political battles of Jackson's presidency was his conflict with the Bank of the United States, which to him represented the plutocratic corruption that he so opposed. In this cartoon, Jackson, assisted by Martin Van Buren and Major Jack Downing (the comic character invented by Seba Smith), battles the bank, personified as the "Many-Headed Monster." Jackson killed the bank by withdrawing government money and depositing it in state banks, which became known as "pet" banks. He vetoed the bill that would have rechartered the bank in 1832, and the charter expired in 1836. I have "fixed my course as firm as the Rocky Mountain . . . Providence has a power over me, but frail mortals who worship Bale [sic] and the golden calf, can have none," he wrote Van Buren.

Fig. 35. *The Modern Balaam and His Ass.* Anonymous. 1837. Hand colored lithograph. 12 3/8 × 16 5/16 in. Courtesy the Library of Congress.

When land speculators began buying public lands with state bank currency at an unprecedented rate in 1835, President Jackson attempted to slow the sales by ruling in 1836 that only hard currency would be accepted for public land (the Specie Circular). Instead of driving the speculators from the market, it enhanced the value of the land they held, because only they would now sell for paper money. This cartoonist pictures Jackson as the Biblical Balaam who rides his jackass to deliver a message from God. Three times the ass sees an Angel and stops, each time Balaam beats him and urges him on. The cartoonist's suggestion is that the Specie Circular (the ass) is being urged on by Jackson despite the warnings of the angel (bank failures, as in the background of the print). The Specie Circular was finally repealed in 1838.

Fig. 36. *Battle of Bexar—Heroism of Col. Crockett.* Anonymous. 1837 in *Davy Crockett's Almanack*. Wood engraving. 6 1/2 × 3 1/2 in. Courtesy Archives Division, Texas State Library, Austin.

The son of a Revolutionary war veteran who ran away from home at age thirteen, David Crockett was elected to the Tennessee Legislature in 1821 and to the United States Congress when he accepted a friend's dare and campaigned for the office. He served three terms, but spent most of his time roaming the backwoods of Tennessee. He reportedly killed 105 bears during one nine-months period. He had little respect for "book-learning" or spelling, which he said were "contrary to nature." When he refused to "gee-woa-haw" to the tune of fellow Tennessean Andrew Jackson, Jackson's candidate defeated Crockett in the next congressional election, and Crockett was off to Texas, where he died heroically defending the "shrine of Texas liberty," the Alamo. Crockett's exploits—real or imaginary—were noted in the various issues of *Davy Crockett's Almanack*, which reached a wide audience whose appreciation of the stories was enhanced by the pictures, such as this humorous portrayal of the tragic defense of the Alamo.

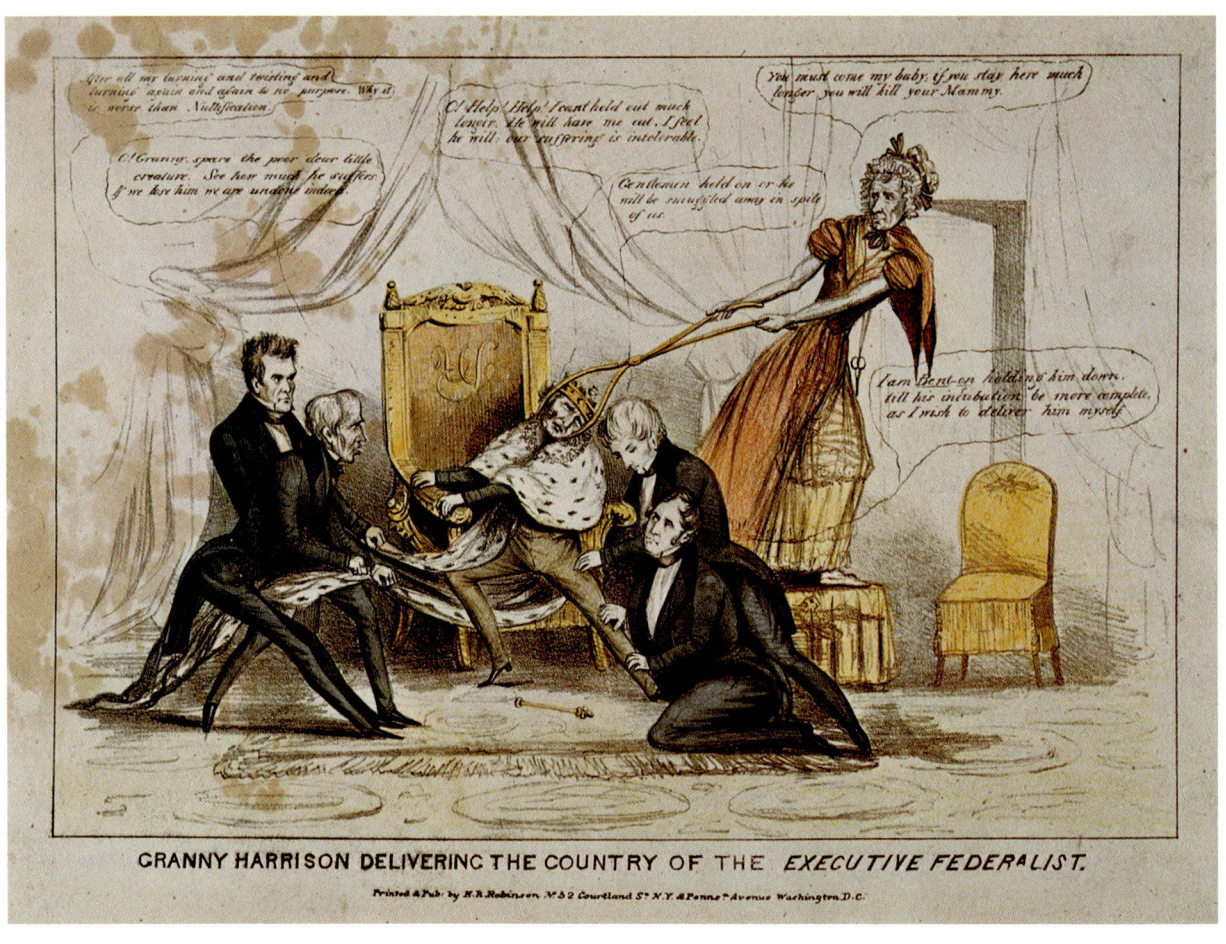

Fig. 37. *Granny Harrison Delivering the Country of the Executive Federalist*. H. R. Robinson. 1840. Colored lithograph. 12 15/16 × 18 1/8 in. Courtesy Smithsonian Institution, Harry T. Peters "America on Stone" Lithography Collection, Washington, D.C.

The Jacksonian Democrats had held onto the presidency for twelve years when General William H. Harrison, called "Granny" because of his sixty-seven years, managed to unseat Martin Van Buren, Jackson's protégé and successor. In this cartoon, John C. Calhoun, Jackson himself, and Thomas Hart Benton attempt to keep Van Buren in the office, while Harrison is successfully pulling him out. Harrison was unable to enjoy his victory, however, as he became ill as a result of the campaign and died after only a month in office.

Fig. 38. *Matty Meeting the Texas Question*. James Baillie. 1844. Lithograph. 13 1/4 × 19 7/16 in. Courtesy Amon Carter Museum, Fort Worth.

Americans had been colonizing the Mexican province of Texas ever since the 1820s. Although they originally intended to become loyal citizens of Mexico, a series of incidents led to their rebellion in 1836 and to the Republic of Texas, which immediately made itself available for statehood. Because of the slavery issue, and not wanting to anger Mexico, President Jackson did nothing about Texas. By the 1844 election, Texas was a potent political question. Jackson is urging Van Buren to "stand up to your lick-log" and accept Texas, while Polk and Dallas, his Vice-Presidential candidate, decide that Dame Texas might not be the worst ally they could find. Polk entered the campaign calling for the annexation of Texas.

Fig. 39. *The Buffalo Hunt*. H. R. Robinson. 1848. Lithograph. 10 3/8 × 15 1/2 in. Courtesy Smithsonian Institution, Harry T. Peters "America on Stone" Collection, Washington, D.C.

The 1848 election was a confused affair with several parties nominating candidates. The Whigs chose war hero Zachary Taylor to bear their banner; the Democrats picked Lewis Cass. Former President Martin Van Buren received support and nomination from the Barnburner and Free-Soil branches of the Democratic Party in a Buffalo, New York, convention. Thus he is shown here astride a buffalo thumbing his nose at Cass and Taylor, something which did not happen, for he received only about ten percent of the total vote cast.

Fig. 40. *An Available Candidate.* [N. Currier?] 1848. Lithograph. 16 × 11 in. Courtesy the Library of Congress.

Political candidates readily acknowledged that a military background helped garner votes. Recalling that the country already had elected Washington, Jackson, and Harrison, President James K. Polk feared the ambitions of General Zachary Taylor and therefore appointed General Winfield Scott to lead the march into Mexico City during the war with Mexico. Still, the fame that Taylor had gained in victories at Palo Alto, Monterrey, and Buena Vista thrust him into the forefront of Whig Party politics, and he received the 1848 nomination, despite this Democratic lithographic comment.

Fig. 41. *The Way They Go to California.* Nathaniel Currier. 1849. Lithograph. 14 × 21 in. Courtesy The Chicago Historical Society.

When it became generally known that John A. Sutter had discovered gold on the American River in California, "forty-niners" began immediate emigration to the West Coast. Because there were no transcontinental roads, they got there the best way they could: overland through the Rocky Mountains, the Southwestern trail through northern Mexico, ship via the Isthmus of Panama, and ship around the Horn. Currier is suggesting even more inventive ways of getting there in this print, while he shows that the conventional means of transportation were full.

Fig. 42. *Defence of the California Bank*. Serrell & Perkins. 1849. Lithograph. 10 3/8 × 14 1/2 in. Courtesy the Library of Congress.

Once Americans had made the long trek to the California goldfields, they became jealous of their opportunity, particularly against foreigners. This cartoon shows Queen Victoria, Louis Napoleon, the Russian Tsar, and a Spaniard coming into San Francisco Bay as a soldier on the shore shouts for them to "keep out of these Diggins." Although the majority of the gold hunters were Americans, Mexicans, Australians, Hawaiians, English, Irish, Chinese, and French also crowded the goldfields.

Fig. 43. *Actionnaires Californiens*. Honoré Daumier. 1850. Lithograph. 9 9/16 × 8 1/2 in. Courtesy Boston Public Library, Print Department.

The gold discovery in California, one of the largest finds of the nineteenth century, attracted attention around the world. Here Daumier pictures two Frenchmen discussing purchase of land in California along the Sacramento River in the gold country. "I invested all the money I owned," says one would-be entrepreneur.

71

Fig. 44. *Lola Has Come!* Anonymous. 1852. Lithograph. 7 1/8 × 11 in. Courtesy Hoblitzelle Theatre Arts Collection, Humanities Research Center, University of Texas, Austin.

A celebrated figure in the nineteenth century, Lola Montez made the most of a confused parentage to play up her supposedly exotic European background, becoming the mistress of, among others, Franz Liszt, Alexandre Dumas, and King Leopold of Bavaria, who made her Countess of Landsfeld and who was forced to abdicate after his attentions toward her were made public. With this reputation preceding her, she arrived in the United States in 1852 billing herself as a Spanish dancer. This cartoon shows Lola dancing in a nearly empty theater (although she most often had a full house). A Quaker peers at her hypocritically from behind spread fingers, while a gentleman reading the New York *Herald* (which gave Lola lots of press) gazes from his box.

Fig. 45. *Wi-Jun-Jon*. George Catlin. 1844. Colored lithograph. 18 1/2 × 23 1/2 in. Courtesy Amon Carter Museum, Fort Worth.

Artist Catlin found *Wi-jun-jon* (as he recorded the name; *Ah-jon-jon* it should have been) along the Upper Missouri River, a proud warrior with great respect among his people, and took him to Washington to meet President Jackson. The Indian quickly assimilated the white man's ways and became a caricature of his former self. "He had . . . exchanged his beautifully garnished and classic costume for a full dress *en militaire*," said Catlin. When he returned to his village his friends and relatives hardly recognized him. Gradually he began to tell stories of his adventure. So preposterous were his tales that his tribesmen killed him as a liar after several months.

Fig. 46. *Young Texas in Repose*. E. Jones. 1852. Lithograph. 14 1/16 × 9 13/16 in. Courtesy Arts of the Book Collection, Yale University Library, New Haven.

The primary political issue of the 1850s was expansion of slavery into Kansas and other territories. Texas was considered a particularly depraved slave-holding state by abolitionists because they felt the 1836 Revolution to be a slave-holder plot to get another slave state into the Union and because it was the fastest growing slave state in the Union throughout the 1850s. Thus this particularly brutal young man sitting on a slave who bears a strong resemblance to a bale of cotton is labeled "Young Texas."

Fig. 47. *A Bad Egg. Fuss and Feathers*. P. Smith. [N. Currier]. 1852. Lithograph. 16 3/8 × 11 in. Courtesy the Library of Congress.

The election of 1852 further cemented the tie between military success and the presidential nomination, with two Mexican War generals, Winfield Scott and Franklin Pierce leading the Whigs and the Democrats respectively. Scott was also supported by the Free Soil Party (thus the "Free Soil Egg" hatched in Baltimore). Fearful that Scott would be influenced by abolitionist William Seward, Southerners were deserting the party. In an effort to stop the desertion, Seward announced that he would accept no favors from Scott, but the cartoonist obviously does not agree.

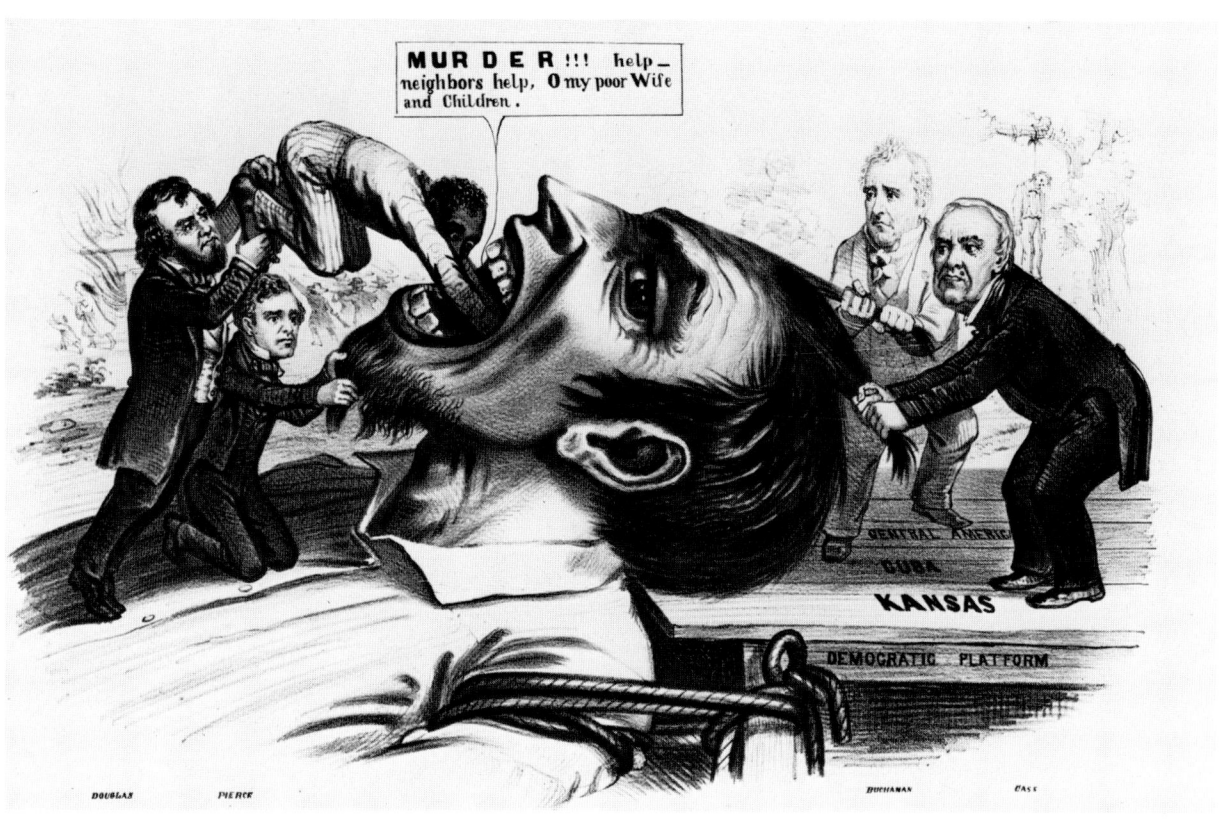

Fig. 48. *Forcing Slavery Down the Throat of a Free-Soiler*. Anonymous. 1856. Lithograph. 12 × 15 3/4 in. Courtesy The New-York Historical Society, New York City.

By 1856 the issue of slavery dominated politics. Senator Stephen A. Douglas of Illinois, a leading Democratic contender, tried to sidestep the issue by leaving it up to the voters of each territory, but this cartoonist sees Douglas' position as one of forcing slavery onto the territories (Kansas, in this instance) because of the effort pro-slavery forces would make to win the elections. James Buchanan is shown holding the free-soiler while Douglas administers the force, a prediction of Buchanan's leaning since he had been away as Minister to England and no one really knew where he stood on the issue.

Fig. 49. *Stephen Arnold Douglas*. Anonymous. 1858. Wood sculpture, polychromed. 18 in. high. Courtesy National Portrait Gallery, Smithsonian Institution, Washington, D. C.

The "Little Giant," as Stephen Douglas was fondly called, was a powerful politician and presidential aspirant during the 1850s. Perhaps most famous for his debates with Abraham Lincoln during the 1858 senatorial campaign, Douglas espoused "popular sovereignty," which held that the states themselves should decide the future of slavery within their boundaries. He ran for President in 1860 as a Democrat but lost much support because the Democratic Party split into northern and southern branches. He died at age 48 of typhoid fever.

Fig. 50. *Abraham Lincoln*. Anonymous. c. 1863. Wood sculpture, polychromed. 17 3/4 in. high. Courtesy Missouri Historical Society, St. Louis.

President Lincoln's leadership during one of the severest crises the country has known endeared him to Americans and made him one of the great figures in our country's history. This anonymous carver seems to have captured Lincoln's dignity and forthrightness. He also tells something about Lincoln by having him pose with his hand near the Bible, which Lincoln often quoted during his speeches.

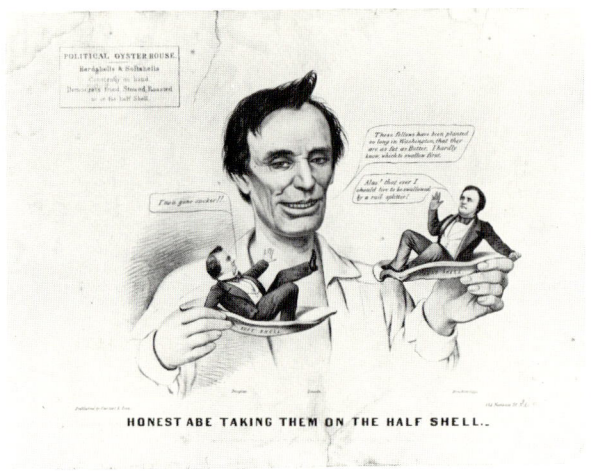

Fig. 51. *Honest Abe Taking Them on the Half Shell*. Louis Maurer. 1860. Lithograph. 13 9/16 × 18 1/16 in. Courtesy The Lilly Library, Indiana University, Bloomington.

Northerners classified Democrats as either "hard-shell" (pro-slavery) or "soft-shell" (moderate on slavery). In this cartoon, the Republican Lincoln is about to swallow his hard-shell and soft-shell Democratic opponents. The sign in the background indicates that this is a Republican "Political Oyster House," where Democrats are served "fried, Stewed, Roasted or on the half Shell."

Fig. 52. *The Political Quadrille. Music by Dred Scott*. Anonymous. 1860. Lithograph. 12 3/4 × 17 7/8 in. Courtesy the Library of Congress.

Dred Scott was a slave whose master had taken him into free territory, then back into slave territory. Scott sued for his freedom, claiming that his sojourn in free territory made him a free man. Chief Justice Roger B. Taney, in his opinion, stated that Scott was a slave and therefore had no right to sue in federal court. Further, he ruled that Scott was property and the slave owner could not be deprived of his property without "due process." This meant that the Missouri Compromise of 1820 was unconstitutional, because it had established certain free territory in which slavery could not exist. Shown in this cartoon are the candidates in the 1860 election, Abraham Lincoln, John Bell, Stephen A. Douglas, and John C. Breckinridge.

Fig. 53. *Dividing the National Map*. Rickey, Mallory & Company. 1860. Lithograph. 13 11/16 × 19 1/4 in. Courtesy The Lilly Library, Indiana University, Bloomington.

Political parties were badly divided as they entered the campaign of 1860. Sectional issues had split the Democrats into Northern and Southern branches, Stephen A. Douglas leaning toward the Northerners and John C. Breckinridge of Kentucky the Southerners' candidate. Remnants of the Whig and Know-Nothing parties united under the Constitutional Union Party banner and nominated John Bell. Lincoln was the candidate of a united but Northern Republican Party. This cartoon shows Lincoln and Douglas struggling for the western section of the map, while Breckinridge captures the South and Bell tries to repair the damage.

Fig. 54. *Virginia Paw-sing*. Anonymous. 1861. Lithograph. 8 1/2 × 14 in. Courtesy The Chicago Historical Society.

Produced in Richmond as the Southern states were seceding, this cartoon shows the order in which the states left the Union, with South Carolina leading the way. It also graphically shows that President Lincoln tried to keep them from leaving. The popular Northern belief that "the Union must and Shall be Preserved" is shown as a dead issue—a decapitated rat.

Fig. 55. *Our National Bird As It Appeared When Handed to James Buchanan. March 4, 1857. The Identical Bird As It Appeared A. D. 1861.* Michael Angelo Woolf. 1861. Lithograph. 7 5/8 × 13 in. Courtesy Boston Public Library, Print Department.

It was President James Buchanan's misfortune to serve during four of the most hectic years our country has known. While it is unlikely that any man could have preserved the Union in 1861, Buchanan had made his share of blunders. He began by announcing that he intended to serve only one term, lessening his influence immediately. He continually called for preservation of the Union, but instituted no measures directed toward that end. In a typical remark, he told Congress that secession was unconstitutional, but that neither the President nor Congress had the power to prevent it.

Fig. 56. *En Amerique*. Charles Henri Amedée, "Cham," Comte de Noé. c. 1862. Lithograph. 10 3/4 × 14 3/16 in. Courtesy Louisiana State Museum, New Orleans, 1956.

To a middle class Frenchman it must have been difficult to tell the difference between the North and the South, for their differences were small by comparison with the peculiarities of France, or Europe in general. Without slavery there would have been too few differences to provoke a bloody Civil War, as this Frenchman seems to understand: "Ah! Devil! I am starting to get mixed up in all this," he says. "Which one is the North? Where is the South? I don't understand anything any more."

Fig. 57. [Lincoln as a Monkey.] David H. Strother [attrib.] Jan. 14, 1863. Pencil on paper. 8 13/16 × 5 1/4 in. Courtesy The Lilly Library, Indiana University, Bloomington.

On March 2, 1862, President Lincoln suggested to Congress a plan whereby slaves in loyal states would be given their freedom and their owners compensated up to an average of $400. Congress took no action regarding the loyal states, but on January 1, 1863, Lincoln issued the Emancipation Proclamation, which granted freedom to slaves in the rebellious states. Few slaves were actually freed until after the war, because Lincoln obviously did not possess the power to free slaves in Confederate-held territory unless the individual slaveholders decided to cooperate. At the conclusion of the war, the Union Army freed slaves as it took possession of territory. Lincoln had feared the Proclamation would be declared unconstitutional, but instead it was validated by the thirteenth amendment.

Fig. 58. *Lincoln and Butler as Don Quixote and Sancho Panza.* Adalbert Volck. 1863. Etching. 6 1/2 × 7 1/2 in. Courtesy The New-York Historical Society, New York City.

Adalbert Volck, a Baltimore dentist and artist, did a number of etchings to accompany verse satirizing the military career of General Benjamin F. Butler, along with Lincoln among the most hated men in the South. Today it may be difficult to understand Butler's prominence in the cartoons of the era, but he was a well-known figure whom many Southerners had thought would fight with them. When he chose to remain with the Union, they considered him a traitor. His command of the Union occupation forces in New Orleans earned him the nicknames "Beast" and "Butcher" before he was finally removed from the command in December, 1862.

Fig. 59. *Lincoln. You'll excuse me Gen. Butler, but as I cant send you everywhere at once, I'll have to take you to pieces.* Thomas Nast [attrib.] n.d. Pencil on paper. 5 7/8 × 6 11/16 in. Courtesy The Lilly Library, Indiana University, Bloomington.

Perhaps Thomas Nast, a loyal Unionist, attempted to answer the Southern caricatures of General Butler with this drawing which seems to say that Butler is so important to Lincoln that the President would like to cut him up and send him to several different locations at once. He was such a poor general, however, Nast might have intended exactly the opposite meaning for his cartoon. Because of Butler's large personal following, Lincoln could not afford to alienate the general and was obliged to give him a field command. Perhaps only in this Nast drawing did Lincoln reveal his true feelings toward Butler.

Fig. 60. *The Miscegenation Ball*. Anonymous. 1864. Colored lithograph. 19 × 23 3/4 in. Courtesy Smithsonian Institution, Harry T. Peters "America on Stone" Collection, Washington, D.C.

Bromley & Company of New York City did several anti-abolitionist cartoons during the Civil War. This one ridicules a Lincoln campaign ball, showing blacks and whites dancing together and in various stages of embrace. Some of the political leaders left the room before the ball began, says Bromley, but many stayed for the party. This print, he claims, is a "perfect facsimile of the room &c. &c."

79

Fig. 61. *Jeff Davis After the Surrender of Fort Sumter, April 13, 1861. Jeff Davis, After the Fall of Fort Sumter, 1863.* David Claypool Johnston. c. 1863. Postcards. 4 1/2 × 2 3/4 in. and 4 1/2 × 2 3/4 in. Courtesy Mr. and Mrs. Draper Hill, Memphis, Tenn.

Jefferson Davis, the President of the Confederate States, was frequently caricatured in the North, particularly after a Northern victory, such as the one alluded to here by Johnston. Fort Sumter was the first Union fort to fall to the rebels as the Civil War began. It was a symbolic victory when the Union won it back in 1863. Shown here are two postcards which can be moved so that Davis is either smiling or frowning. The event shown below the title also changes as the card is maneuvered.

Fig. 62. *Satan Tempting Booth to the Murder of the President*. J. L. Magee. 1865. Lithograph. 10 1/2 × 8 3/4 in. Courtesy Collections of The Library Company of Philadelphia.

On the afternoon of April 14, 1865, President Lincoln told his cabinet that, "I hope there will be no persecution, no bloody work after the war is over. No one need expect me to take any part in hanging or killing those men, even the worst of them. . . . We must extinguish our resentments if we expect harmony and union." That night he was assassinated by actor John Wilkes Booth, a demented Southern sympathizer, as he relaxed at Ford's Theater in Washington.

Fig. 63. *John Brown Exhibiting his Hangman*. G. Querner. 1865. Lithograph. 16 3/8 × 12 1/4 in. Courtesy The New-York Historical Society, New York City.

John Brown, an abolitionist who had incited rebellion and murdered five slave owners, had been hung for his excesses in 1859 by the State of Virginia. Embittered and enraged by the Civil War experience many Northern sympathizers came to liken Brown to an Old Testament prophet who called violence down upon the heads of the sinful, slaveholding South. This cartoon, executed soon after the war, depicts Brown as a vengeful spirit pointing an accusing finger at Jefferson Davis. Davis is depicted as a woman holding Eve's apple of sin and is suspended above the heads of the emancipated slaves for their ridicule.

Fig. 64. *The Massacre at New Orleans*. Thomas Nast. 1867. Oil on canvas. 7 ft. 10 3/4 in. × 11 ft. 6 1/2 in. Courtesy The Swann Collection of Caricature and Cartoon, New York City.

In the summer of 1867 Thomas Nast, by then a well known cartoonist for *Harper's Weekly*, began work on his Grand Caricaturama, which was exhibited in Dodworth Hall, New York City, in December, 1867. The Caricaturama consisted of thirty-three "Grand Historical Paintings." Shown here is his depiction of the New Orleans riot of July 30, 1866, in which thirty-seven Negroes and three white sympathizers were killed. The riot started when police attacked a number of Negroes participating in a Radical Republican meeting, which was designed to help the Radicals take over the state from the Johnson Republicans. Combined with riots in Memphis and Vicksburg, the New Orleans riot gave Northerners the impression that Southerners were taking out their frustration on the Negroes, and Nast blamed President Johnson.

Fig. 65. *The Reconstruction Policy of Congress, as Illustrated in California.* Anonymous. 1867. Lithograph. 14 3/8 × 10 1/2 in. Courtesy the Library of Congress.

In 1867 George C. Gorham was nominated for governor of California by the Republican Party convention. A man who made no secret of his ambitions, Gorham is here satirized as a tool of the Radicals who uses the "machine" votes of Negroes, Chinese, and Indians to gain election. There was so much protest over his selection that the Republicans held another convention and the nomination was offered to John Bidwell, who turned it down. Finally, Caleb T. Fay was nominated, but he was beaten by Democrat H. H. Haight.

Fig. 66. *The Smelling Committee.* John Cameron. 1868. Lithograph. 8 1/2 × 14 1/2 in. Courtesy Boston Public Library, Print Department.

During March, April, and May of 1868 the Senate sat as a jury in the impeachment trial of President Andrew Johnson, who faced eleven charges of high crimes and misdemeanors in office. When the first ballot was taken, the Radical Republicans who had instigated the impeachment proceedings were shocked to find that they had lost by one vote. They recessed for ten days to try to marshal the votes necessary for conviction, but when they reconvened, they were again defeated. Seven Republicans (the "fatal number") voted with the Democrats to acquit Johnson. The impeachment managers, John A. Logan, T. Williams, George S. Boutwell, J. F. Wilson, Ben Butler, Thaddeus Stevens, and J. A. Bingham, encircle a dead horse, "Impeachment," in this cartoon. Butler suggests that Thurlow Weed, Republican political boss of the 1840s who sanctioned bribery and legislative trading as legitimate political tools, is causing the bad smell. But Johnson, at right, corrects him by pointing out that it is impeachment that is dead and decaying.

Fig. 68. *Horace Greeley*. Thomas Nast. June 20, 1872 in *Vanity Fair*. Watercolor on paper. 12 1/8 × 7 1/4 in. Courtesy National Portrait Gallery, Smithsonian Institution, Washington, D. C.

Perhaps most famous for his admonition to young men to "Go West," Horace Greeley was the influential founder and editor of the New York *Tribune* and a candidate for president in the controversial 1872 election, which also included the first woman candidate for that office (fig. 71). He had been a supporter of Grant, but later denounced that corrupt administration, split from the Republican Party, and helped form the Liberal Republican Party. More a social reformer than a politician, Greeley actually thought he had a good chance to be elected. Overwhelmed by Grant's crushing victory, Greeley died a short time after the election.

Fig. 67. *To the White House, March 4th 1869*. Auguste Peyrau. 1869. Bronze. 10 5/8 in. high. Courtesy Museum of Fine Arts, Boston: M. and M. Karolik Collection.

The Civil War hero Ulysses S. Grant was elected President in 1868 to succeed the ineffective Andrew Johnson. Grant's Vice-President was Schuyler Colfax.

Fig. 69. *Earth Quakey Times, San Francisco, Oct. 8, 1865*. Edward Jump. 1865. Lithograph. 14 3/16 × 19 7/8 in. Courtesy Collections of the California Historical Society, San Francisco.

This print "celebrates" the earthquake that shook San Francisco on October 8, 1865. Jump has taken a tragic situation and by means of skillful pen and imagination turned it into a humorous lithograph with eccentric people and buildings braving the quake.

85

Fig. 70. *The Age of Brass. Or the Triumphs of Woman's Rights*. Currier & Ives. 1869. Lithograph. 18 3/4 × 13 3/8 in. Courtesy the Library of Congress.

Woman's crusade for equal rights predates this Currier & Ives print, but the Civil War made the issue timely again. Women took on many roles that were not necessarily theirs by routine during the war—running farms or plantations, organizing charities, hospitals, etc. on the home front. After the war they were not anxious to give up their newly won privileges, privileges they proved they could handle during the war. Currier & Ives are only predicting what most men thought would be the logical end of such nonsense.

Fig. 71. *"Get thee behind me, (Mrs.) Satan!"* Thomas Nast. Feb. 17, 1872 in *Harper's Weekly*. Wood engraving. 15 15/16 × 11 in. Courtesy Amon Carter Museum, Fort Worth.

Victoria Claflin Woodhull was an unconventional woman's rights agitator whose antics continually shocked and disturbed nineteenth century America. She was alleged to be the offspring of a one-eyed backcountry drifter and an Ohio saloonkeeper's daughter. At age fifteen Victoria married the elderly Dr. Canning Woodhull. They separated, and she divorced him to marry Col. James Harvey Blood. With Col. Blood she became involved in the nineteenth century fad of spiritualism, a profession which introduced her to railroad magnate Cornelius Vanderbilt. With Vanderbilt's money and advice Victoria and her sister, Tennessee, established a prosperous brokerage firm. The next male bastion the intrepid Mrs. Woodhull assaulted was politics. In her *Origin, Tendencies and Principles of Government*, first printed as articles in the New York *Herald* in 1870, she espoused free love and communal property. On April 2, 1870, buoyant on the waves of her notoriety, she declared her candidacy for President of the United States. Her highly unconventional views and colorful background made her appear in most Victorian eyes as a female antichrist rather than a potential national leader.

Fig. 72. [Andrew Johnson caricature with a donkey]. Thomas Nast. c. 1876. Pastel on paper. 51 1/2 × 40 1/2 in. Courtesy National Portrait Gallery, Smithsonian Institution, Washington, D. C.

Fig. 73. *The Third-Term Panic*. Thomas Nast. Nov. 7, 1874, in *Harper's Weekly*. Wood engraving. 11 × 15 15/16 in. Courtesy Amon Carter Museum, Fort Worth.

To Nast Andrew Johnson represented tyranny in the Executive Office. "King Andy" as Nast portrayed him, is confronted here with the whimsical donkey scarecrow, which Nast used to symbolize President Grant's alleged "Caesarism." Throughout Grant's second term the press had accused him of arrogance and vaunting political ambition, speculating that he would seek a third term to satisfy this lust for power. Nast, ever defensive of Grant despite the scandals and political debacles of his administration, portrayed this supposed threat as a make-believe jackass, thus juxtaposing the "real" tyrant Johnson (in Nast's opinion) with the unreal threat of Grant's Caesarism created by the hostile press.

While continuing to counter the charge of President Grant's "Caesarism," Nast inadvertently invented the Republican elephant. In this cartoon the New York *Herald*, which had been vociferously denouncing what it thought were Grant's intentions of running for a third term, is shown as an ass masquerading in a lion's skin scaring off all the other newspapers (the frightened animals, in this reference to one of Aesop's fables). The elephant symbolizes the massive Republican vote, which Nast fears is about to be duped by the *Herald's* charges (portrayed by the trap the elephant is about to fall into). The Democratic Party is the fox in this picture, the donkey having been assigned to the *Herald*.

87

Fig. 74. *America*. G. Bridgman. 1870s. Hand-colored lithograph. 16 1/2 × 10 15/16 in. Courtesy Amon Carter Museum, Fort Worth.

The American businessman of the 1870s confronted the world, confident of his ability, riding the railroad of "Progress," and spreading "Greenbacks" wherever he traveled in search of new materials and markets. The greenbacks owed their popularity to the political party of the same name, which campaigned in 1876 for the issue of more paper money. Peter Cooper ran for president, but received only 80,000 votes. Two years later the party drew more than two million votes, but in the following years merged itself with other inflationist groups and disappeared. Bridgman's caricature of the American businessman represents the vigor with which the new merchants hit the world's economy following the Civil War and the expansive period of industrialization in this country.

Fig. 75. *The Commercial Vampire*. Leon Barritt. 1898 in *Vim*. Chromolithograph. 11 1/4 × 18 in. Courtesy The Chicago Historical Society.

Known as "Palaces of Consumption," the department stores revolutionized consumerism in the United States at the turn of the century. By locating in large buildings, the department stores were able to centralize distribution of associated merchandise and lower the price to a set, non-negotiable figure. Barritt shows, by the skulls and bones of bankrupt dry goods merchants, bicycle dealers, and "segar" dealers, that the department stores drove many smaller merchants and clerks out of business. "N. B.," he adds to the caption, "This picture will not be found on the bargain counter."

Fig. 76. *The Slave Market of Today*. Bernhard Gillam. Jan. 2, 1884, in *Puck*. Chromolithograph. Approx. 14 1/2 × 20 1/2 in. Courtesy The Chicago Historical Society.

One of the raging issues of the 1880s was whether the United States would adopt a high tariff on foreign goods. Throughout most of the decade the country did erect a protectionist shield, behind which labor struggled to organize but was virtually at the mercy of industry. "Surely there should be some consideration for the workman, who, although he may not be aware of it, is nevertheless bound hand and foot, and is of necessity the abject slave of the Protectionist," commented the *Puck* editors.

Fig. 77. *The American River Ganges. The Priests and the Children.* Thomas Nast. Sept. 30, 1871, in *Harper's Weekly.* Wood engraving. 11 × 15 7/8 in. Courtesy Amon Carter Museum, Fort Worth.

A common fear throughout the nineteenth century on the part of "Americans" was that their standards would be lowered by the horde of immigrants. The article accompanying this powerful Nast cartoon bemoans the decline in the public school system because of Irish Catholic influence. "To destroy our free schools, and perhaps our free institutions, has been for many years the constant aim of the extreme section of the Romish Church." Some even believed that the radical Catholics in New York City wanted to deliver that city into the Pope's hands because they controlled the elected and appointed governing offices (through Tammany Hall). Strongly anti-Catholic himself, Nast shows the Catholic assault on "our children" in this cartoon.

Fig. 78. *The Great Fear of the Period: That Uncle Sam May be Swallowed by Foreigners*. White and Bauer, pubs. 1860s. Pen lithograph. 23 1/8 × 25 in. Courtesy the Library of Congress.

Several years of free immigration into the United States led many "natives" to fear that they would be overcome by the newcomers. Immigration into California was particularly large as a result of the gold rush. Friction between the "natives" and the immigrants was a regular feature, with some 300,000 Chinese being tormented, mobbed, stoned, and their businesses burned by laborers who feared that the industrious Chinese would drive them out of work. The Exclusion Act of 1882 limited immigration, as did the ban on importation of contract labor in 1885. Limitation of immigration continued to be popular until the twentieth century, supported by organizations like the American Protective Association, established in 1887.

Fig. 79. *Barsqualdi's Statue. Liberty Frightening the World. Bedbugs Island, N. Y. Harbor*. Thomas Worth. 1884. Lithograph. 15 3/8 × 10 1/8 in. Courtesy the Library of Congress.

The many corruptions in the administration of New York Harbor led Thomas Worth to produce this racist picture for Currier & Ives showing Liberty as a symbol of the corruption and the abusive treatment of immigrants rather than the symbol of freedom to all the world.

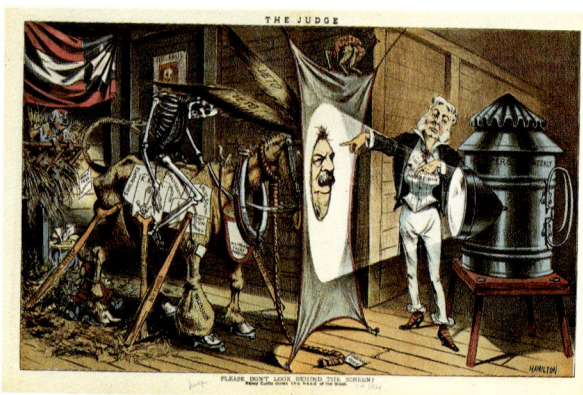

Fig. 80. *A Group of Vultures Waiting for the Storm to "Blow Over." —"Let Us Prey."* Thomas Nast. Oct. 1871, in *Harper's Weekly*. Wood engraving. 15 15/16 × 11 in. Courtesy Amon Carter Museum, Fort Worth.

Thomas Nast undertook his most famous crusade in 1871 when the corruption in the Court House of New York City became known. William M. Tweed, the Tammany Hall boss, had been doling out millions of dollars to himself and his cronies for several years. When the corrupt practices became known, 31-year-old Nast began a series of cartoons that literally ran Tweed out of town. After the scandal had become public, Tweed and his henchmen hoped the storm would blow over, but Nast kept the public aware of the crime with his pictures. In a famous statement, Tweed commented that he did not care what the newspapers wrote, because most of his supporters could not read. But "them damn pictures," which they could understand without reading were hurting him.

Fig. 81. *Please Don't Look Behind the Screen*. Grant Hamilton. Oct. 18, 1884, in *Judge*. Chromolithograph. 13 5/8 × 20 3/4 in. Courtesy The Chicago Historical Society.

When Grover Cleveland was proposed as a presidential candidate, the editors of *Puck* quickly let it be known that they were against him. Even his friends admitted that he had no outstanding record of achievement, commented the editors, but they did propose him as "the great moral reformer." After investigation, however, even that disappeared. "Then . . . came the terrible story of Maria Halpin to scatter all his pretentions of morality to the winds," charged the editors. One of the most memorable campaign slogans of our history came out of Cleveland's alleged involvement with Miss Halpin: "Ma, Ma, where's my pa?"

Fig. 82. *The Religious Vanity Fair.* Joseph Keppler. Oct. 22, 1879, in *Puck*. Chromolithograph. 12 × 18 1/2 in. Courtesy Boston Public Library, Print Department.

Indigenous American religious movements, combined with the varieties of religious practice imported with the immigrants, produced a true "Vanity Fair" of religion in the last quarter of the nineteenth century. Here the *Puck* editors comment that one can consult *Cook's Tourist Guide* to find any spot on the globe, but when one seeks "to soar beyond this habitable sphere" the "routes and guides are so many, so contradictory, and so confusing, that the poor man, who would be *en route* for Heaven gets himself completely mixed and finds himself at a standstill." This Keppler print exaggerates the religious situation of the day, but makes reference to several of the newsworthy events of the day such as "Beecher's only love road to Heaven."

Fig. 84. "*Mark Twain*." Max Beerbohm. 1908. Pencil and watercolor on paper. 8 1/4 × 6 3/8 in. Courtesy The Iconography Collection, Humanities Research Center, University of Texas, Austin.

Fig. 83. *Parade for Causes*. Frederick Opper. c. 1890. Pen and ink on paper. 17 × 25 in. Courtesy The Swann Collection of Caricature and Cartoon.

As Americans became aware of the problems of their society, and as society itself became more complex, reforms defending virtually any group or cause organized to achieve their ends, as Opper illustrates here.

Mark Twain (whose real name was Samuel Langhorne Clemens) was one of the leading writers and humorists of the nineteenth and early twentieth centuries, and one of America's greatest prosemen. Immortalizing his boyhood on the Mississippi River in such works as *Life on the Mississippi* (1883), *The Adventures of Tom Sawyer* (1876), and *The Adventures of Huckleberry Finn* (1884), he was a respected critic and literary figure whose opinions were widely sought and published. Today he is one of the most recognizable American literary figures around the world.

Fig. 85. *The Poker Game* and *Not a Chinaman's Chance*. Charles M. Russell. 1893. Bronze (cast in 1966). 6 3/4 in. high. 10 1/2 in. high. Courtesy Amon Carter Museum, Fort Worth.

Charlie Russell, the "cowboy artist," delighted in caricaturing the stereotypes of the West. Here he shows a cowboy, an Indian, and a Chinese playing poker. According to the Helena, Montana *Weekly Herald* (Dec. 28, 1893), "The Chinaman has the best of the layout as far as the game has progressed." In the second sculpture, the cowboy has pulled a gun on the Oriental and is raking in the stakes. "The observer can only conjecture whether the wily Oriental was caught dealing from the bottom of the deck or had an ace up his sleeve, but it is obvious that 'he didn't have a Chinaman's chance' against two such adversaries." The editor of the newspaper did not suggest that the cowboy might have lost the game and pulled the gun to recoup his losses.

95

Fig. 86. *Hanna: That Man Clay was an Ass. It's Better to be President than to be right!* George Luks. Mar. 13, 1899 in *The Verdict*. Lithograph. 12 7/16 × 9 1/2 in. Courtesy the Library of Congress.

A Cleveland coal, iron, and newspaper millionaire, Marcus A. Hanna, was a shrewd power broker who early spotted William McKinley as a vote-getter. Coaching McKinley to stay at home and make only carefully-rehearsed speeches to selected visitors, Hanna carried on the battle against Democratic nominee William Jennings Bryan from his New York office. Assessing corporations and big banks one quarter of one percent of their capital funds, shaking down insurance companies and railroads, he amassed one of the largest campaign funds in history. With his money Hanna hired an army of 1,400 speakers to follow Bryan around the country and refute his speeches; he mailed more than 100 million pieces of campaign literature; and sponsored a "sound money" parade in New York the Sunday before the election. The Democrats countered as best they could. *The Verdict*, a quarto-size magazine published by Alfred Henry Lewis with brilliant cartoonists such as George Luks, was one of the more effective publications they issued for the campaign of 1900. Hanna is actually reported to have made the remark that Luks attributes to him in the cartoon.

Fig. 87. *A Cry for Help*. Homer Davenport. 1890s. Ink on paper. 22 × 21 9/16 in. Courtesy the Library of Congress.

America's moral conscience was active during the reform years following the Civil War and settlement of its corruption. With liberties firmly entrenched at home, Americans looked around the world and saw the home of liberty, Greece, threatened by Turkey, and Cuba, an island that always would have made a profitable annexation, plundered and enslaved by the Spaniards. Davenport is suggesting that Uncle Sam cannot hold up his head until he takes the musket down from the wall and defends liberty wherever it is threatened.

Fig. 88. *Santiago Bay Pop*. Anonymous. 1898–1901. Gouache on paper. 26 × 22 in. Courtesy the Georgia Historical Society, Savannah.

The last major battle of the short Spanish-American War was the destruction of the Spanish fleet in Santiago Harbor. With the battleships *Indiana*, *Iowa*, *Massachusetts*, *Oregon*, and *Texas*, and cruisers *New York* and *Brooklyn*, Rear Admiral William T. Sampson had trapped Spanish Admiral Pascual Cervera y Topete's fleet in Santiago Bay. When the *Infanta María Theresa*, the *Cristobal Colón*, the *Furor*, the *Plutón*, the *Admirante Oquendo*, and the *Vizcaya* tried to escape on the morning of July 3, 1898, Admiral Sampson's ships destroyed them. "If I were to live a thousand years and a thousand centuries never should I forget that 3d day of July 1898," said one of Cevera's officers, "nor do I believe that Spain will ever forget it."

Fig. 89. *Who Gets the Ballot, Philippines or Negro?* Homer Davenport. 1900. Ink on paper. 25 7/16 × 21 7/8 in. Courtesy the Library of Congress.

As a result of the Spanish-American War, the United States acquired the Philippine Islands. There was much discussion as to what kind of colonial policy the country should develop, with Senator Albert J. Beveridge speaking out strongly in favor of territorial expansion: "[God] has made us . . . the master organizers of the world to establish system where chaos reigns . . . He has made us adept in government that we may administer government among savage and senile peoples. . . . And of all our race, He has marked the American people as His chosen Nation to finally lead in the regeneration of the world." Davenport is obviously puzzled by the person who would extend the vote to the recently dominated natives of the Philippines and not to the American Negro of the South, who at that time was suffering from widespread moves to disenfranchise him.

Fig. 90. [Teddy Roosevelt as a pirate.] Frank A. Nankivell. 1906. Ink on paper. 22 1/2 × 13 5/8 in. Courtesy The Swann Collection of Caricature and Cartoon.

When President William McKinley was assassinated, Theodore Roosevelt, who called the office a "bully pulpit" and soon "preached from it," became President. His image as a courageous and adventuresome leader was enhanced when, during the 1904 Republican Convention, he responded swiftly to ransom demands from a Moroccan bandit named Raizuli who had captured an American citizen, Ion H. Perdicaris. "We want Perdicaris alive or Raizuli dead," Roosevelt ordered. The convention talked of nothing else for days as Roosevelt was overwhelmingly nominated for a second term. His popularity increased even more when Perdicaris was safely returned to the American consul. Perhaps it was the aura of the Barbary Coast that led Nankivell to picture Roosevelt as a pirate.

Fig. 91. *It's That Roosevelt Kid Again*. Frank A. Nankivell. 1906. Ink on paper. 19 7/8 × 16 5/8 in. Courtesy The State Historical Society of Missouri, Columbia.

Although Roosevelt talked much about breaking up the trusts, thereby disturbing the conservative elements in both parties, he really did little to disrupt them, trying instead the countervailing power of government to keep them from abusing their privileges. Until businessmen learned that they had little to fear from him, they considered him an upstart and something of a radical.

Fig. 92. *The Sirens Try to Lure Teddysses to the Rocks*. Otho Cushing. May 16, 1907, in *Life*. Ink on paper. 18 7/8 × 22 1/4 in. Courtesy The State Historical Society of Missouri, Columbia.

One of a series of drawings done for the original *Life* magazine, *The Teddyssey* depicts Roosevelt as Ulysses tied to the mast of his ship while the sirens, John D. Rockefeller, J. P. Morgan, and Andrew Carnegie, three of the wealthiest men in the world in 1907, try to lure him from his stated policy of regulation of trusts. Like Ulysses, Roosevelt might have thought that such a close encounter with the sirens would strengthen him.

Fig. 93. *Design for a Union Station*. Luther Daniels Bradley. 1907. Ink on paper. 17 × 13 7/8 in. Courtesy The Swann Collection of Caricature and Cartoon.

Edward H. Harriman was one of the ablest and most practical railroad men of his generation. The son of a clergyman, he started in business as a runner on Wall Street, and owned a seat on the Stock Exchange by age 22. Entering railroading seriously, he revamped the weak Illinois Central, then turned his attention to the near-bankrupt Union Pacific. In 1901 he bought the Southern Pacific, gaining control of the principal system of transportation between Kansas City and California. Here Luther D. Bradley, a brilliant cartoonist for the Chicago *Daily News*, graphically depicts Harriman's one-man control of the railroads.

Fig. 94. *Scarecrow of the Pacific.* John S. Pughe. Oct. 16, 1907, in *Puck*. Pen, ink, blue chalk on paper. 17 1/2 × 27 1/2 in. Courtesy The Metropolitan Museum of Art, Fletcher Fund, 1942.

In 1907 amid anti-American agitation in Japan and anti-Japanese demonstrations on the West Coast of the United States, President Roosevelt announced that the entire American fleet would move from the Atlantic to the Pacific, stimulating rumors that hostilities between the United States and Japan were about to begin. As the fleet reached the Pacific, however, Roosevelt talked of a "good will cruise" and soon announced that the "Great White Fleet" would actually visit Japan. The show of force had its effect, as the Japanese welcomed the Americans, and anti-Japanese and anti-American demonstrations ceased. The "big stick" had carried the day again.

Fig. 95. *That Western Corn. The Western Farmer—"Wot'd' I care about the price of coal?"* Albert T. Reid. Aug. 29, 1902, in the Kansas City *Journal*. Pen and ink on paper. 18 × 11 5/8 in. Courtesy Kansas State Historical Society, Topeka.

By the turn of the century the urban centers of the nation had developed serious problems directly traceable to overcrowding, sanitation, and high prices. With thousands of people leaving the farms for the cities, a feeling of competition between farm and city developed. Albert T. Reid, the famous Missouri cartoonist, has captured that feeling of competition as the prosperous farmer counts his blessings compared to the tribulations of the city-dwellers. This situation did not last long, for the farmers were among the first to feel the effects of the depression that eventually engulfed all the world in 1929.

Fig. 96. *Ye Scoldes*. Joseph Keppler, Jr. 1908 (?) in *Puck*. Ink and crayon on paper. 22 1/8 × 14 3/8 in. Courtesy The Swann Collection of Caricature and Cartoon.

During his last term in office, Roosevelt had a Congress more conservative than himself. A good democratic politician, he had been watching the rise of liberalism throughout his career, feeling in 1908 that the socialist movement was more significant than the Populists. As he was going out of office in January, 1908, Roosevelt sent Congress the most radical message of his entire eight years. He blasted the federal courts (one of his measures had just been declared unconstitutional) and big business, and demanded regulation of Stock Market "gambling," which he claimed was no different from gambling with machines or cards. Roosevelt did not long remain locked in the stocks with Congress, for his term ended when he turned the presidency over to William Howard Taft in 1909.

Fig. 97. *The Old Woman and the Shoe*. John S. Pughe. March 25, 1908 in *Puck*. Ink and blue chalk on paper. 17 × 27 in. Courtesy The Swann Collection of Caricature and Cartoon.

The enormous industrial capacity the United States had developed during the nineteenth century was organized under such wizards of industry as Morgan, Rockefeller, Carnegie, and Vanderbilt in the early twentieth century into trusts and monopolies. Little had been done to insure free exchange, but the legal machinery existed: the Sherman Antitrust Act, 1890. Roosevelt recognized that the "tremendous and highly complex industrial development" presented the country with "very serious social problems," and he got indictments against forty-two trusts during his eight years in office. In four years, however, Taft prosecuted even more trusts than Roosevelt had.

Fig. 98. [William Howard Taft.] Anonymous. c. 1908. Printed postcard, cloth, paper and brass. 5 1/2 × 3 1/2 in. Courtesy University of Hartford, DeWitt Collection, West Hartford, Conn.

A huge man of conservative mind, William Howard Taft only desired a seat on the Supreme Court. Three times Roosevelt offered that seat to him, but three times he declined, the last time because Mrs. Taft so badly wanted her husband to be President. When Roosevelt decided not to seek a third term, he chose Taft as his successor. Taft had been a loyal administrator under Roosevelt, but his own views were more conservative, and he did not trust the progressives and reformers who gathered around Roosevelt. Naturally the Taft administration was more conservative than Roosevelt's, leading Teddy to repudiate his hand-picked successor and seek reelection on his own in 1912.

Fig. 99. *Howdy, Brother!* Jay Norwood Darling ("Ding"). May 9, 1909, in the Des Moines *Register*. Pen and ink on paper. 22 1/2 × 18 1/2 in. Courtesy The University of Iowa Libraries, Iowa City.

American pride soared with the Wright brothers, Orville and Wilbur, when they successfully tested their four-cylinder engine with a twelve-second flight at Kitty Hawk, North Carolina, in 1903. By 1905 they had made a twenty-four mile flight from Dayton, Ohio. In 1909 their patented machine was adopted by the United States Army in time to have planes ready for the Mexican intervention in 1916 and World War I in 1917. Wilbur died in 1912 at age forty-five, but Orville lived until 1948 and reigned as the elder statesman of aviation.

Fig. 100. [William Randolph Hearst.] A. Redfield. n. d. Ink on paper. 15 × 11 1/8 in. Courtesy Collection of Morris George Hecht.

An ambitious young man who had taken over his father's failing San Francisco *Examiner* in 1887, William Randolph Hearst realized the success of Joseph Pulitzer's New York *World* could also be his. He bought out the New York *Journal* and began to out-sensationalize Pulitzer. With colored comic strips, bold headlines trumpeting the day's news, and full-page editorials, Hearst soon attracted attention. He provoked much of the public sentiment behind the Spanish-American War, calling it "the *Journal's* war." His estimated worth in 1935, the depths of the depression, was more than $200 millions, and he built an extravagant castle, San Simeon, in California. He died in 1951.

Fig. 101. *The Fool Pied Piper*. Ehrhart. June 2, 1909, in *Puck*. Ink and blue chalk on paper. 16 3/4 × 27 1/2 in. Courtesy The State Historical Society of Missouri, Columbia.

Much of the anti-immigration feeling of the early twentieth century was attributable to the belief that most immigrants were associated with the Black Hand, a secret society which began in Italy in 1868 and apparently bore some resemblance to the present-day Mafia. It turned up in Spain and Serbia associated with anarchists and nationalists. Here Ehrhart shows Europe glad to be rid of the bad elements of society that Uncle Sam, in the form of the Pied Piper, is not only accepting but luring away.

Fig. 102. *Uncle Sam: "They say he needs it, but he doesn't look sick to me."* Joseph Keppler, Jr. Mar. 17, 1909, in *Puck*. Crayon on paper. 13 1/2 × 19 3/4 in. Hand colored print. 14 1/4 × 20 1/4 in. Courtesy The Murray A. Harris Collection of Graphic Art, North Hollywood, Calif.

America has traditionally been a high-tariff nation, favoring home industry and passing laws favorable to its development. The tariffs rose from 1861 until 1909, when the hugeness of the trusts finally made politicians realize that American business no longer needed protection. A protective tariff is nothing more than "a tax on commerce, forcing the body of citizens to pay tribute to producers at home," said David Starr Jordan, president of Indiana University and later Stanford University. "To guarantee anyone a reasonable profit is to do so at the expense of the rest." Both the Democrats and the Republicans campaigned for lower tariffs in 1908. Exhibited here are the original drawing and the proof made for *Puck*.

Fig. 103. *I'm Not a Member of the Legislature*. Boardman Robinson. c. 1912. Black crayon, ink wash, white highlights on paper. 19 1/2 × 14 1/2 in. Courtesy Grunwald Center for the Graphic Arts, University of California, Los Angeles.

The thousands of non-English-speaking immigrants who entered the country each year participated in politics by means of the "boss system," that is, a neighborhood boss took care of them, provided them with a job, insured that their needs were fulfilled in return for their votes. New York City built the most durable political machine, Tammany Hall, which controlled an annual city payroll of more than $12 millions after 1880. Charles Francis Murphy led Tammany from 1902 to 1924, controlling the state legislature and lining his pockets with what Richard Croker called "honest graft"—taking advantage of inside knowledge to buy the right stocks, real estate, etc., and kickbacks, which were illegal.

Fig. 104. *Miss Democracy's Valentine*. C. K. Berryman. 1912. Ink on paper. 14 15/16 × 14 1/8 in. Courtesy the Library of Congress.

William Jennings Bryan had led the Democratic Party to national defeat three times before 1912. He was the titular head of the party as the 1912 election approached, but most of the country felt the party had to be reorganized to get some new faces before the electorate to try to stop the Republican sweep, which had lasted since 1896. Bryan is leaving his "valentine" in front of Miss Democracy's door, but Hiram W. Johnson, Judson Harmon, and George Gray, watching from behind the fence, remark on his persistence. They plan to unseat him as head of the party.

Fig. 105. *Time Will Tell*. Carey Orr. 1912. Ink on paper. 24 3/4 × 18 in. Courtesy Jonson Collection, University of New Mexico, Albuquerque.

In September, 1912, the Senate Committee on Privileges and Elections conducted hearings on Roosevelt's political campaign contributions in the elections of 1904, 1908, and 1912. Allegedly involving John D. Archibold of Standard Oil Company, the investigations held potential embarrassment for Roosevelt, although nothing was ever proved. Senator Boies Penrose was one of the sponsors of the resolutions sponsoring the hearings in the Senate.

Fig. 106. *Keep Off! Munroe Doctrine*. T. E. Powers. 1912. Ink on paper. 14 1/2 × 10 3/4 in. Courtesy The Swann Collection of Caricature and Cartoon.

When Americans realized in 1911 that a Japanese syndicate was negotiating for purchase of a large tract of land along the West Coast of Mexico on Magdalena Bay, Baja California, the State Department registered its disapproval and Senator Henry Cabot Lodge introduced legislation in the Senate stating that the United States viewed with "grave concern" the possession of strategic areas in the Americas by any foreign country or company. This became the Lodge Corollary to the Monroe Doctrine.

Fig. 107. [Uncle Sam shooting dice with Carranza.] C. K. Berryman. Jan. 4, 1917, in the Washington *Evening Star*. Ink on paper. 12 1/8 × 14 1/16 in. Courtesy the Library of Congress.

When Mexican bandits under Pancho Villa raided the town of Columbus, New Mexico, on the night of March 9, 1916, President Woodrow Wilson ordered General John J. Pershing and 7,000 American troops to pursue the bandits into northern Mexico. Pershing marched more than 300 miles into Mexico in what to President Venustiano Carranza was an invasion. He vehemently protested, threatening even to attack the Americans unless they were immediately withdrawn. Soon more than 100,000 American troops and National Guardsmen lined the border to prevent another raid.

Fig. 108. *A Quieter Spot for Him*. Luther Daniels Bradley. c. 1915. Ink on paper. 13 1/4 × 21 3/4 in. Courtesy The Swann Collection of Caricature and Cartoon.

When the British transatlantic steamer *Lusitania* was sunk by a German U-boat off the Irish coast on May 7, 1915, 128 Americans were killed. President Wilson drafted a protest note for Secretary of State William Jennings Bryan's signature, demanding that Germany abandon unrestricted submarine warfare, disavow the sinking of the *Lusitania*, and pay reparations for the loss of American lives. Wilson regarded the response as evasive and drafted another note, which Bryan refused to sign because he felt it might provoke Germany to war. The pacifist Bryan resigned on June 7.

Fig. 109. *In the White House Attic—a Find*. Luther Daniels Bradley. 1916. Ink on paper. 13 × 22 1/4 in. Courtesy The Swann Collection of Caricature and Cartoon.

President Roosevelt not only talked about a "big stick," but he wielded one while he was in office. Woodrow Wilson hoped for a different approach. "Many of us thought that peace could be achieved by processes which would permit us to split the big stick into kindling for the hearth fire, or cut it into gavels for purposes no more belligerent than registering decisions at meetings," commented Mark Sullivan (*Our Times, 1900–1925* [New York: Scribner, 1936], IV, 136). But as German aggression continued, even Wilson realized that the big stick was useful.

Fig. 110. *William, you dont mean to say that you are really going to do something?* Louis Raemaekers. 1917. Pencil and watercolor on paper. 17 × 13 in. Courtesy Hoover Institution on War, Revolution, and Peace, Stanford University, Palo Alto, Calif.

Had the Kaiser been more familiar with the chivalrous "code of the American West," he might not have been so surprised at President Wilson. In asking Congress for a declaration of war on April 2, 1917, Wilson couched his message in the moralistic, idealistic terms so pervasive in American society: "The world must be made safe for democracy. Its peace must be planted upon the tested foundations of political liberty. We have no selfish ends to serve. We desire no conquest, no domination. We seek no indemnities for ourselves, no material compensation for the sacrifices we shall freely make. We are but one of the champions of the rights of mankind. . . . We shall . . . observe with proud punctilio the principles of right and of fair play we profess to be fighting for."

Fig. 111. *White House or Bust*. John Clubb. 1916. Ink on paper. 19 × 14 in. Courtesy The Swann Collection of Caricature and Cartoon.

Lusting for office and detesting Wilson's 1916 slogan, "He Kept Us Out of War," Roosevelt tried to arrange for the Republican Party to draft him for the nomination. But the Republicans were not interested in the Bull Moose Party candidate of 1912 and chose instead Charles Evans Hughes. Convinced that Hughes was overcautious, Roosevelt nevertheless decided to support him rather than split the Republican vote by again seeking office on a third party ticket. He might have exercised more real influence in the party and the election if he had remained the aloof elder statesman in retirement at his home at Sagamore Hill.

Fig. 112. *I Want You for U. S. Army*. James Montgomery Flagg. 1917. Colored poster. 40 × 29 3/16 in. Courtesy the Library of Congress.

The classic image of Uncle Sam is this Flagg poster that was published for World War I recruiting. It has been revived numerous times and used by the Army. It is probably a self-portrait of Flagg.

Fig. 113. *Army Medical Examiner: "At Last a Perfect Soldier."* Robert Minor. July, 1916, in *The Masses*. Magazine page. 12 1/2 × 10 in. Courtesy Ben Goldstein, New York City.

Robert Minor was among the small number of liberal artists who contributed cartoons to the outspoken leftist magazine *The Masses*, which actually was banned from the mail by the Postmaster General during World War I. This cartoon is representative of a number of pacifist caricatures which appeared in the United States prior to America's entry in the war and that pointed out the degradation of the intellect and the personality by the military and by war.

Fig. 114. *"War is Hell isnt it?"* Dalrymple. c. 1898. Ink on paper. 18 1/8 × 18 3/4 in. Courtesy The Swann Collection of Caricature and Cartoon.

Rather than a poke at the farmers, who were providing ample food for the country and the war effort, this cartoon probably is an attack on war resisters and draft dodgers. The slightly picturesque garb of the characters might indicate that they are recently-arrived European immigrants, who were almost universally suspected of unpatriotic if not traitorous sentiments by an overzealous American public.

Fig. 115. *Chess Players*. Boardman Robinson. [1917.] Lithograph. 8 3/16 × 11 13/16 in. Courtesy Fogg Art Museum, Harvard University, Cambridge, Mass., Gift of James N. Rosenberg.

Although Lenin, Wilson, Lloyd George, and Georges Clemenceau never met in a four-way conference, this Boardman Robinson cartoon probably expresses the threat the Allied leaders felt as Lenin was negotiating a separate peace with Germany in March, 1918, freeing the Germans to fight only on the Western front. The international Communist movement threatened the United States, Britain, and France, giving Lenin the somewhat sinister air associated with the "Bolshevik Menace."

Fig. 116. *The Hold-Up*. Edward Kemble. 1919. Ink wash on paper. 15 1/8 × 12 1/8 in. Courtesy The Swann Collection of Caricature and Cartoon.

The return of the railroads to private hands after World War I was a controversial problem. To facilitate prosecution of the war the government had taken over the railroads. The Transportation Act of 1920 returned the roads to private companies, but also widened the powers of the Interstate Commerce Commission, enabling the Commission to consolidate the railroads into a small group of companies exempt from antitrust laws. The companies claimed that the government had not kept up the roads during the War, that they would be required to spend millions of dollars to put them back in order, etc. Many of today's railroad problems might be traced to the ill-will resulting from the government takeover of World War I.

Fig. 117. *A Ticket to Normalcy*. John Tinney McCutcheon. Aug. 12, 1921. Ink on paper. 23 1/4 × 14 5/8 in. Courtesy The Lilly Library, Indiana University, Bloomington.

Employing President Harding's famous phrase "normalcy," a term he used in his 1920 presidential campaign to indicate a swift national recovery from World War I and a return to life and business as usual, John McCutcheon calls attention to the plight of the railroads following government operation of them during the war. "I want a ticket to Normalcy," says Uncle Sam. "Can't let you have one till the Road is repaired," answers the stationmaster.

Fig. 118. *Washington Conference*. Boardman Robinson. 1921. Ink and pastel on paper. 14 1/2 × 15 in. Courtesy The Swann Collection of Caricature and Cartoon.

President Harding at the request of Senator Borah issued a call to all major powers, except Russia, to attend the Washington disarmament conference in August, 1921. Secretary of State Charles Evans Hughes startled the conferees in his opening remarks by suggesting that they not only limit future armaments, but scrap large portions of those already constructed. Under Hughes' skillful leadership the delegates agreed to a limit for future construction along with a host of other treaties regarding warfare and colonial disagreements. The tonnage of capital ships in the future was limited to the ratio of five for the United States and Britain, three for Japan, and 1.67 for France and Italy.

Fig. 119. *How Happy I Could Be with Either if They'd Let Me Run Things*. C. K. Berryman. 1924. Ink on paper. 12 3/16 × 14 3/16 in. Courtesy the Library of Congress.

Perhaps the most ardent Progressive of all was Robert M. La Follette, Senator from Wisconsin, who entered the 1924 election as the head of a third party, the Progressive Party. Berryman is pointing out in this cartoon that La Follette would have worked with either party if they had turned more toward progressivism, and that either party would have liked to have had La Follette's progressive followers vote for them.

Fig. 120. *In the Yellowstone*. C. K. Berryman. 1927, in the Washington *Evening Star*. Ink on paper. 13 1/2 × 14 1/4 in. Courtesy National Park Service Archives. Harper's Ferry, W. Va.

An aloof and austere man who made a point of honesty and propriety, President Calvin Coolidge loved the simple things of life. He was on a fishing trip with his father in Vermont when President Harding died in San Francisco. Coolidge was also well known for being a man of few words, a virtue that Berryman obviously thinks Coolidge would have appreciated in Congress.

Fig. 121. *Negro Jazz Band*. Jan Matulka. 1920s. Black ink, pencil and white highlights on paper. 25 × 19 1/8 in. Courtesy St. Louis Art Museum: Friends of the St. Louis Museum Fund.

Nothing expresses the spirit of the 1920s better than jazz. It began to emerge from the Black enclaves of America's cities during the early years of World War I and burst onto the national scene along with bobbed hair, short skirts and joy rides. This vital expression of the emotional extremes of Black life is one of America's most important contributions to twentieth century music and is destined to endure, according to Leopold Stokowski, "because it is an expression of the times, of the breathless, energetic, superactive times in which we are living. . . ."

Fig. 122. *Indian Detour*. John Sloan. Sept. 24, 1927. Etching. 9 13/16 × 12 5/8 in. Courtesy Amon Carter Museum, Fort Worth.

The tourists have crowded around the corn dance at Santo Domingo Pueblo. In this print Sloan is satirizing the Fred Harvey Indian Tour. "Busses take the tourists out to view the Indian dances, which are religious ceremonials and naturally not understood as such by the visiting crowds," he wrote.

Fig. 123. *National Park as the People Inherited It*. Herbert Johnson. 1920s. Ink, gouache, crayon on paper. 13 1/2 × 18 in. Courtesy National Park Service Archives.

Industry and manufacturing were growing with phenomenal speed during the decade of the twenties, and in many cases this growth was labeled as "progress" in spite of detrimental effects it might have had on the environment. Here Herbert Johnson expresses the fear that, unless checked, these industries could end up destroying all the beautiful areas set aside as national parks.

115

Fig. 124. *I Won't Workers*. John Clubb. 1914. Ink on paper. 17 3/4 × 13 5/8 in. Courtesy The Swann Collection of Caricature and Cartoon.

One of the more radical labor unions in America's history, the Industrial Workers of the World was founded in June, 1905, in Chicago. Advocating abolition of the wage system and formation of industrial unions, the I. W. W. opposed America's entry into World War I, but was itself eliminated as a powerful labor force in the West between 1918 and 1920 by government prosecution. Their most influential leader, William D. ("Big Bill") Haywood, led them in several successful strikes when laborers were badly needed in the expanding economy, but was himself jailed during the war.

Fig. 125. *Celebration of Highways*. Winsor McCay. n.d. Pen and ink on paper. 6 7/8 × 23 in. Courtesy The Chesler Collection, Library, Fairleigh Dickinson University, Florham-Madison Campus.

In 1908 Henry Ford produced the design for his Model T motor car. It outperformed anything then on the road and at a price affordable to the general public. Automobiles were at first greeted by jeers, jokes, and often angry protest by a horse-drawn society which considered the car unsafe, uncomfortable, unaesthetic, and unpractical. But by 1920 about four million were rattling down American roads, that is, where roads existed. In 1921 the Federal Highway Act began financing a national highway program. Backwoods villages gained access to cities, the East Coast was joined to the West, the North to the South by a mesh of roads and highways. And these highways provided an enormous stimulus to travel and transportation for business and pleasure. People, goods, and ideas traveled and circulated across the land as never before.

Fig. 126. *Almost Thru the Dark Alley*. Kenneth Chamberlain. 1919 in the Cleveland *Press*. Black crayon, pen, and ink on paper. 22 × 17 in. Courtesy Grunwald Center for the Graphic Arts, University of California, Los Angeles.

Women were finally granted the right to vote on June 4, 1919, when Congress passed the nineteenth amendment to the Constitution stating that no one could be denied their political rights because of sex. It was a long-overdue victory heralded by the Kansas City *Star* as "not just a victory for women alone" but "a victory for democracy and the principle of equality upon which the nation was founded." But "Uncle" Joe Cannon, Speaker of the House, did not see how anything would be different. He pointed out that he had been influenced by five generations of women and that he was the result of their molding. They did not have to have the vote to have influence. Many observers, however, expected that women would be a powerful force for honest government.

Fig. 127. *Playing Horse with Him*. Rollin Kirby. 1921. Lithographic pencil washed with tusche on cardboard. 19 7/8 × 14 7/8 in. Courtesy The Metropolitan Museum of Art, Gift of Rollin Kirby, 1944.

After the eighteenth amendment went into effect, Congress passed the National Prohibition Enforcement, or the Volstead, Act to enforce the amendment. President Wilson, in one of his last acts as President, vetoed the act on October 27, 1919, but Congress passed the law over his veto. A multi-million dollar business was immediately declared illegal and went underground. "Bootleggers" supplied forbidden liquor to rural and urban areas alike, and "speakeasies" became as numerous and as popular as saloons had been. Uncle Sam was saddled with prohibition, a sentiment given classic expression by Kirby's "Mr. Prohibition."

Fig. 129. *Hic Jacet John (Hic) Barleycorn.* Ralph Barton. 1920s. Ink and blue wash on paper. 8 × 10 in. Courtesy The Swann Collection of Caricature and Cartoon.

Fig. 128. *"So long as the dry farce lasts, a girl who sips ice-water is looked upon as 'freezing the party.'"* John Held, Jr. June, 1928, in *Harper's Bazaar.* Ink on paper. 7 3/4 × 8 1/16 in. Courtesy the Library of Congress.

Born in Salt Lake City in 1889, John Held, Jr., the "Mormon Kid," was the artist who gave the 1920s one of their most memorable images—the flapper. The flapper seemed to capture the spirit of "The Era of Wonderful Nonsense." In this drawing, which accompanied Emily Post's article entitled "How to Behave," Held has combined two of his images, the flapper and the college kids, all of whom are enjoying the forbidden delights of prohibition.

Shortly after the enactment of the eighteenth amendment, Rev. Billy Sunday held a mock funeral for "John Barleycorn," complete with a twenty-foot coffin and horse-drawn hearse. In his eulogy he denounced John Barleycorn as "God's worst enemy" and "Hell's best friend," but now with the advent of Prohibition, "The slums soon will be only a memory. We will turn our prisons into factories and our jails into storehouses and corncribs." But crime and corruption did not cease. On the contrary, Ralph Barton shows it rising from Barleycorn's grave as a gangster who drives the Puritans away to gain profit and power from the sale of illegal spirits.

Fig. 130. *The Only Thing They Fear*. John Tinney McCutcheon. 1929. Pen and ink on paper. 18 3/4 × 14 5/8 in. Courtesy The Chicago Historical Society.

On January 1, 1920 Attorney General A. Mitchell Palmer began a crackdown on "foreign subversives." The Great Red Raid resulted in two thousand arrests in thirty-three cities across the U.S.A. Fears aroused by Russia's Bolshevik Revolution and the general xenophobia and super-patriotism engendered during the First World War culminated in this attack on aliens, socialists, and other political and social non-conformists. Answering charges that the United States was behaving autocratically in deporting these "trouble-makers," Attorney General Palmer replied, "that in our determination to maintain our government we are treating our alien enemies with extreme consideration. To deny them the privilege of remaining in a country which they have openly deplored as an unenlightened community, unfit for those who prefer the privileges of Bolshevism, should be no hardship."

Fig. 131. *The Darwin Club*. Rea Irvin. 1914 in *Life*. Ink and wash on paper. 15 1/2 × 13 in. Courtesy The Swann Collection of Caricature and Cartoon.

As Darwin's concept of evolution spread, it had great impact on the intellectuals, many of whom tried to adapt it to society in general. They reasoned that if natural selection worked among the animals, the same sort of procedure was working in human society at a more refined level. Herbert Spencer coined the term that seemed to sum up Darwin's ideas for many people: the survival of the fittest. Rea Irvin seems in this drawing to be asking who the fittest really are, or at least what kind of behavior would characterize a member of the fittest.

Fig. 132. *The Special Prosecuting Attorney*. Daniel Robert Fitzpatrick. May 14, 1925. Crayon on paper. 26 × 21 7/16 in. Courtesy The State Historical Society of Missouri, Columbia.

A Tennessee state statute of 1925 forbade any public educational institution from teaching the "theory that denies the story of the divine creation of man as taught in the Bible." Thinking this law unconstitutional, John T. Scopes purposely taught the theory of evolution and was tried the following July for violation of the act. His case attracted nation-wide attention, and William Jennings Bryan and Clarence Darrow came to Tennessee to represent the prosecution and the defense. "Civilization is on trial," said Darrow as the trial began. The trial climaxed when Darrow called Bryan to the stand to testify as an expert on the Bible. Scopes was convicted, but the fine was set aside because the trial court had authorized a fine larger than the law permitted.

Fig. 133. *Billy Sunday*. George Bellows. 1923. Crayon and ink wash on paper. 15 × 28 1/2 in. Courtesy Boston Public Library, Print Department.

William Ashley Sunday, better known as Billy, was a professional baseball player from Chicago before he was ordained as a Presbyterian minister in 1903. Then he became one of the most famous revivalists of the 1920s, holding meetings across the nation as Americans were returning to "that Old Time Religion," enforcing prohibition, and denouncing evolution. According to one historian, Billy Sunday was one of the "big time operators" with "hard-sell showmanship, mass soul-saving, and massive profits."

Fig. 134. *Men, We've Got to Improve Our Image*. Jon Kennedy. 1960s. Crayon on paper. 13 3/4 × 10 11/16 in. Courtesy The State Historical Society of Missouri, Columbia.

The Ku Klux Klan, an organization founded in the South during Reconstruction, returned to power during the 1920s, organizing around anti-Catholic, anti-Semitic, anti-immigration, anti-Negro, and enforcement of prohibition stands. So strong in 1924 that it split the Democratic Party, the Klan was soon discredited and lost most of its members. It was virtually destroyed when the Baltimore *Sun* ran a series of stories on its illegal activities, and the Indiana Grand Dragon was convicted of murder.

Fig. 135. *Michael! Where's That Air Coming From?* Peter Arno. Nov. 26, 1932, in *The New Yorker*. Ink and wash on paper. 21 × 14 in. Courtesy The Swann Collection of Caricature and Cartoon.

A dropout from Yale in 1923, Peter Arno understood New York City's café society as well as anyone. A member of a respected New York family who changed his name so as not to embarrass them, he was also a member of the world of flappers and speakeasies and bandleader in a nightclub called The Rendezvous. When Harold Ross started *The New Yorker* magazine, Arno, with pictures like this, helped him create a magazine definitely not intended for Ross' imaginary "old lady in Dubuque."

Fig. 136. *Head of Sinclair Lewis*. Boardman Robinson. 1923. Ink and red crayon on paper. 8 7/8 × 7 in. Courtesy The Minneapolis Institute of Arts, the John De Laittre Fund.

In the twenties and thirties many young American writers and artists fled the puritanical structures of American society for the freedom of the Bohemian life in European cities. But Sinclair Lewis remained in America to write about Americans. His great novels, *Babbitt*, *Arrowsmith*, *Elmer Gantry* and *Dodsworth* laid bare the hypocrisy and shallowness of American middle-class values and culture. In 1930 he was awarded the Nobel Prize for Literature, the first American author to be so honored.

Fig. 137. *Mayor Walker, Welcome to New York*. Miguel Covarrubias. 1920s. Tempera and watercolor on paper. 16 × 11 in. Courtesy The Nikolas Murray Collection, The Iconography Collection, Humanities Research Center, University of Texas, Austin.

The man who seemed to lead New York City in the ways of the 1920s was Mayor Jimmy Walker, a rather average fellow but one who could translate the increasingly complex problems of the nation's largest city into terms the common man could understand. Mayor Walker also fitted in. His racy, big-city ways attracted many votes. He kept show girls on the side, although he was married. He took seven vacations during his first two years in office, although New York City was beset with problems. And he hastily resigned in 1932 after several charges of corruption were leveled against his administration. He lived in Europe for several years, then returned to New York to live out his years as president of a record company.

Fig. 138. *Let the "Swatting" Begin*. John Clubb. 1927. Ink and brush on paper. 19 × 14 7/8 in. Courtesy The Murray A. Harris Collection of Graphic Art, North Hollywood, Calif.

In the twenties sports, particularly spectator sports, captured the American public interest as never before, and baseball became the "national pastime." This interest was fanned by a new breed of journalist, the sportswriter, and the radio as well as the newspaper spread the sports news. This new breed included such notables as Damon Runyon, Grantland Rice, and Ring Lardner. Other writers had their comments too. George Bernard Shaw described baseball as a combination of "cricket . . . , puss-in-the-corner, and Handel's *Messiah*." In 1927, the date of this cartoon, the World Series pitted the New York Yankees against the Pittsburgh Pirates. That year Babe Ruth hit his peak, knocking a record sixty home runs. Uncle Sam is shown turning his attention away from a desk full of urgent national matters to enjoy instead America's national sport.

Fig. 139. *Enrico Caruso*. James Montgomery Flagg. Apr. 25, 1914, in *Harper's Weekly*. Dry brush, ink, tempera, wash on paper. 24 × 17 1/4 in. (sight). Courtesy Mr. and Mrs. Draper Hill, Memphis, Tenn.

Born in Naples, Italy, in February, 1873, Enrico Caruso swept into New York City to perform in the Metropolitan Opera in 1903, which he called "the goal of every opera singer's desire." Here he is pictured as Pagliacci in the fifth of a series called "Captains of Industry" done for the cover of *Harper's*. Widely loved for his sense of humor, his generosity, and his beautiful voice, Caruso became a popular performer with an international reputation. Flagg himself was proud of this caricature.

Fig. 140. *John D. Rockefeller, Sr., a caricature.* Erik Johan Smith. 1923. Pencil and ink on paper. 23 1/2 × 13 1/2 in. Courtesy Jonson Collection, University of New Mexico, Albuquerque, Gift of Mrs. Jerome Frank.

John D. Rockefeller was one of the first great, wealthy men of the United States. A deeply religious man who began his career by becoming a partner in a produce commission business in 1859, Rockefeller soon got into oil refining. In 1870 he and his associates organized Standard Oil Company of Ohio, which he developed into a company that dominated the oil refining industry. In 1892 he was forced to break up his holdings because of an adverse Supreme Court decision, but he continued to manage his vast empire through the holding company, Standard Oil of New Jersey, which the Supreme Court dissolved in 1911. Late in life Rockefeller developed a passionate interest in philanthropy and gave away over one-half billion dollars through the world-famous Rockefeller Foundation before his death in 1937.

Fig. 141. *At Least One Senator Now Knows What the President Meant by Choose.* Jay Norwood Darling. October 22, 1927, in the Des Moines *Register*. Pen and ink on paper. 28 1/2 × 22 1/2 in. Courtesy The University of Iowa Libraries, Iowa City.

When President Calvin Coolidge announced in 1927 that "I do not choose to run for President in 1928," he left many observers wondering if that meant that he would accept a draft. Ohio Senator Simeon Davison Fess, who was temporary chairman of the Republican National Convention and made the keynote address, apparently thought so and intended to nominate Coolidge at the end of his speech. But his hopes were "doused" by Coolidge's adamant refusal to accept.

Fig. 142. *But Isn't It Kind of Dangerous?* Jay Norwood Darling. June 1, 1926. Pen and ink on paper. 22 1/2 × 14 1/2 in. Courtesy The University of Iowa Libraries, Iowa City.

A veteran of the New York State legislature and Tammany Hall, Alfred E. Smith ran for President in 1928 on a platform featuring repeal of prohibition. "Ding" Darling realizes that Smith is on dangerous ground, as did H. L. Mencken: "Those who fear the Pope outnumber those who are tired of the Anti-Saloon League." Despite his charm and poise, Smith embarrassed the Democrats by clinging to his Lower East Side pronunciation of words like "raddio."

Fig. 143. [Caricature of Herbert Hoover.] Emidio Angelo. 1940 in the Philadelphia *Inquirer*. Ink on paper. 13 × 13 in. Courtesy Herbert Hoover Presidential Library, West Branch, Iowa.

Herbert Hoover carried the aura of "Coolidge prosperity" to the Presidency in 1928, but the Great Depression marked him indelibly as a Depression President. Known as an able engineer, businessman, and administrator, Hoover thought the Depression to be only temporary and never expended the creative energy he had lavished on the Belgian relief effort and U. S. Food Administration during World War I. He oversaw the Reconstruction Finance Corporation, but his conservative faith in individual initiative prevented him from forcefully using it.

Fig. 145. *Oct. 29. Dies Irae*. James Rosenberg. Lithograph on colored paper. 13 3/4 × 10 1/2 in. Courtesy Philadelphia Museum of Art, Carl and Laura Zigrosser Collection.

In September, 1929, the stock market began to ease downward, then it dropped sharply—and did not surge back. Foreign investors began to withdraw their money; prudent Americans began to wonder. Thursday, October 24, sent them into panic as millions of shares of stocks changed hands, and prices fell uniformly. But the following Tuesday was disastrous. No one knows how many shares really were sold, although the official total is in excess of sixteen millions. By the end of 1929 more than $30 billions, a sum equal to twice the national debt, had disappeared. It would be years before the country realize the magnitude of the disaster.

Fig. 144. *N. Y. Stock Ex*. Reginald Marsh. 1929. Crayon and ink on paper. 6 1/2 × 7 1/2 in. Courtesy the Library of Congress.

The 1920s were a zany, get-rich-quick era in which millions of Americans "played" or watched the Stock Market. The vice-president of General Motors summed it up well: "Everybody ought to be rich." Others saw the Stock Market as the national passion. Some play the horses, some gamble, some play Wall Street.

Fig. 147. *Franklin D. Roosevelt*. Miguel Covarrubias. 1930s. Pen and ink wash on paper. 13 3/4 × 9 1/2 in. Courtesy The Nikolas Murray Collection, The Iconography Collection, Humanities Research Center, University of Texas, Austin.

Franklin Delano Roosevelt was not an economist, but he was a political genius. Realizing that the country needed at least the semblance of action, he began his administration with a dramatic speech, then moved into a legislative program the likes of which the country had not seen. "First of all, let me assert my firm belief that the only thing we have to fear is fear itself—nameless, unreasoning, unjustified terror . . . . We are stricken by no plague of locusts. . . . Plenty is at our doorstep, but a generous use of it languishes in the very sight of the supply." The government and the people would now have an opportunity to remedy the ills of the nation because "the money changers have fled from their high seats in the temple of our civilization." With that he moved into the famous 100 days, which saw enactment of most of the New Deal legislative program.

Fig. 146. *Unemployed*. William Gropper. 1930. Mixed media on paper. 18 × 13 in. Courtesy William Gropper.

As the Great Depression was felt throughout the nation, millions lost their jobs. The United States had seen depression before, but never one that continued year after year and spread worldwide. No one really knew how many Americans were out of work—between twelve million and sixteen million. Perhaps the most damage, however, was done to the psyche. "'Depression' shows man as a senseless cog in a senselessly whirling machine which is beyond human understanding and has ceased to serve any purpose but its own," said Peter F. Drucker.

Fig. 148. *"You Know the Way Back Do You, Herbert?"* Daniel Robert Fitzpatrick. Nov. 19, 1935. Crayon on paper. 23 1/2 × 20 in. Courtesy The State Historical Society of Missouri, Columbia.

Among the most graphic reminders of the depression and its havoc were the "Hoovervilles," shanty-towns where the unemployed and poor lived in slum conditions. "I had not the stomach to stay long at the Hoovervilles I came upon here and there," wrote Matthew Josephson; "they were sores on the body politic, and they stank. Here was the unsanitary by-product of our freewheeling economy, with its haphazard institutions of private charity and its limited local relief." As the Hoovervilles spread, former President Hoover's promise of two chickens in every pot and a car in every garage sounded hollow. "Hoover blankets" were newspapers, broken down mule-drawn wagons were "Hoover wagons," and pockets turned inside-out were "Hoover flags." Fitzpatrick suggests in this cartoon that the Republican elephant will have to find his way back to the White House through the Hoovervilles.

Fig. 149. *Technocracy Devouring the City*. Winsor McCay. n. d. Pen, ink, colored pencil on paper. 11 × 22 in. Courtesy The Chesler Collection, Library, Fairleigh Dickinson University, Florham-Madison Campus.

Although there were few workable ideas that President Roosevelt could employ in combating the Depression, one that gained overnight popularity, except with skeptics like McCay, was "Technocracy," an idea unveiled in an article by Howard Scott of New York in December, 1932. His idea was that national affairs would be regulated by experts rather than by elected officials. His plan was novel but broke down when applied to something as vague as the price system. Technocracy fitted the mood of the early thirties and many grasped at it as the solution to the country's problems, but practical men only smiled. "Nobody could really make anything out of technocracy and Howard Scott," commented the New York *World Telegram*, "but they find it's a great thing to think about."

Fig. 150. *When Al Capone's Attorney Finished His Address to the Jury.* C. K. Berryman. 1931. Ink on paper. 12 9/16 × 14 1/8 in. Courtesy the Library of Congress.

The Big Guy of all the organized mobsters was Al Capone of Chicago, who had fought his way up through the organization from a New York slum. Devoting his time to organizing the gangsters, Capone soon had the largest mob in Chicago, and operated primarily by guaranteeing the illegal establishments in his district "protection" from police raids or raids by rival gangs. Capone collected an income from each of them and kept himself "clean." By 1929 he was worth probably $20 millions. But the gangster who was too big for local and state government was not too big for the federal government. In 1931 he was tried for income tax evasion, then was indicted for 5,000 separate charges of bootlegging. He was sentenced to eleven years in prison. He got out in eight, with time off for good behavior, but he was a broken man. He died in 1947 at age 48.

Fig. 151. *Another of Those Feasts of Love.* Dorman H. Smith. June 29, 1940 (?). Ink on paper. 21 11/16 × 20 3/16 in. Courtesy Mr. and Mrs. Draper Hill, Memphis, Tenn.

As manipulator of Franklin D. Roosevelt's political fortunes, James Farley impressed many people as the Tammany tiger run amuck—trampling over Jeffersonian democracy in the form of the lady who has just been devoured. Farley was credited with being an astute supporter whose skillful politics led to Roosevelt's presidential nomination in 1932.

Fig. 152. *"Come Up and See Me Sometime."* William Gropper. 1934. Ink on paper. 17 × 12 1/2 in. Courtesy William Gropper.

This anti-Roosevelt cartoon by Gropper pictures the President as temptress Mae West wearing the NRA eagle as a bauble and receiving love letters from supporters of labor interests such as William Green (president of the American Federation of Labor) and Senators Robert Wagner (sponsor of the Wagner Bill, which established the National Labor Relations Board) and Joe Robinson (who literally died trying to support Roosevelt in his later battles with the Supreme Court). At the same time he is receiving tokens from the bankers of Wall Street.

Fig. 153. [Caricature of J. P. Morgan, John D. Rockefeller, Henry Ford, and William R. Hearst as thugs.] William Gropper. Ink and crayon on paper. 14 1/4 × 11 1/8 in. Courtesy Collection of Morris George Hecht.

The so-called Robber Barons ruled the age of industrialism but came face to face with economic disaster and a growing federal government during the Depression. Able to have their way so long as the government did not intervene, the "captains of industry" had to yield to the force applied by the countervailing power of government regulation. "I do not believe that in the name of that sacred word, individualism, a few powerful interests should be permitted to make industrial cannon fodder of the lives of half the population of the United States," President Roosevelt announced as he noted the collapse of "equality of opportunity" and the control of the economic system by some 600 corporations. He called for a more equal distribution of the wealth as well as a change in the nature of the economic institutions that permitted such inequality.

Fig. 154. *Strike-breaking*. William Gropper. 1930s. Brush and ink on paper. 14 × 11 in. Courtesy William Gropper.

Due largely to the tireless efforts of John L. Lewis, American labor made large legal gains that permitted men to join unions and use the unions to bargain with their bosses. Putting these rights into practice, however, was more difficult. Some employers still hired strike-breaking crews or hired guns. A strike might get a union man injured or killed. In this cartoon Gropper belittles the government enforcement agencies who go looking for insects while major crimes are being committed. "Labor, like Israel, has many sorrows," said Lewis in an eloquent summary. "Its women weep their fallen and they lament for the future of the children of the race."

Fig. 155. *The State Department*. William Gropper. c. 1937. Crayon, ink, and white highlights on paper. 14 1/16 × 11 in. (sight). Courtesy William Gropper.

As it became more evident that Europe was headed for war and that America was entrenching in isolationism, President Roosevelt, in the words of King George VI, "led public opinion [toward involvement] by allowing it to get ahead of [him]." In this cartoon Gropper personifies the attitude of the State Department in leading the public. Die-hard isolationists, which before 1940 counted many progressives among their ranks, saw Roosevelt and his advisors, especially the "Brain-Trusters," as disregarding the will of the people in most matters.

Fig. 156. *Monkey-Glands for the N. R. A.* William Gropper. 1930s. Ink on paper. 14 3/4 × 10 3/4 in. Courtesy Collection of Morris George Hecht.

The National Recovery Administration (NRA) was created in 1933 by executive decision, approved by Congress. It was intended to regulate wages, working hours, and, indirectly, prices. Director Hugh Johnson energetically applied himself to his task, but businessmen damned it as "creeping socialism," and labor leaders called it "business fascism." The Hearst newspapers claimed that NRA really stood for "No Recovery Allowed." This cartoon by Gropper was probably done before the Supreme Court invalidated it in May, 1935, during an era in which William Green, president of the A. F. of L., and Roosevelt were still hopeful that the agency would perform the economic miracles they had hoped.

Fig. 157. *The Upturn*. James Thurber. 1934. Pen and ink on paper, glued to portion of wastebasket. 9 × 12 in. Courtesy Ohio State University Libraries, Columbus.

In the summer, 1933, most everyone agreed that the worst of the depression was over. Business confidence had returned, and people assured each other that prosperity was on its way. The Stock Exchange showed some life as the Dow-Jones index turned upward and the volume of trading topped any month's performance since October, 1929. But the situation had not really changed. "The Upturn" was as dead as Thurber depicts here. Factories still stood idle. Purchases were not up. The poor did not have jobs. There was more to conquer than the fear that President Roosevelt had warned about.

Fig. 158. *Slap Stic Comedy*. Jack Patton. 1933. Ink with white highlights on paper. 12 3/4 × 11 1/8 in. Courtesy Collection of Joel Rosen, Fort Worth.

Capitalizing on the confusion, despair, and frustration following defeat in World War I, Adolf Hitler gained political power in Germany and quickly abolished the Republic and established the Third Reich. Cartoonist Jack Patton shows Hitler in the guise of Charlie Chaplin, the master clown of American slapstick comedies, tossing a pie in the face of the Weimar Republic. In 1933 the world could still regard Hitler as something of a joke, as Chaplin often did in his routine. By 1939, however, Hitler had proved his diabolical characteristics were real.

Fig. 159. *The Four Dictators*. Miguel Covarrubias. 1930s. Watercolor on cardboard. 17 1/2 × 15 in. Courtesy The Swann Collection of Caricature and Cartoon.

The 1930s is often referred to as the decade of the dictators. Here Miguel Covarrubias has depicted three well-known ones with one aspirant. Joseph Stalin, Benito Mussolini, and Adolf Hitler are shown with Huey P. ("Kingfish") Long of Louisiana, who, until his assassination in the State Capitol building of Louisiana, was a radical threat to President Franklin D. Roosevelt.

Fig. 160. *"Some Folks Might Prefer the Horse & Buggy Era."* Henry I. Cobb, 1935–1936. Charcoal on paper 20 × 29 7/8 in. (irregular). Courtesy Collection of Paulette Greene, Rockville Centre, New York.

The New Deal, a dramatically different approach to government, shocked American society with its introduction of scores of novel social legislative measures, including the Social Security Act, minimum wage and hour principles, and the Federal Deposit Insurance Corporation. People acknowledged that the New Deal started the country moving again, but the foremost question in everyone's mind, including FDR's, was "to where?"

Fig. 161. [Roosevelt in *Alice in Wonderland*.] Gregory Duncan. 1930s. Watercolor on paper. 12 1/2 × 8 3/4 in. (image). Courtesy The Swann Collection of Caricature and Cartoon.

In Duncan's parody of one of John Tenniel's famous *Alice in Wonderland* illustrations, Franklin Roosevelt, as the cook, stirs a pot of money which he hopes will quiet the squalling "Administration Mistakes." Jim Farley, a Democratic politico and one of Roosevelt's presidential advisers, is portrayed as the irascible Duchess. The ever-changeable Cheshire Cat is Secretary of the Interior, Harold Ickes, a former Republican who abruptly switched his support to Roosevelt and the Democrats in 1932.

Fig. 162. *The West is in the Saddle*. John Tinney McCutcheon. 1936 in the Chicago *Tribune*. Ink on paper. 21 × 14 in. (sight). Courtesy The Newberry Library, Chicago.

In 1936 the Republicans selected Alfred Landon and Frank Knox to challenge the incumbent Roosevelt. Both were Mid-Westerners, which was unusual since a sectional mix is usually sought for a presidential ticket, but the G. O. P. had great hopes for Governor Landon of Kansas. Landon had an appealing, down-to-earth personality and had implemented the state's recovery programs without incurring debt. He had no chance, however, as he was overwhelmed by Roosevelt's New Deal programs.

Fig. 163. *New Deal Plan for Enlarged Supreme Court*. C. K. Berryman. Feb. 10, 1937. Ink on paper. 12 1/4 × 14 1/8 in. Courtesy the Library of Congress.

In 1935 and 1936 the Supreme Court declared several New Deal programs unconstitutional and the Administration was furious at what it considered impediments to national progress and recovery from the Depression. On February 5, 1937, Roosevelt sent a bill to Congress to replace six Supreme Court Justices and forty-four federal judges with younger, more able men. Roosevelt's "Court Packing" plan caused great contention among congressional Democrats and caused many people to question Roosevelt's motives and political integrity. In Berryman's cartoon Harold Ickes, Administrator of Public Works, is shocked by Roosevelt's judicial building plans.

Fig. 164. *"But It Would Make Such a Nice Scoop if You'd only Tell Me, Franklin."* Jacob Burck. May, 1940, in the Chicago *Times*. Ink and crayon on paper. 22 1/2 × 15 1/4 in. Courtesy Franklin D. Roosevelt Presidential Library, Hyde Park, New York, Gift of the Armand Hammer Foundation.

Eleanor Roosevelt was one of America's most active First Ladies. Her intense concern for social welfare took her from city slums to the wastes of the Dust Bowl. And she wrote a syndicated column, "My Day," which reported her observations and concern for what she saw. This cartoon, which was one of her personal favorites, shows her wishing that her husband would reveal to her his intention regarding a third term in 1940.

Fig. 165. *Listening to the Radio*. Perry Barlow. 1930s. Ink and wash on paper. 20 × 17 in. Courtesy The Swann Collection of Caricature and Cartoon.

The radio, like the automobile, was a sweeping technological advance of the twentieth century and had enormous social implications. The radio industry began with the tinkering of a few hobbyists on homemade sets after the First World War. In 1920 Westinghouse built the first broadcasting station in Pittsburgh. By 1927 there were seven hundred stations in the United States, and the radio was standard furniture in the American home. It provided news, information, culture, and entertainment instantaneously, at all hours, to all sectors of the population.

Fig. 166. *Martha Graham*. Miguel Covarrubias. 1930s. Pencil on paper. 8 × 5 in. Courtesy The Swann Collection of Caricature and Cartoon.

One of America's greatest contributions to the arts of the twentieth century has been the development of modern or interpretive dance. Early in the century American dancers such as Isadora Duncan, Ruth St. Denis, and Ted Shawn eschewed the strictures of classic ballet, seeking a freer expression of emotion and ideas by movement. Martha Graham, a student of St. Denis and Shawn, developed a new technique of dance based on sudden and subtle contraction and release which gave the dancing of her company and students from 1929 to the present a distinctive power of movement and expression.

Fig. 167. *Ernest Hemingway*. Albert Hirschfeld. 1930s. Gouache on paper. 12 1/4 × 8 1/4 in. Courtesy The Iconography Collection, Humanities Research Center, University of Texas, Austin.

Ernest Hemingway, one of America's greatest authors, spent much of his life as an expatriate, and most of his writings deal with disaffected Americans adrift among other cultures and peoples. Hemingway eschewed intellectual or social pretensions and, though in the vanguard of twentieth century literary developments, cultivated a rugged anti-intellectual image. Hirschfeld depicts him reading James Joyce's *Ulysses* in the Stork Club, a book that had been banned in the United States as obscene until 1934. It was this kind of narrowminded prudishness that had driven the young Hemingway abroad. After achieving international fame, however, he returned home to be lionized by New York nightclub society. Here we see the burly Hemingway enjoying success, social prominence, and a masterpiece of modern literature.

Fig. 168. *Sultan o' Swat*. Leo Hershfield. Apr., 1933. Pen and ink on paper. 12 3/4 × 9 3/4 in. Courtesy National Baseball Hall of Fame and Museum, Inc., Cooperstown, New York.

George Herman ("Babe") Ruth was one of America's greatest and most beloved sports heroes. After beginning as a pitcher with the Boston Red Sox, Ruth batted his way to fame with the New York Yankees. As a member of one of the most formidable Yankee teams of all time, Ruth helped bring seven pennants to New York between 1921 and 1932. When Yankee Stadium was built in 1923, it was dubbed "the house that Ruth built." It was built for him, too, with a specially-designed short right field fence that helped him on his way to a record sixty home runs in 1927. Babe was the second player voted into the Baseball Hall of Fame in 1936.

Fig. 169. *Dispossessed*. Rollin Kirby. Jan. 29, 1931. Pencil, black ink, blue crayon on paper. 16 1/4 × 12 1/4 in. Courtesy Dartmouth College Library, Hanover, N. H.

When *Literary Digest* polled almost five million people in 1930 it found more than fifty percent either against prohibition or in favor of some kind of modification. The Wickersham Commission, assigned to study prohibition, soon reported the same ambivalent conclusions in January, 1931. Of the eleven members, two favored repeal, four modification, and five further experiment. The commission concluded that prohibition was not working, but that it should be continued. Here Kirby shows that "bone dry enforcement" is a thing of the past although the country is still "saddled" with Mr. Prohibition. That too was removed in December, 1933.

Fig. 170. *But Only God Can Make a Tree*. Reginald Marsh. 1930s. Ink, crayon, and Chinese white on paper. 20 1/2 × 13 5/8 in. Courtesy the Library of Congress.

In the fall of 1937 the stock market took another nose-dive, wiping out gains made during the first five years of the Roosevelt administration. The New Deal had not cured all the nation's ills, or even most of them. Lewis Mumford concluded that, "Our metropolitan civilization is not a success. It is a different kind of wilderness from that which we have deflowered." Naturalist Joseph Wood Krutch commented that it was a "gloomy vision of a dehumanized world."

Fig. 171. *The Hanged Man* (from the portfolio *The American Scene*, No. 1). José Clemente Orozco. 1933–1934. Lithograph. 12 3/4 × 8 15/16 in. Courtesy The Museum of Modern Art, New York City, Gift of Abby Aldrich Rockefeller.

The great Mexican muralist Orozco here has turned his attention to the American landscape, attempting to graphically illustrate the staggering statistics on lynching in the United States. Between 1885 and 1950 more than 4,000 persons were lynched, more than 3,300 of them Negroes. In 1935 alone it has been estimated that lynchings were occurring at the rate of one every three weeks. The Great Depression drove millions of people out of work and pushed their families below the poverty line. Under such circumstances Negroes especially suffered, because the racial hatred only increased. Amid such conflicting values, Orozco has made an eloquent comment on the "land of the free" where "liberty and justice for all" prevails.

Fig. 172. *Massachusetts—There She Stands!* Rollin Kirby. Apr., 1937. Black crayon, black ink, blue pencil heightened with white wash on paper. 17 7/8 × 11 3/4 in. Courtesy Fogg Art Museum, Harvard University, Cambridge, Mass., Gift of Mrs. Frederic T. Lewis in memory of Dr. Frederic T. Lewis.

In 1935 widespread legislation supported by the Daughters of the American Revolution, the American Legion, the Hearst newspapers, and the Elks was introduced requiring teachers and professors (in many states those in private and parochial as well as public schools) to take oaths of loyalty to their state and the national constitutions. Opposition to these teacher's oath laws was equally widespread; in Massachusetts it was led by Harvard President J. B. Conant. Conant and his supporters fought for a repeal of the measure for two years, until such was passed by the Massachusetts legislature on April 1, 1937. The next day, contrary to expectations, Governor Hurley surprised everyone by vetoing the measure.

Fig. 173. *Learn to Dance "The Big Apple" in One Easy Lesson.* Reuben ("Rube") Goldberg. Dec., 1937. Pen, ink, and watercolor on paper. 14 1/2 × 21 in. Courtesy The Swann Collection of Caricature and Cartoon.

As *Time* magazine explained in 1937, "the Big Apple" is "danced in a circle by a group." As in a Virginia reel, one dancer calls the steps, which produces a lot of "floating power and fannying." "The Big Apple invariably ends upon a somewhat reverent note, with everybody leaning back and raising his arms heavenward," the "Praise Allah" movement. Goldberg, famous for his crazy inventions, devised a foolproof method of Big Apple instruction.

Fig. 175. *U. S. Supporting Chiang Kai-Shek against China*. William Gropper. 1938. Ink on paper. 14 × 10 in. Courtesy William Gropper.

One of President Truman's great problems immediately following World War II was the Chinese situation. For years Nationalist President Chiang Kai-Shek had been waging a losing battle against Mao Tse-Tung and the Communist rebels. Three times the pair met under American auspices to try to work out an agreement, but Mao knew he could win, and Chiang would sacrifice nothing to gain a settlement. Even General George C. Marshall gave up in disgust. Secretary of State Dean Acheson issued a Truman administration "white paper" in 1949 acknowledging that China had been "lost."

Fig. 174. *The Fuehrer Wallace*. C. K. Berryman. Feb. 16, 1938. Ink on paper. 12 1/4 × 14 1/16 in. Courtesy the Library of Congress.

For his Secretary of Agriculture, President Roosevelt picked Henry A. Wallace, a man who had successfully edited *Wallace's Farmer* and had built a respectable business producing and selling hybrid seed corn. As head of the Agricultural Adjustment Administration, Wallace went through a political metamorphosis and became an ardent socialist. He ran against Truman and Dewey for President in 1948, then reversed himself and published "*Why I Was Wrong*" late in life.

Fig. 176. *Gone With the Wind . . . .* Antonio Arias Bernal. 1940. Watercolor on paper. 20 1/2 × 15 1/2 in. Courtesy The Swann Collection of Caricature and Cartoon.

By the summer of 1940 the Fascists controlled all of Europe except hard-pressed Great Britain. Still professing neutrality, President Roosevelt took steps to aid the Allies. In spite of vocal isolationist opposition, he urged an unprecedented arms production build-up and supported the Act of Havana (July, 1940), a defense agreement which provided that America would defend Latin America in case of Fascist aggression there. In September he instituted the first compulsory peacetime draft in American history. In Argentinean Arias' cartoon, South America, which enjoyed cordial relations with both the United States and Germany, watches Uncle Sam's pledges of neutrality and isolationism blow away as he pours funds and energy into armaments.

Fig. 177. *John L. Lewis vs. Congress.* Lute Pease. 1944 (?) in Newark *Evening News*. Charcoal, pencil, and ink on paper. 15 1/4 × 19 1/4 in. Courtesy Rutgers University Library, New Brunswick, N.J.

During the Second World War American labor honored a "no-strike" pledge. An exception occurred in 1943 when John L. Lewis, leader of the United Mine Workers, called for a walk-out. An angry Congress passed the Smith-Connally Act, overriding a presidential veto. The Act authorized the president to seize strike-bound factories, compelled "cool off" periods before walk-outs, and prohibited union contributions to political campaigns. The cartoon by Lute Pease depicts the head-on confrontation of John L. Lewis and the Congress, which was in no mood for reformist or social legislation. In 1944, as President Roosevelt put it, "Dr. New Deal" had to give way to "Dr. Win-the-War."

Fig. 178. *Albert Einstein, Citizen of the New World*. Daniel Robert Fitzpatrick. Oct. 4, 1940. Crayon on paper. 23 15/16 × 19 15/16 in. Courtesy The State Historical Society of Missouri, Columbia.

Albert Einstein was the director of theoretical physics at the Kaiser Wilhelm Institute in Berlin and had received the Nobel Prize for Physics in 1921 for his Theory of Relativity. However, the Nazis were more interested in his Jewish parentage than his accomplishments and reputation. They confiscated his property and revoked his German citizenship in 1934. He subsequently immigrated to the United States, assuming a post at the Institute for Advanced Study at Princeton, where he continued to pursue his research until his death in 1955.

Fig. 179. *Didn't Know What He Uncorked*. Daniel Robert Fitzpatrick. 1942. Watercolor, crayon, and ink on paper. 20 × 17 5/8 in. Courtesy The Murray A. Harris Collection of Graphic Art.

The United States watched the European war and prepared for ultimate involvement, but still clung to neutrality as late as December, 1941. Noting the strong isolationist tendencies and believing that America would be drawn into the war anyway, Japanese strategists decided that a surprise attack might keep America out of the war altogether by strengthening the isolationists, and at the very least would give Japan the advantage of choosing the point at which to begin the war in the Pacific. Although the attack on Pearl Harbor was more successful than the Japanese had even hoped, it served to unify the divided Americans and permitted them to enter the conflict determined to win, to gain revenge for the "sneak attack."

Fig. 180. [Chinese leaflet of an American pilot.] Anonymous. 1945. 14 × 7 1/2. Colored woodcut. Photographic copy courtesy American Heritage Publishing Company. Courtesy the Library of Congress.

This Chinese likeness of an American pilot was passed out during World War II in an effort to help Americans shot down by Japanese planes over Mainland China. The script at the bottom asks the Chinese should help any American pilot looking like the caricature, and that they should not let the Japanese occupation forces see the leaflet or they would be tortured.

Fig. 181. *"I'll be damned. Did you know this can opener fits on the end of a rifle?"* Bill Mauldin. 1940s. 4 13/16 × 3 7/8 in. Book page. Courtesy Fred White, Jr., Bryan, Tex.

Too often the history of World War II merges into a glorious battle waged by America after being deceitfully attacked by the Japanese at Pearl Harbor. Historians emphasize the tremendous war effort, the unprecedented production, the success of American arms. Bill Mauldin, the "G. I. cartoonist," effectively presents the common soldier's view of the war. The individual had not changed, although war had been taken over by engineers. Willie and Joe became the symbol of every American G. I. in the war.

Fig. 182. *Tokio Here We Come*. Jay Norwood Darling. c. 1944. Pen and brush on paper. 28 5/8 × 22 3/4 in. Courtesy William A. Farnsworth Library and Art Museum, Rockland, Me.

Fig. 183. [Teheran Conference.] Anonymous. 1943. Colored postcard. 4 × 5 in. Courtesy Franklin D. Roosevelt Presidential Library, Hyde Park, N. Y.

The Japanese attack on Pearl Harbor inspired an immediate change in the American opinion toward the war. The country immediately mobilized, both public opinion and military forces. By 1943 American factories were producing 40% of the world's total arms supply with fifteen million citizens in the armed forces. Until the defeat of Germany, however, the brunt of this effort was focused on Europe. With the situation in hand there, Americans turned their fury toward the Pacific, and headed for the Japanese home islands.

In November and December, 1943, Prime Minister Churchill, President Roosevelt, and Premier Joseph Stalin met in the Iranian capital for the first of several three-power conferences. The main topic of conversation was the projected British-American invasion of Western Europe, supported by a flanking invasion in southern France and a Soviet counter-offensive against Germany from the east. Stalin reaffirmed his promise to enter the war, and the three leaders laid plans for an international peace-keeping organization to be established after the war.

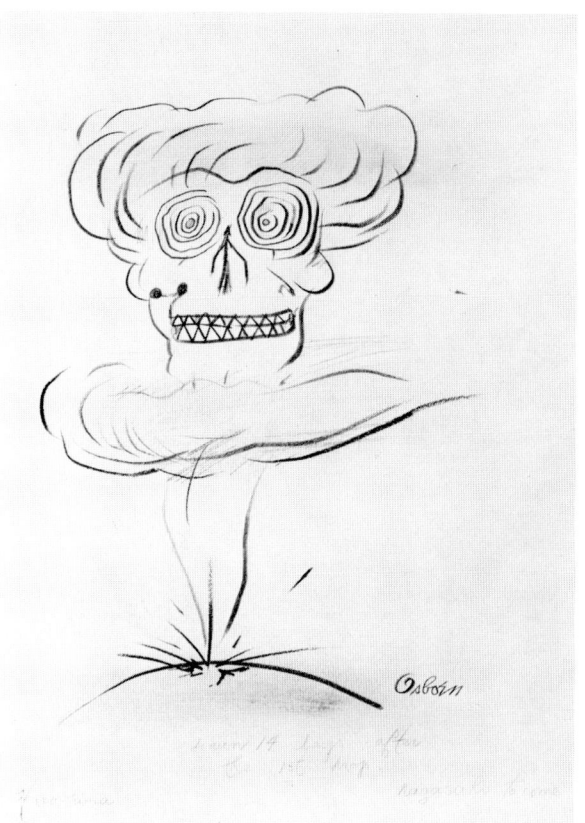

Fig. 184. *Hiroshima*. Robert Osborn. 1945. Crayon and pencil on paper. 13 1/4 × 10 in. (with text). Courtesy the Library of Congress.

The climax of the war against Japan was the dropping of the first atomic bomb on the Japanese city of Hiroshima in August, 1945. With an explosive force of more than 20,000 tons of TNT, the bomb destroyed over four square miles of the city and killed or injured more than 160,000 persons. Osborn did the drawing fourteen days after the devastation of Hiroshima.

Fig. 185. *For Whom the Bell Tolls*. Fred O. Seibel. Aug. 10, 1945, in Richmond *Times–Dispatch*. Pen and ink on paper; caption in pencil. 23 1/8 × 14 7/16 in. Courtesy University of Virginia Library, Charlottesville.

With the dropping of the second atomic bomb on Nagasaki, Fred O. Seibel produced this cartoon pointing out that the bell was tolling for the Japanese even if they did not know it. There was some doubt in the United States that the Japanese would surrender when they did not immediately give up after the first bomb was dropped, but it was a difficult decision for a split government to reach. The Japanese had sent a team of physicists to Hiroshima to determine whether it was really an atomic bomb. By the time the scientists had returned to Tokyo, made their report, and the government considered its decision, the Americans had already dropped the second bomb, which brought complete surrender.

A NEW ERA IN MAN'S UNDERSTANDING OF NATURE'S FORCES
—*President Truman.*

TUESDAY, AUGUST 7, 1945.

Fig. 186. *A New Era in Man's Understanding of Nature's Forces.* Daniel Robert Fitzpatrick. Aug. 7, 1945, in the St. Louis *Post-Dispatch*. Crayon on paper. 14 1/8 × 11 in. Courtesy The State Historical Society of Missouri, Columbia.

With the dropping of the atomic bomb on the Japanese city of Hiroshima, the world entered the atomic age, and Fitzpatrick saluted this new power the following day with this cartoon. Albert Einstein had urged that the bomb be developed only because he feared that Germany was developing it. Now he was concerned that the bomb would be misused. Although there were immediate questions concerning the welfare of a Europe devastated by warfare, the greater question that is still not satisfactorily solved is how the nations will handle atomic power.

Fig. 187. *Hot Piano*. Ben Shahn. 1948. Watercolor on paper. 23 1/2 × 15 1/2 in. Courtesy Harry S. Truman Library and Museum, Independence, Mo.

President Harry S Truman guided the United States during the first faltering steps of the atomic age with unusual decisiveness. He was rudely introduced to the atomic age with President Roosevelt's sudden death, but quickly absorbed the necessary information to make required decisions. He became well-liked through his first term in office because of his directness, his "down to earth" personality, and his affinity with the common people. His performances at the piano became his trademark, and his familiar rendering of *The Missouri Waltz* became his campaign song. Ben Shahn did this watercolor in preparation for a larger study of Truman and Thomas Dewey, the Democratic and Republican candidates in the election of 1948.

Fig. 188. *There's No Free Election in Poland*. William Gropper. 1948. Mixed media. 9 1/2 × 9 3/4 in. Courtesy William Gropper.

Churchill and Franklin Roosevelt agreed to permit the Soviet Union to occupy and dominate Poland after World War II, with the Soviet promise that they would allow free elections in Poland so the Polish government-in-exile could be properly represented. When the naïve Allies realized that Poland was now a Soviet satellite, they grew bitter. Gropper points out in this cartoon that while Russia was crushing political liberty in Poland, Eugene Talmadge was being elected governor of Georgia after a recount in which enough votes to give him the victory had been "found." He might well have added Texas, for it was in 1948 that Lyndon B. Johnson won his disputed race for the U. S. Senate.

 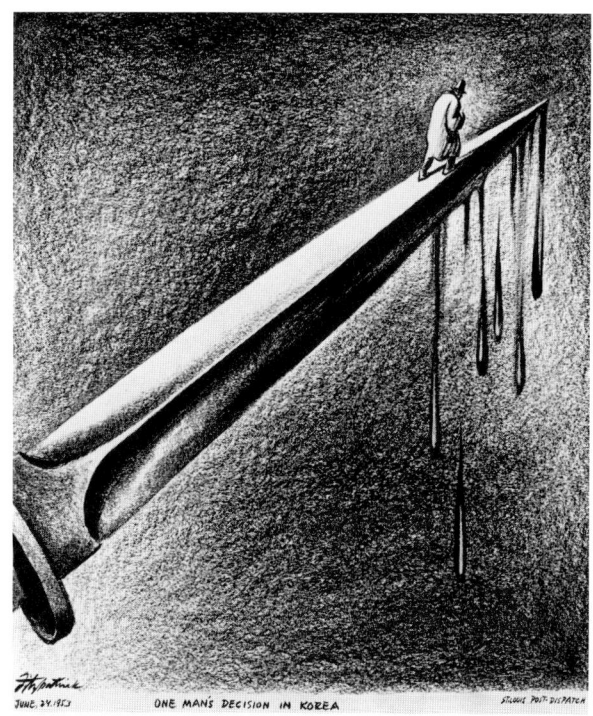

Fig. 189. *Step by Step—Where Are We Going?* Don Hesse. 1950s. Ink, crayon, and pencil on paper. 11 1/4 × 9 in. Courtesy the Library of Congress.

When Secretary of State John Foster Dulles announced that the United States would depend less on traditional arms and more on the "deterrent of massive retaliatory power," the United States and the Soviet Union, both of whom possessed the superbomb, or hydrogen bomb, were locked in an unending arms race. Both countries experimented with larger and more powerful bombs, invested more in "defense," and entered every confrontation with the threat of nuclear disaster prominent. Both countries were trying for, in the words of the day, a "bigger bang for the buck."

Fig. 190. *One Man's Decision in Korea*. Daniel Robert Fitzpatrick. June 24, 1953, in the St. Louis *Post-Dispatch*. Ink, crayon, and gouache on paper. 15 3/8 × 13 1/8 in. Courtesy the Library of Congress.

On June 25, 1950, the North Korean Communists attacked South Korea, and President Truman committed U. S. forces with the sanction of the United Nations but without congressional authorization. Truman organized a wartime cabinet, placed the United States on a semi-wartime status, and declared a national emergency. He later sought and received congressional support for his actions, but he had involved the United States in the Korean War by virtually a one-man decision.

Fig. 191. *Taft-Hartley Act*. Jim Berryman. 1948 in the Washington *Evening Star*. Pen and ink on paper. 12 5/8 × 13 5/8 in. Courtesy Harry S. Truman Library and Museum, Independence, Mo.

Returning the nation to peacetime economic conditions following the war was difficult at best. Truman's unwillingness to abandon price controls was blamed for a wave of strikes that swept the country in 1945–1946 and led to sweeping Republican victories in the 1946 congressional elections. Using the votes as a mandate, Congress moved toward more conservative measures including the Taft-Hartley Act in 1947. Called the "slave labor law" because it forced men to work against their will (during the sixty-day "cooling-off" period before a strike is permitted), the Act probably unified and strengthened unions because of their unanimous opposition to it and assured President Truman's surprising victory in 1948.

Fig. 192. " . . . that we here highly resolve that this nation, under God, shall have a new birth of freedom . . ." A. Lincoln, Gettysburg Address. Leslie Illingworth. Mar. 17, 1954, in *Punch*. Scratchboard and pen. 14 1/4 × 11 in. Courtesy Mr. and Mrs. Draper Hill, Memphis, Tenn.

Another shock of the post-war era was the Cold War that the United States and the Soviet Union slipped into almost unnoticed until the lines were clearly drawn across Europe and Asia. The confrontation included an atomic arms race (punctuated by spies, investigations, and executions), the "loss" of China, and active intervention in Korea. Crediting virtually all the country's problems to Communist infiltration in the State Department and other branches of government, Senator Joseph McCarthy of Wisconsin began a one-man campaign to "clean out" the government. Thrashing about aimlessly—not one of his charges resulted in a conviction—McCarthy attracted widespread attention among countrymen who also were groping for answers in the increasingly complex world.

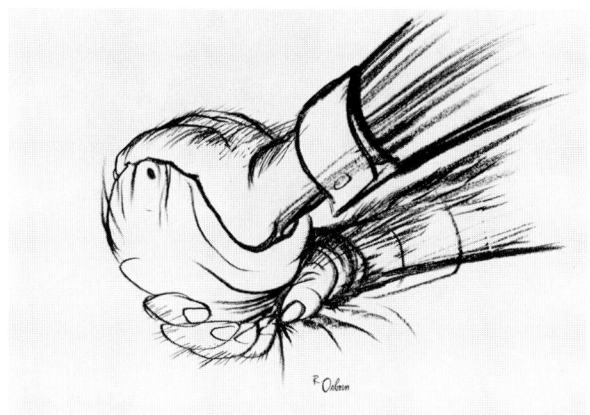

Fig. 193. *Sacco and Vanzetti*. Ben Shahn. 1952. Ink on paper. 5 3/4 × 8 3/8 in. (sight). Courtesy Fogg Art Museum, Harvard University, Cambridge, Mass.

Although anarchists Sacco and Vanzetti were convicted and executed for murder in 1927, Ben Shahn, who was convinced of their innocence, continued to draw and paint them and scenes from their trial. As the McCarthy mania gripped the country, Shahn and other artists like William Gropper looked to our history to find examples that became articulate reminders of other miscarriages of justice, a comment that they could make with a historical figure without fear of reprisal from McCarthy.

Fig. 194. *If You Differ With Me We Will Silence You*. Robert Osborn. 1954. Ink and crayon on paper. 14 15/16 × 21 in. Courtesy The Swann Collection of Caricature and Cartoon.

Robert Osborn was more direct, depicting the fear and lack of freedom of speech that prevailed during McCarthy's reign. After a televised appearance in which McCarthy accused an army dentist of being "pink," the public began to see him as dictatorial and cruel, and he lost influence. In September, 1954, the Senate censured him, and he vanished from the national scene almost as quickly as he had arrived. He died in 1957.

Fig. 195. *"Please understand there is no depression in this house, and we are not interested in the possibilities of defeat. They do not exist."* (Queen Victoria). Leslie Illingworth. Mar. 19, 1958, in *Punch*. Pen and brush on paper. 13 9/16 × 10 3/4 in. Courtesy Mr. and Mrs. Draper Hill, Memphis, Tenn.

When the economy plunged and unemployment soared (ending the post-war prosperity) in 1957, President Eisenhower forestalled tax cuts and refused substantial federal subsidies to stimulate economic recovery. The situation was first called a "recession," Eisenhower's administration preferring not to use the dreaded term "depression." Illingworth here comments on the President's apparent belief that the economic threat will vanish if he does not recognize it.

Fig. 196. *Braggers*. Nasu. 1957. Ink on paper. 7 9/16 × 10 11/16 in. Courtesy The State Historical Society of Missouri, Columbia.

As the United States and the Soviet Union continued their arms race, developing increasingly larger bombs and more powerful carriers, the disarmed Japanese grew more discontent. In this cartoon the Japanese artist Nasu shows President Eisenhower and Soviet Premier Nikita Khrushchev bragging about their missiles. The Japanese are particularly sensitive to nuclear confrontations as a result of their being the only nation in the world to have felt the devastation of an atomic bomb.

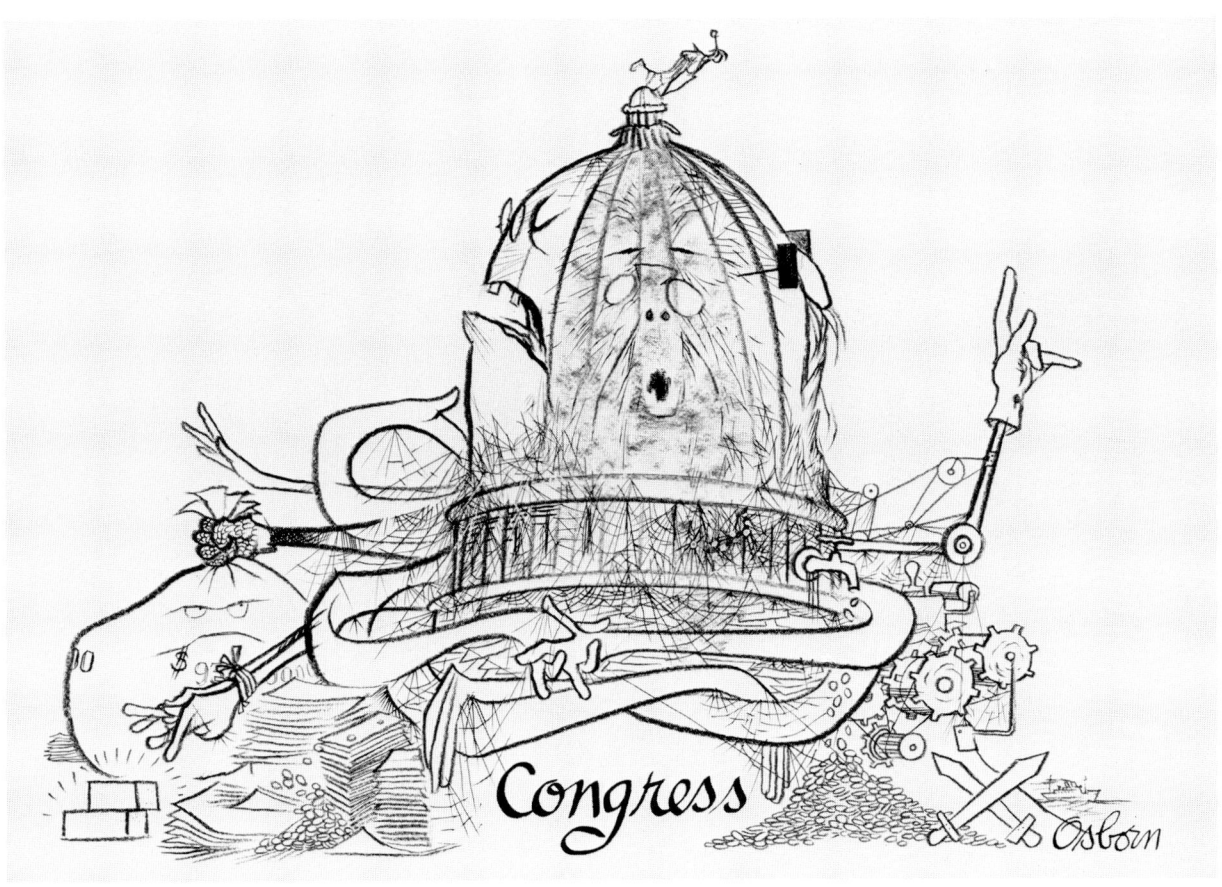

Fig. 197. *Congress*. Robert Osborn. 1950s. Ink and crayon on paper. 14 13/16 × 20 9/16 in. Courtesy The Swann Collection of Caricature and Cartoon.

Congress developed a bad reputation during the late 1940s and 1950s. President Truman had a Republican Congress and blamed virtually all the failures of his administration on the "do nothing 80th Congress." Eisenhower had Democratic Congresses, so he also had a convenient excuse for any administration shortcomings.

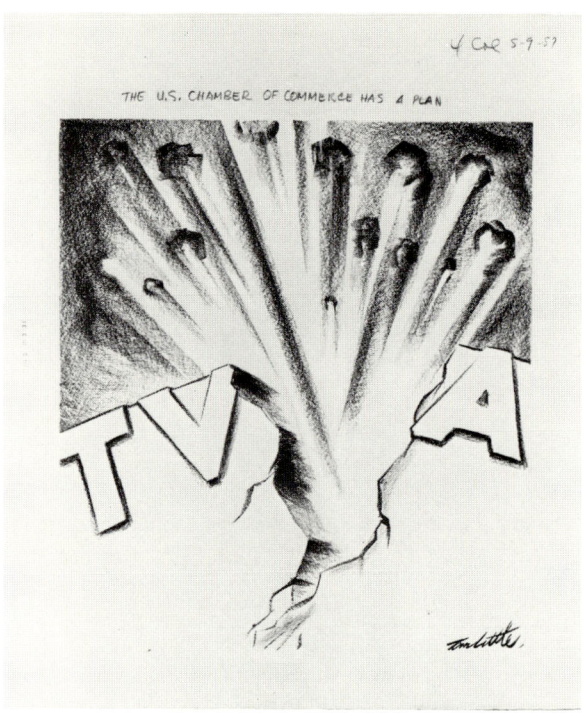

Fig. 198. *The U. S. Chamber of Commerce Has a Plan*. Tom Little. May 9, 1957, in the Nashville *Tennessean*. Charcoal on paper. 20 × 23 in. Courtesy Tom Little Cartoon Collection in Special Collections, Joint University Libraries, Nashville, Tenn.

The Tennessee Valley Authority was a giant undertaking designed to harness the powerful Tennessee River to provide power for the more than 4.5 million people living in its valley. A success under President Roosevelt's New Deal, the TVA found disfavor under Republican President Eisenhower, who favored private development of power and attempted to circumvent the TVA by allowing private businesses to develop plants on the Mississippi River. Eisenhower referred to TVA as "creeping socialism," but quickly rescinded the words as many supporters of TVA protested. The U. S. Chamber of Commerce, of course, sided with private businessmen in the development of power.

Fig. 199. *This Is My Territory*. Fred O. Seibel. Sept. 6, 1957, in the Richmond *Times-Dispatch*. Pen and ink on paper; caption in pencil. 20 × 15 1/16 in. Courtesy University of Virginia Library, Charlottesville.

In the wake of the 1954 Supreme Court decision declaring that "separate but equal" school facilities were unconstitutional, the Little Rock, Arkansas, school system was preparing to desegregate Central High School. The incident probably would have passed unnoticed had not Governor Orval Faubus, needing an issue for his third campaign, decided to send in National Guardsmen to "grease the way." Although the Guardsmen were sent largely for a political end, the incident was widely regarded as being in opposition to the Supreme Court's ruling when it occurred, as Seibel shows in this cartoon.

Fig. 200. *"You should have been here in the old days, before the budget cutbacks.... There were cops and fire engines and planes buzzing around...."* Mike Peters. 1975. Brush and ink on chemical board. 6 × 10 in. Courtesy Mike Peters. © *Dayton Daily News.*

The increasing number of people who moved from the inner city to the suburbs caused mounting problems for the city, such as an inadequate tax base to support the normal city services. Here Mike Peters dramatizes New York City's problems by depicting the return of King Kong, the monster who drew such attention during his first fictitious visit to the city.

Fig. 201. *The Space-Age Toy Shop.* A. Kovarsky. 1950s. Watercolor on paper. 23 3/4 × 17 3/4 in. Courtesy The Swann Collection of Caricature and Cartoon.

Kovarsky's cartoon reflects modern society's fascination with the technology of destruction and violence as the children gaze at a fantastic array of destructive gadgetry available for their Christmas selection. The toys, of course, merely reflect the time, money, and energy adults pour into the proliferation of space-age engines of war.

155

Fig. 202. *History of Man*. Robert Osborn. 1950s. Crayon on paper. 11 1/2 × 15 1/16 in. Courtesy The Swann Collection of Caricature and Cartoon.

The Cold War, the arms race, and constant confrontation convinced many Americans that World War III was just around the corner. Urged by various government agencies to prepare, thousands of citizens constructed their own bomb shelters to protect them from the "ultimate blast." To cartoonist Osborn this was the ultimate state of man, as he has traced civilization in this drawing from cave-dwellers, through classical Egypt, through Classical Antiquity, the Middle Ages, and the Modern Age, to the present century. Apparent is his question as to whether this civilized age is any better than the age of the cave-dwellers.

Fig. 203. *Inflation*. Robert Osborn. 1950s. Crayon and watercolor on paper. 17 5/16 × 13 3/16 in. Courtesy The Swann Collection of Caricature and Cartoon.

Making earnings stretch to meet expenditures in a time of inflation seems a perennial problem in American society, and Robert Osborn captured graphically the situation that existed for many families in the 1950s.

Fig. 204. *Smaller Does Not Mean Better*. André François. 1970s. Ink on paper. 11 3/4 × 9 1/2 in. (sight). Courtesy John Locke. © André François in the New York *Times*.

Inflation did not disappear with the 1950s, as André François shows in this cartoon first reproduced on the Op-Ed page of the New York *Times*. It increased to double-digit proportions and became one of the leading domestic problems in the 1970s.

Fig. 205. *Uncle Sam and Santa Claus as Don Quixote and Sancho Panza*. Saul Steinberg. 1959. Ink on prepared paper. 14 1/2 × 23 1/4 in. Courtesy Fogg Art Museum, Harvard University, Cambridge, Mass., Purchase—Gifts for Special Uses Fund through Mrs. Ernest Angell.

In this cartoon Steinberg mixes Abraham Lincoln with Uncle Sam in the figure of Don Quixote, and Santa Claus is Sancho Panza. Perhaps he is suggesting that the United States is ready to defend (or dominate) the world with force and dollars.

Fig. 206. *Beatniks*. William Steig. 1950s. Ink and wash on paper. 10 × 8 in. Courtesy The Swann Collection of Caricature and Cartoon.

After the disillusioning experience of Korea, some young Americans rebelled against the pervasive conformity of the fifties. The "Beat Generation," or "beatniks" (a play on the word, Sputnik), emerged in San Francisco and Los Angeles in beards, berets, and black leotards and studying Zen Buddhism. In their special jargon, borrowed primarily from jazz musicians, they espoused a cynical, but passive philosophy which sought to establish a subculture, rather than exert change on society at large.

Fig. 207. *Benny Goodman*. Ronald Searle. 1950s. Ink on paper. 13 1/4 × 7 in. Courtesy The Iconography Collection, Humanities Research Center, University of Texas, Austin.

In the 1930s the popular jazz style began to acquire a "new" sound. It coupled a unique syncopated energy with a full orchestration requiring a "big band." This was "swing" and it was to make the music industry big business. The radio, records, and movies blared its catchy rhythms across the nation, and American troops took it with them in World War II. Benny Goodman formed his first band in 1934 and two years later had already acquired Gene Kruppa, Teddy Wilson, and Lionel Hampton, the great swing musicians who formed the core of his orchestra. Goodman's ability to spot and hold talent, along with his showmanship, managerial ability, as well as his musical virtuosity, earned him the well deserved title, "King of Swing."

Fig. 208. *Groucho Marx*. Anonymous. c. 1955. Hair, wire, glass, painted stones and plaster. 16 in. high. Courtesy Herbert Waide Hemphill, Jr. New York City.

As television became an increasingly popular American pastime during the 1950s, certain personalities developed as the old *Amos 'n' Andy* radio show had developed during the 1930s. Groucho Marx, a member of the famous Marx brothers comedy team that had made several movies during the 1930s, became one of the best known quiz show hosts, conducting *You Bet Your Life* with a combination of jokes, ad libs, and zany questions, the most famous of which is "Who is buried in Grant's Tomb?"

Fig. 209. *The Lives of Great Men*. Victor Weisz ("Vicky"). Sept. 29, 1960, in the London *Evening Standard*. Pen, brush, opaque white, blue pencil on paper. 15 1/8 × 18 1/2 in. Courtesy Mr. and Mrs. Draper Hill, Memphis, Tenn.

The presidential candidates in the 1960 campaign were both much younger than their recent predecessors in that office. Many voters also felt that both Kennedy and Nixon were motivated by personal ambition rather than ideological conviction and that neither was really adequate for the job. In their televised debates Kennedy was prone to invoke the memory of Franklin Roosevelt while Nixon recalled Abraham Lincoln to dignify and sanction their respective political philosophies and attitudes towards issues of the day. This cartoon contrasts the insignificant figures and footprints of the two presidential hopefuls with the enormous historical impressions of the former leaders they sought to follow.

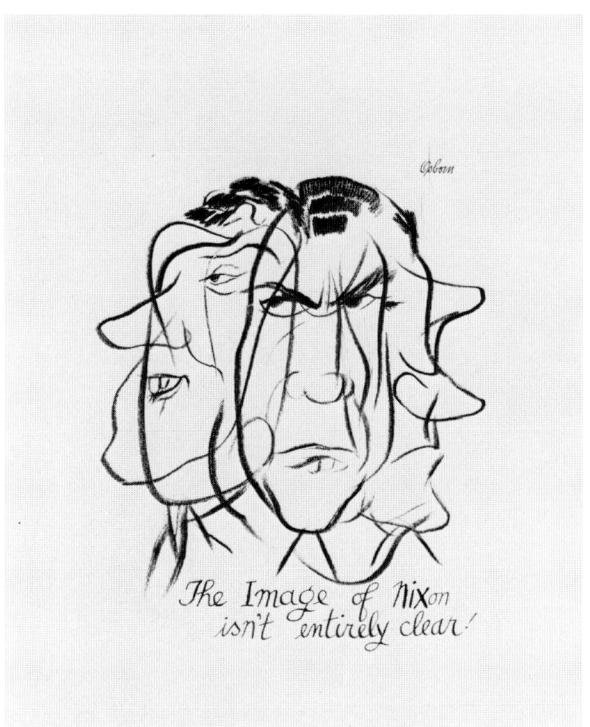

Fig. 211. [Kennedy and exploding Cuban cigar.] Leslie Illingworth. Apr. 21, 1961. Scratchboard. 11 3/16 × 8 13/16 in. Courtesy The National Library of Wales.

Castro had seized power in Cuba during Eisenhower's term, and shortly before he left office, Eisenhower broke diplomatic relations with the Cuban government because of Castro's Communist leanings. When President Kennedy learned of the plans to invade Cuba from Central Intelligence Agency officials, he thought it unwise to change them since he had taken such a hard line on Cuba during the campaign. In April, 1961, some 1,500 Cuban exiles and Americans landed at the Bay of Pigs. The badly-planned assault immediately collapsed and 1,200 of the invaders were taken prisoner. The United States had denied having anything to do with the invasion, but when it miscarried so badly, Kennedy shouldered the blame.

Fig. 210. *The Image of Nixon Isn't Entirely Clear*. Robert Osborn. 1960 (?). Crayon and ink on paper. 14 15/16 × 11 7/8 in. Courtesy The Swann Collection of Caricature and Cartoon.

President Nixon was the target of many critical remarks during his unsuccessful 1960 campaign against John Kennedy. Perhaps the most famous question posed to the electorate is, "Would you buy a used car from this man?" But the most prophetic, in hindsight, is probably this caricature by Osborn showing that Nixon was not being as straightforward even then as he claimed to be.

Fig. 212. *Cuban Missile Showdown*. Leslie Illingworth. Oct. 24, 1962, in the London *Daily Mail*. Brush and pen on paper. 12 1/2 × 14 1/8 in. Courtesy The Swann Collection of Caricature and Cartoon.

Perhaps President Kennedy's most famous personal confrontation with another foreign leader was his Vienna meeting with Soviet Premier Nikita Khrushchev. Khrushchev tested the young President, hoping to uncover a weak spot or lack of character, which he would soon try under international pressure. The Soviet leader thought Kennedy would not oppose the installation of Soviet missiles in Cuba after the embarrassment of the Bay of Pigs, but he was mistaken. Upon receiving word that missiles were being installed, Kennedy placed a naval blockade around Cuba on October 22, 1962.

Fig. 213. *"You're using the wrong kind of plow, neighbor!"* Richard Yardley. 1962 in the Baltimore *Sun*. Ink with white highlights on paper. 18 15/16 × 14 7/8 in. Courtesy Fort Worth Art Museum.

Competition in the Cold War reached new proportions when Premier Khrushchev visited the United States in 1959. During the course of his tour he made his now-famous "we will bury you" remark, which the American propaganda machine turned into one of the most effective anti-Soviet campaigns of the Cold War. Khrushchev claimed that he meant that Communists would "bury" Capitalists economically, but most Americans felt certain that he meant militarily. Khrushchev's boast looked particularly hollow after Soviet agriculture performed so disastrously during the 1960s. This Yardley cartoon comments on the competition between farmer Uncle Sam and the Communists.

Fig. 214. *"You ain't gaining much altitude holding me down."* Bill Mauldin. Oct. 10, 1962. Ink and crayon on paper. 13 × 9 1/2 in. Courtesy Collection of Bill Mauldin.

The public reaction to the 1954 Supreme Court decision which outlawed the segregation of public education (*Brown vs. Board of Education Topeka*) resurrected the specter of racial prejudice which has haunted American society since its beginnings. The Court's recognition of the advantages enjoyed by whites under the "separate but equal" doctrine seemed to signal a major breakthrough in the civil rights struggle, but many areas in the deep South openly resisted the order. The *de facto* segregation of the North also became apparent. Progress has been made slowly, and Mauldin's cartoon is as pertinent today as it was in 1962.

Fig. 215. *Bookmark*. Bill Mauldin. 1967. Ink on paper. 18 × 14 in. (sight). Courtesy Collection of Joel Rosen, Fort Worth, Tex.

As President Kennedy was preparing for the 1964 presidential campaign by making a political "fence-mending" trip to Texas, he was tragically assassinated by Lee Harvey Oswald. The special investigating committee, headed by Chief Justice Earl Warren, concluded that Oswald was acting alone in killing the President and wounding Texas Governor John Connally, but after the commission report was made public numerous critics have claimed that the investigation was not thorough enough, and that there are complicating factors that point to conclusions other than those the panel reached.

Fig. 216. *Martin Luther King*. Ben Shahn. 1965. Pen and ink wash on paper. 26 1/4 × 20 1/4 in. Courtesy Amon Carter Museum, Fort Worth.

Martin Luther King was the most outstanding civil rights advocate of the 1960s. Using mass demonstrations of passive resistance, he attracted international attention and sympathy for the battle against the political, economic, and social inequality of the Negro in America. For his effective yet nonviolent efforts he was awarded the Nobel Peace Prize in 1964. In 1968 he was gunned down in a Memphis motel, setting off a chain of riots in the black ghettos of cities across the nation. When King saw this drawing on the cover of *Time* magazine, he reportedly remarked, "There is a little racism in all of us."

Fig. 217. *The Eyes of GM Are Upon You*. Jon Kennedy. c. 1966–1967. Ink and crayon on paper. 13 11/16 × 11 1/8 in. Courtesy The State Historical Society of Missouri, Columbia.

In 1959 General Motors began to market a new automobile, the Corvair, which won awards and enjoyed phenomenal sales in the early sixties. Then auto industry critic Ralph Nader wrote a book, *Unsafe At Any Speed*, attacking the Corvair as dangerous. In an effort to discredit him and prove him untrustworthy, General Motors harassed Nader with their "gumshoes," according to Nader. But their efforts failed to save the Corvair. In 1969, with economic pressures slowing the sales, GM announced that the Corvair would be discontinued. Nader, meanwhile, had become the country's leading consumer watchdog.

Fig. 218. *It failed as a moon vehicle but as sculpture it wins an award*. Garrett Price. 1960s. Ink on paper. 9 × 11 1/2 in. Courtesy Nelson-Atkins Museum, Kansas City, Mo., Gift of the artist.

After the Soviet Union launched "Sputnik" and initiated the American-Soviet space race, the American public was deluged with a barrage of extraterrestrial equipment as bizarre and baffling to them as the new trends in the arts, which had by the 1960s left many traditionalists wondering what had become of the fundamental values and standards. Artists turned "found objects" into imaginative creations, giving many of their works a "common touch" that some viewers could not understand, for they had always thought of art in terms of the "uncommon." Mechanical art also was popular among the artists. Such a state of affairs obviously confused many, including the two ladies at this art show.

Fig. 219. *Caricature of Louis Armstrong*. Makoto Wada. 1968. Watercolor on paper. 13 1/2 × 11 in. Courtesy The Swann Collection of Caricature and Cartoon.

Louis "Satchmo" Armstrong was born on the Fourth of July in the slums of New Orleans. He learned to play the cornet in the Negro Waifs' Home there, and music, jazz, became his career. In 1924 he switched to the trumpet and became an internationally acclaimed master of the horn. Whether improvising in the style of pure jazz or performing a popular tune, "Satchmo" stamped his music with his personal mark, as distinctive as the clenched-tooth grin, white handkerchief, and expansive gesture by which the Japanese cartoonist Makota Wada identifies him.

Fig. 220. *LBJ*. Marisol [Escobar]. 1967. Painted wood construction. 80 × 27 7/8 × 24 5/8 in. Courtesy The Museum of Modern Art, New York City, Fractional gift and extended loan from Mr. and Mrs. Lester Avnet, 1968.

Marisol, the pop artist, is known for her life-size three-dimensional representations of both the known and the anonymous people of society and her portrayal of them, via carving, casting, assemblage, and painting, in their characteristic if often ridiculous situations. Here she depicts President Lyndon B. Johnson with his family in his hand: wife Lady Bird and daughters Luci Baines and Lynda Bird. The sheer size of the LBJ statue in comparison with the depictions of the women captures the massiveness, domination, and overpowering qualities that he continually exhibited.

Fig. 221. *Howdy Arts*. Tomi Ungerer. c. 1965. Watercolor on paper. 13 1/2 × 11 11/16 in. Courtesy Galerie Daniel Keel, Zurich, Switzerland.

On June 14, 1965 President Johnson sponsored the White House Festival of the Arts which included the exhibition of American painting and sculpture, performances by American singers, dancers, musicians and actors, and readings by American dramatists and authors from their works. The press hailed it as "a salute to the creative people of the nation." Tomi Ungerer conveys the same message in his cartoon as he contrasts Johnson's Western background with the cultural sophistication that he was trying to bring to the White House.

Fig. 222. *LBJ Armwrestling Big Steel*. Ken Alexander. c. 1965. Ink on paper. 14 3/8 × 11 in. Courtesy The Lyndon Baines Johnson Library Collection, Austin, Tex.

In the summer of 1965 President Johnson intervened in a deadlocked struggle between the steel workers' union and the steel industry. The union was to strike on September 1 and implications for the national economy were dismal if the issues could not be settled. "Come let us reason together," pleaded Johnson in his invitation to the chief negotiators. He first got the union to push back the strike date, then managed by using the powers of persuasion at the command of the President to get a settlement before Labor Day.

Fig. 223. *"Where I come from, we call it 'Cultural Revolution.'"* Corky Trinidad. 1967. Ink on paper. 10 1/2 × 14 3/8 in. Courtesy The Lyndon Baines Johnson Library Collection, Austin, Tex.

The decade of the sixties witnessed an important tactical shift in the civil rights movement. Along with the rise of new leaders and ideologies in the black community, a series of spontaneous riots shook many metropolitan areas: Watts, a Negro suburb of Los Angeles, was the scene of the first riot in 1965, followed by outbreaks in Newark and Detroit in 1967. Riots also convulsed many cities in Communist China during the sixties, but they resembled the American phenomena only in that they were chiefly instigated by militant young activists against the established power. Trinidad contrasts the reactions of the shaken Johnson, who watched the riots demolish his dreams of a "Great Society," and the inscrutable Chairman Mao, who simply placed himself at the ideological head of the movement and declared that society should be "renewed" so it will not depart from its founding principles.

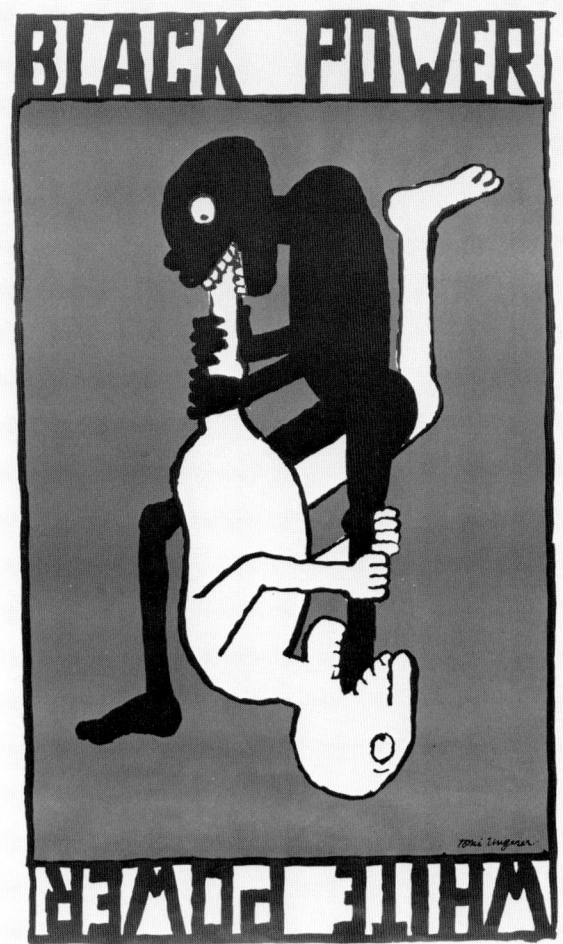

Fig. 224. *Black Power/White Power*. Tomi Ungerer. 1967. Colored poster. 28 × 20 in. Courtesy The International Poster Museum; collection of Mr. Jack Rennert.

"Black Power"—a catch-phrase of the mid-sixties—was a subtle concept with far-reaching implications because it signaled a fundamental change in the attitude of the black man toward himself, his race, and American society. In the popular mind, Black Power acted as an umbrella under which many different philosophies were combined. It included everything from the "Black is beautiful" concept to the manifestos of the militants. Here Ungerer reflects upon the recent violent urban riots and the growing "white backlash" in reaction to them and depicts the black and white separatist movements as destructive of each other and society.

Fig. 225. [LBJ suit at the Chinese Laundry.] Blaine MacDonald. c. 1967. Ink on paper. 14 1/2 × 11 3/4 in. Courtesy The Lyndon Baines Johnson Library Collection, Austin, Tex.

On August 5, 1964, the Vietnamese conflict was escalated by President Johnson's retaliation against North Vietnam for attacks on American P. T. boats in the Bay of Tonkin. Johnson pursued a punitive policy toward North Vietnam for the next four years, incorporating routine saturation bombing of Hanoi and other major cities in an attempt to break down the morale and resistance and the ability to prosecute the war in South Vietnam. Canadian cartoonist MacDonald Blaine depicts Ho Chi Minh as a laundryman who, instead of finding loose change, finds bombs in LBJ's trouser pockets.

Fig. 227. *The Time Machine*. Leslie Illingworth. Sept. 13, 1967, in *Punch*. Scratchboard. 15 1/4 × 12 1/2 in. Courtesy The Lyndon Baines Johnson Library Collection, Austin, Tex.

Fig. 226. [LBJ and Vietnam Specters.] Paul Szep. 1960s in the Boston *Globe*. Scratchboard. 15 × 14 7/8 in. Courtesy The Swann Collection of Caricature and Cartoon.

President Johnson's main interest while in office was his domestic program. Johnson yearned to do something for the nation's poor and to equalize educational opportunities. However, most of his attention was devoted to foreign issues, with the Vietnam policy leading them all. He inherited his commitment from President Kennedy but increased it, hoping to end the war quickly. The South Vietnamese rebels and North Viet Nam supporters were much stronger than American military advisors had thought, however, and the war outlasted Johnson's terms in office. Thus Szep has caricatured him haunted by the ghosts of Vietnam.

As the 1968 presidential election approached, it became evident that unless President Johnson could dramatically end or downgrade the Vietnam war, his chances of being reelected would be greatly hampered. The public clamored for an end to the war, either by victory or withdrawal. Senator Eugene McCarthy served as a unifying factor for the anti-war forces, drawing an embarrassingly large percentage of the vote in the first presidential primary, considering that he was not really a serious candidate. Johnson pressed the Vietnamese to negotiate, saying that American diplomats would go anywhere in the world to meet. Still there was no positive reaction from Hanoi. As the election primaries drew near, Johnson announced that he would not run, that he would devote the remainder of his term to trying to settle the war issues.

Fig. 228. *Mayor Daley's Gesture*. Jack Levine. 1969. Drypoint and aquatint. 14 7/8 × 23 1/2 in. Courtesy New Jersey State Museum Collection, Trenton, Gift of Mr. and Mrs. David Deitz, 1969.

In some ways Mayor Richard Daley of Chicago overshadowed all other figures at the 1968 Democratic convention, held in his city. In an attempt to prevent the nomination of Hubert Humphrey, thought to be aligned with Johnson's Vietnamese policies, tens of thousands of protesters demonstrated in the streets. Daley directed his 12,000 policemen and 5,000 National Guardsmen in brutal suppression of the demonstrators. Prominent politicians and delegates expressed disgust at the mayor's "police state" tactics, and Chicago became a symbol during the election. Richard Nixon so narrowly defeated Humphrey that many observers commented that Daley's action probably cost the Democrats the presidency.

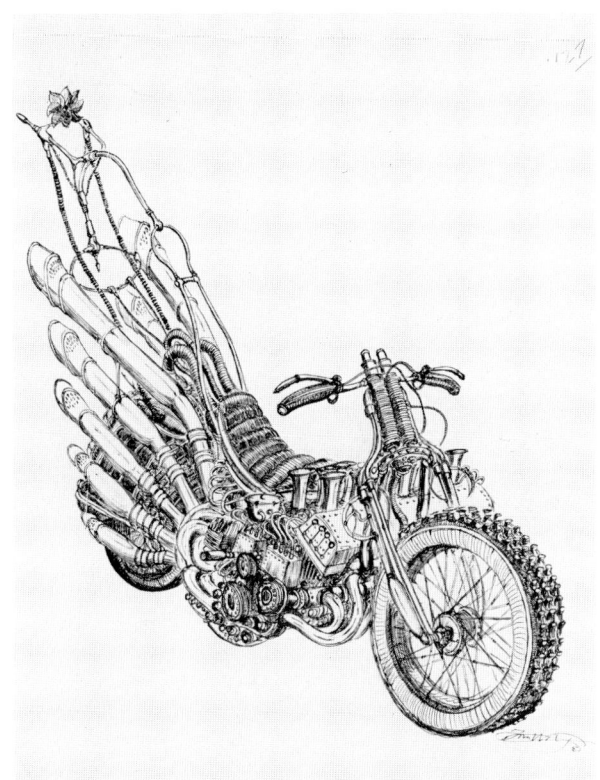

Fig. 229. *The Hilton Hotel*. Tom Wolfe. 1968 in *The Pump House Gang*. Colored crayon on paper. 14 × 11 1/8 in. Courtesy The Tunnell Gallery at Karl Mann Associates, New York City.

This comment by Wolfe points out how much our society is a youth-oriented culture. Even obviously richer and older men and women feel obligated to dress, and presumably to act, in the mode of the "younger generation" in order to maintain their "Beautiful People" status. Wolfe could also be commenting on the commercialism rampant in our society; assuming that this pair could afford designer clothes, their studded, faded denim jeans are probably *haute couture* products that cost thousands, yet poorer, younger kids around the country make the same products out of ragged, naturally faded products for a few dollars. Because some people need to have their taste certified by both the mark of a designer and youth, however, the designers are able to market such items.

Fig. 230. *Motorcycle*. Tom Wolfe. 1968 in *The Pump House Gang*. Ink on paper mounted on cardboard. 20 × 15 1/4 in. Courtesy The Tunnell Gallery at Karl Mann Associates, New York City.

The anti-hero and the counter-culture emerged as products of American life during the 1960s. Expressions of uniqueness and alternative life-styles gained currency. The motorcycle became an ideal symbol for the new non-conformists; it could be mechanically and visually altered to display personal taste, and it carried ready-made associations with radicalism. Best of all, when its owner could no longer cope, he could (in the tradition of that Great American Individual, the Cowboy) simply take to the open road and ride off into the sunset.

Fig. 231. *Nixon. Nov., 1962. "You won't have me to kick around anymore." (His Last Words).* Paul Szep. 1969 in the Boston *Globe*. Pen, dry brush, charcoal on paper. 14 × 15 1/2 in. Courtesy Boston Public Library, Print Department.

As Eisenhower's Vice-President, Richard Nixon enjoyed the benefits and power of high office, and was deeply hurt and humiliated when he lost the 1960 Presidential race to John Kennedy. Realizing that he had to keep politically active, he returned to his home state of California and challenged incumbent Edmund Brown for the governorship. When he lost that contest, he sank to the depths of despair and embarrassment, and his bitterness manifested itself in his famous "last press conference," in which he lashed out at the reporters for causing his defeat: "you won't have me to kick around anymore." When Nixon reappeared to run for the presidency in 1968, cartoonist Szep showed him emerging from his self-dug grave.

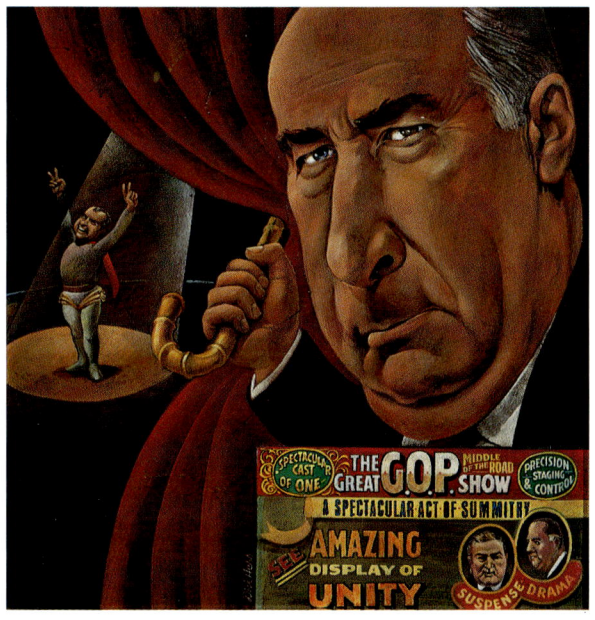

Fig. 232. *The Great G. O. P. Middle of the Road Show*. Richard Hess. 1972. Oil on canvas. 12 × 12 in. Courtesy The Swann Collection of Caricature and Cartoon.

Hoping to capitalize on public sentiment for order and leadership in a tumultuous period, the Republican Party staged an amazing show of order and unity at its 1968 convention. Potential Nixon opponents agreed to serve as chairmen, Governor Nelson Rockefeller agreed to nominate Nixon, and the emphasis was placed on getting most of the party's business handled during prime-time television hours. Nixon's ensuing campaign was managed by John Mitchell, who had a good Wall Street reputation. Recalling the television debates, which turned the 1960 election in favor of John Kennedy, Mitchell allowed Nixon to be seen in only the most favorable situations—before favorable audiences or in carefully managed television appearances. Several critics remarked that Nixon was "packaged" just like a commercial product and sold to the voters.

Fig. 233. *The Blind Leading the Blind*. David Levine. 1971. Ink on paper. 11 × 14 in. Courtesy Forum Gallery, New York City. © by NYREV, Inc., 1971.

As the true nature of the conflict in Vietnam became known, and as more Americans poured into that small Southeast Asian country, many Americans began looking for answers to such perplexing questions as how and why America got involved in the beginning. The search led to an equivocal commitment made by President Eisenhower before he left office. The commitment was increased by President Kennedy and enlarged into a major conflict by President Johnson. President Nixon finally brought most of the American troops home, but not until he had widened the target of bombings to include neutral Cambodia. Thus Levine pictures four American Presidents as being blind on the same issue.

173

Fig. 234. [Spiro Agnew]. Nguyen Hai Chi ("Choé"). 1973. Ink on paper. 11 1/4 × 5 5/8 in. Courtesy The Swann Collection of Caricature and Cartoon.

Vice-President Spiro Agnew was the leading spokesman in the Nixon administration in favor of "law and order." Disgusted with Nixon's stalling tactics in the Watergate case, most Americans greeted Agnew's full-face confrontation of the charges brought against him—bribery, income tax evasion, and others—with relief, thinking that that was the way an innocent man should react. Agnew then surprised them when, overwhelmed by the evidence produced by the Justice Department pertaining to corruption in his governorship of Maryland as well as during his Vice-Presidency (he apparently received at least $50,000 illegally from one firm alone in a six year period), he pleaded *nolo contendere* to a single charge of income tax evasion and resigned his office. He was fined $10,000, but never served a jail term, as indicated by the South Vietnamese cartoonist "Choé," as his three year sentence was suspended. He had, however, removed himself from the line of Presidential succession, an important fact to Attorney General Elliot Richardson, who oversaw the prosecution of the case.

Fig. 235. *Une Grande, Une Immense Mayorité Silencieuse*. Vázquez de Sola. 1970s. Ink on paper. 6 1/4 × 8 5/8 in. Courtesy The Swann Collection of Caricature and Cartoon.

Nixon liked to claim early in his presidency that he had the support of America's "silent majority," which he interpreted to mean the mass of middle-America as opposed to the vocal leftists who marched and staged demonstrations. Vázquez de Sola, an Argentine artist, has interpreted the phrase a bit differently, indicating the thousands of Americans who had died, presumably in Vietnam, since Nixon had taken office. "A large, a huge silent majority," Nixon proclaims to his listeners.

Fig. 236. *The Peaceable Kingdom*. Richard Hess. 1972. Oil on canvas. 15 × 11 in. Courtesy The Swann Collection of Caricature and Cartoon.

The 1972 Presidential election saw a different kind of campaign by Senator George McGovern, the minister's son from South Dakota. Calling for tax reform, an end to corporate privilege, for breaking up monopolies, for a quick end to the Vietnam war, McGovern gathered liberals and young people around himself for an almost evangelical campaign. Parodied here as an innocent child in the style of one of Early American painter Edward Hicks' allegorical renderings of *The Peaceable Kingdom*, McGovern was often accused of naïveté and unrealistic idealism because of his pacifistic attitude toward the war and his proposed social and economic reforms. Nixon won easy reelection.

Fig. 237. [Sam Yorty and Tom Bradley.] Peter Green. 1972. Crayon on paper. 23 9/16 × 18 11/16 in. Courtesy The Swann Collection of Caricature and Cartoon.

In 1969 city councilmember and former policeman Thomas Bradley decided to challenge incumbent Sam Yorty in the Los Angeles mayoral race. In a fourteen-candidate primary Bradley emerged with forty-two percent of the vote from an electorate only seventeen percent Negro, but Yorty, with twenty-six percent, qualified for the run-off. After waging a particularly ugly contest, Yorty won, but in a 1973 rematch, Bradley became Los Angeles' first black mayor.

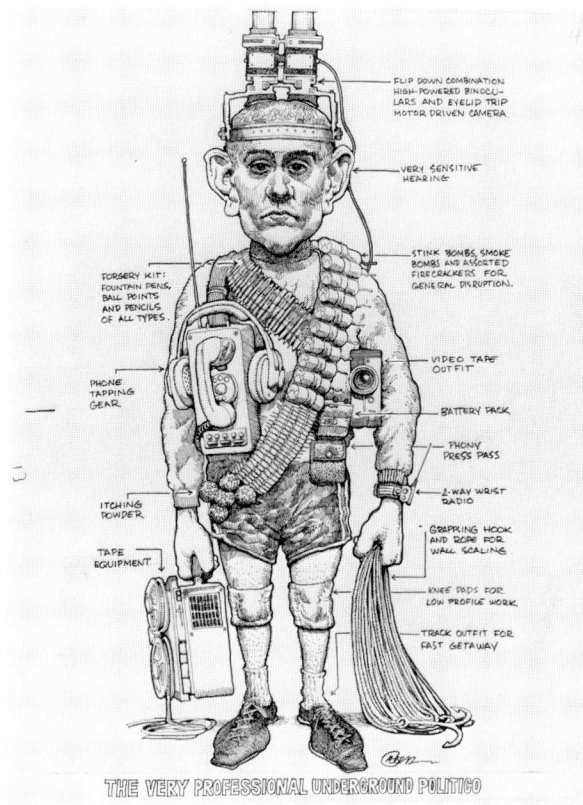

Fig. 238. *Caricature of George and Cornelia Wallace*. Edward Sorel. 1973. Ink on paper. 25 × 19 in. Courtesy The Swann Collection of Caricature and Cartoon.

"I thank God for George Wallace of Alabama," said former Mississippi Governor Ross Barnett as he introduced Wallace to a meeting. "He is a true son of the South." Despite his identification with the South and his strong Southern accent, Wallace managed to become a national candidate by appealing to racism and issues that affected the common man: law and order, tax reform, and the spreading bureaucracy. Wallace almost threw the presidential election of 1968 into the House of Representatives. In 1972 he appeared to be an even better candidate, moving more gracefully before crowds with his beautiful new wife, Cornelia. But an intended-assassin forced him from the race with an almost-fatal wound while he was speaking in Baltimore. Now paralyzed from the waist down, Wallace is still a strong political force in the nation.

Fig. 239. *The Very Professional Underground Politico*. Peter Green. 1973. Ink and gouache on paper. 23 7/16 × 8 13/16 in. Courtesy The Swann Collection of Caricature and Cartoon.

With exposure of the Watergate burglary, public attention was focused on the intelligence-gathering activities of political parties, businesses, and finally of governments. Peter Green here spoofs the spy activities of politicians such as the "White House plumbers," who broke into several private offices and files in search of politically damaging evidence that Nixon could use to harm his political enemies.

Fig. 240. [Kissinger and Le Duc Tho.] Nguyen Hai Chi ("Choé.") 1973. Ink on paper. 8 3/8 × 7 5/8 in. Courtesy The Swann Collection of Caricature and Cartoon.

Americans began withdrawing from South Vietnam after Secretary of State Henry Kissinger and North Vietnamese Chief Negotiator Le Duc Tho began discussions in 1972. But the fighting did not stop. Both sides violated the cease-fire, and the Communists eventually moved in for a final victory with the fall of Saigon in 1975. The award of the 1973 Nobel Peace Prize to Kissinger and Tho had aroused an unprecedented storm of protest. Even the Nobel committee, which officially awards its prizes by unanimous consent, split, with three out of the five members voting for Kissinger and Tho. "Choé" captures that sentiment here, showing Kissinger and Tho feeding uncomfortably off the dove of peace.

Fig. 241. *My Dad's Bigger Than Your Dad*. Wally Fawkes ("Trog"). Sept. 4, 1970, in the London *Daily Mail*. Ink, gray tempera, with opaque white on paper. 6 5/8 × 15 1/2 in. Courtesy Mr. and Mrs. Draper Hill, Memphis, Tenn.

In October, 1956 Israel invaded Egypt's Sinai Peninsula to regain access to the Suez Canal, beginning a series of hostilities which erupted into war on June 5, 1967. Thereafter Egypt's President Gamal Abdel Nasser acquired a substantially increased arsenal of Soviet armaments, military expertise and economic aid. Golda Meir, Israel's premier, received a comparable supply from the United States, and the stage was set for a major power confrontation in the Mid-East.

Fig. 242. *"Your Money or Your Way of Life."* Draper Hill. Jan. 5, 1975, in the Memphis *Commercial Appeal*. Brush, pen and ink on toneboard. 15 5/8 × 11 3/16 in. Courtesy Draper Hill, Memphis, Tenn. © *The Commercial Appeal*, Memphis.

Draper Hill has captured the reluctance with which the American public has faced the oil crisis, as Henry Kissinger thinks it over, Jack Benny fashion, before announcing his decision.

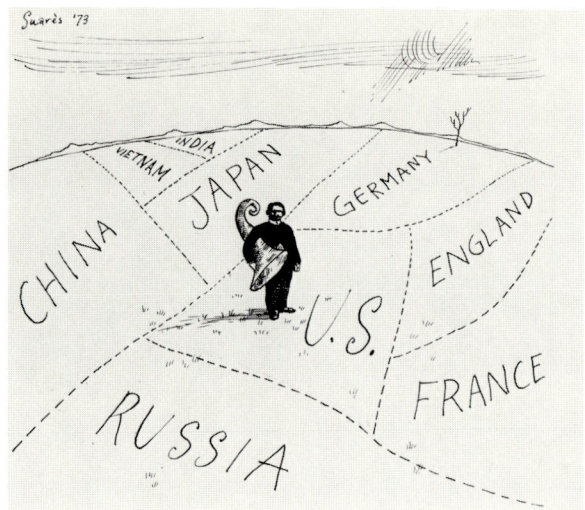

Fig. 243. *Horn of Plenty*. Jean-Claude Suarès. April 14, 1973, in the New York *Times*. Ink on paper. 7 1/2 × 8 in. Courtesy The Swann Collection of Caricature and Cartoon.

This cartoon of a nineteenth century gentleman standing on an international patchwork map accompanied a group of letters to the editor of the New York *Times* concerning capitalism. Some debated that U. S. capitalism had fed the world, others that it had bled it. Suarès cartoon is an equivocal statement taking neither side. The cornucopia could be empty because it has nothing to offer the world or because it has already poured forth its contents to it.

Fig. 244. *Milhous I*. Edward Sorel. Mar. 14, 1974 in *Rolling Stone*. Ink, watercolor, paste-up on paper. 18 1/2 × 14 in. Courtesy The Swann Collection of Caricature and Cartoon.

When President Nixon first took office, reporters began to notice several touches which they compared to the trappings of monarchy: the change in the uniform of the White House guards, the atmosphere in the White House, the aloofness surrounding the President and his aides. When Nixon reacted in the Watergate affair as if he were above the fray, Edward Sorel was inspired to draw him as "Milhous I," a comparison to the autocrat Louis XIV of France and an eloquent comment on a situation that reporters were having difficulty explaining to their listeners and readers without sounding personally offended.

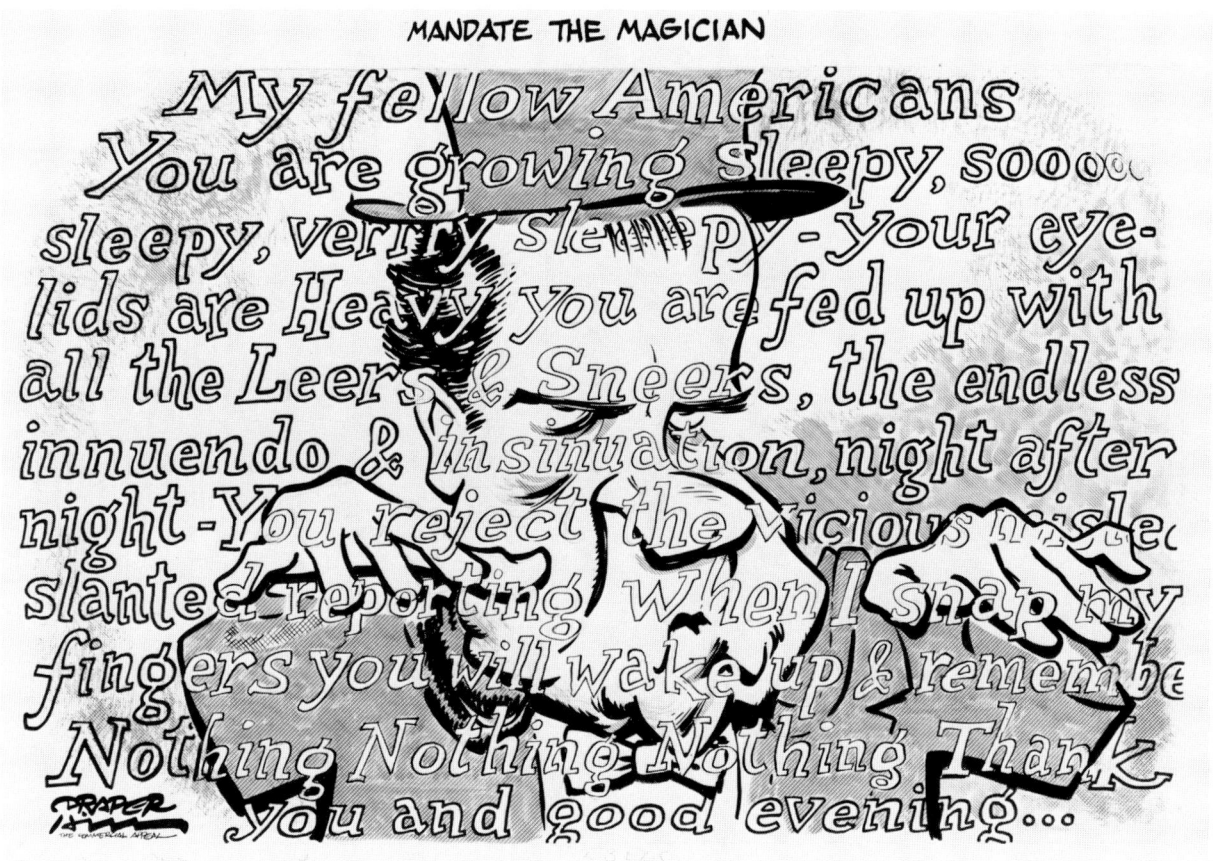

Fig. 245. *Mandate the Magician*. Draper Hill. Jan. 16, 1974. Brush, pen and ink on chemical toneboard. 11 × 16 1/16 in. Courtesy Draper Hill, Memphis, Tenn. ©*The Commercial Appeal*, Memphis.

At several points during the Watergate affair, President Nixon went on national television to "clear the air." Each time he seemed to make new revelations while insisting that the Watergate scandal had been solved, that no other administration officials were involved, and that he had not known about it. Draper Hill has combined this television image of Nixon with the "mandate" from the people that he continually talked of to produce "Mandate the Magician," a caption inspired by the well-known *Mandrake the Magician* comic strip.

Fig. 246. *Rose Mary's Baby*. Richard Hess. Mar. 18, 1974 in *New York*. Acrylic on canvas. 14 × 12 in. Courtesy Richard Hess, New York City.

This picture, which has already become a political classic, suggests that Nixon's personal secretary and loyal staff member Rose Mary Woods, who gave a very suspect explanation of how she accidentally erased a crucial and probably incriminating passage from one of the Watergate tapes that the investigating Grand Jury had subpoenaed, is in fact taking care of Nixon as would the mother of a bungling child. The title is adapted from the film *Rosemary's Baby*.

Fig. 247. *Nixon in a Tape Web*. Robert Pryor. 1974. Ink on paper. 12 × 11 in. Courtesy The Swann Collection of Caricature and Cartoon.

Nixon fought hard to keep the White House tape recordings from being turned over to the Watergate Grand Jury, but once the Supreme Court had rejected his contention that the tapes could be kept secret because of "national security" and executive privilege, he yielded first the White House Transcripts (typewritten transcripts of the recordings), then the tapes themselves. The House Judiciary Committee investigating impeachment then listened to the tapes and was able to understand some damaging passages that the White House Transcripts had listed as inaudible, etc. Thus Nixon really was caught in a web of tape, as Robert Pryor illustrates here.

Fig. 248. *Watergate*. Miles B. Carpenter. 1974. Wood, metal and paper. 13 in. high. Courtesy Herbert Waide Hemphill, Jr., New York City.

With the pervasiveness of the "Watergate affair," the term "Watergate" came into the American dialect as an expression meaning "dirty tricks." Its widespread acceptance is illustrated in the ease with which the entire affair was connected with other bits of American folklore: Every Milhous [millhouse] has a watergate, went one joke. The sculptor has worked other bits of the Nixon scandal into this carving: the income tax evasion, the questionable funding for his San Clemente house.

Fig. 249. *"I think I've seen enough mud."* Pat Oliphant. 1975. Ink on paper. 11 5/8 × 17 5/8 in. Courtesy Pat Oliphant, Washington *Star*, Los Angeles *Times* Syndicate.

Here cartoonist Oliphant comments on President Ford's criticism of Congress for "mudslinging." Originally cautious of criticizing the Congress because of his connections and sympathies there, Ford rapidly concluded that Congress was not cooperating with his administration as best it could.

Fig. 250. *In the Presidential Chair*. David Levine. 1974. Ink on paper. 14 × 11 in. Courtesy Forum Gallery, New York City. © by NYREV, Inc., 1974.

David Levine characterized Gerald Ford as the man who had never aspired to an office higher than the Speaker of the House and the man who had seriously thought of retiring after completing over two decades as congressman. Ford was selected by Nixon to replace Spiro Agnew and elevated to the presidency when Nixon resigned. Levine is suggesting that the presidency (represented by the chair) is probably too big an office for Ford, and Ford himself admitted that the job was more difficult than he had anticipated.

Fig. 251. *Arabian Knights*. Draper Hill. Sept. 29, 1974, in Memphis *Commercial Appeal*. Brush, pen and ink on chemical toneboard. 12 7/16 × 17 9/16 in. Courtesy Draper Hill, Memphis, Tenn. © *The Commercial Appeal*, Memphis.

When the Arab nations increased the price for crude oil, the Western nations were thrown into an economic crisis, complicated by the oil boycott that the Arabs then imposed. Secretary of State Kissinger darkly hinted that in bygone years such a monopolistic action would have been adequate to start a war. Here Draper Hill suggests that Ford and Kissinger are tilting windmills in the tradition of Don Quixote and Sancho Panza in battling the increasing prices.

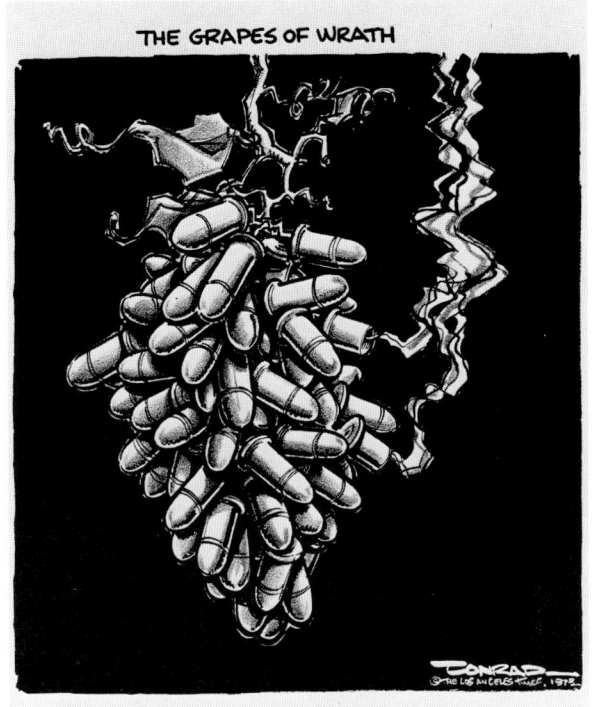

Fig. 252. *Sic Transit Gloria*. Edward Sorel. 1974. Ink on paper. 17 7/8 × 13 1/8 in. Courtesy Edward Sorel.

Woman's liberation leader and feminist writer Gloria Steinem helped raise the consciousness of women in all walks of life to some of the discrimination experienced by women as a class. *Life* magazine revealed, for example, that a woman must have a college degree to earn as much as a man with an eighth grade education. Some of the more militant feminists, like Ti-Grace Atkinson, were anti-men, but Steinem, contrary to the viewpoint in this Sorel caricature, was not among them. She much more opposed unequal pay for equal work and other rational complaints popularized because of the woman's movement.

Fig. 253. *Grapes of Wrath*. Paul Conrad. 1974 in the Los Angeles Times. Ink wash on paper. 13 1/2 × 11 in. Courtesy The Swann Collection of Caricature and Cartoon.

Employing a title historically connected with migrant labor en route to California during the Dust Bowl years of the 1930s, Paul Conrad has adapted the analogy to the bitter confrontation between Mexican-American laborers and farmers and ranchers today in California.

Fig. 254. *"When Johnny Comes Marching Home."* Anita Seigel. 1974 in the New York *Times*. Ink and collage on paper. 8 1/4 × 11 in. Courtesy The Swann Collection of Caricature and Cartoon.

This cartoon uses the picture of Washington from the dollar bill surrounded with a collage of weapons, military paraphernalia, death images, gears and springs, and the title of a popular Civil War marching song to comment on the militaristic character of American political policies in the past and the present.

Fig. 255. *Disarmament Talks*. Ralph Steadman. 1971 in the New York *Times*. Pen and ink on paper. Approx. 12 × 18 in. Courtesy Ralph Steadman.

When both the United States and the Soviet Union developed nuclear weapons, each possessed the capacity to destroy the world. With that realization, both nations began a series of disarmament talks aimed at reducing the tensions and the dangers of the arms race. The SALT (Strategic Arms Limitations Talks) Talks began in 1963 and offered hope that both nations would add to their initial nuclear test ban agreements, but Ralph Steadman sees such conference participants as ever willing to negotiate but refusing to relinquish any power.

Fig. 256. *The Junkie*. Brad Holland. 1970s. Ink on paper. 14 1/4 × 16 1/2 in. Courtesy Brad Holland, New York City.

Here Brad Holland depicts the plight of the junkie, the heroin addict who is the slave of a drug that he must inject into his veins in ever increasing amounts in order to prevent the violent physical and psychological withdrawal. The size of the drug problem in New York City can be seen in the fact that more than 32,000 addicts were put on the relief rolls as "disabled" to keep them from robbing and stealing to support their habit. Law enforcement officers estimate that heroin addiction is the major cause of increased crime in the cities, where addicts concentrate because of the availability of the drug. This drawing is a caricature of one of the artist's friends, who died of an overdose a few days after the picture was finished.

Fig. 257. *Cupid and the Cop*. Paul Psorakis. 1970s. Watercolor on paper. 14 1/2 × 11 1/2 in. Courtesy The Swann Collection of Caricature and Cartoon.

Perhaps the antagonism between authority and the youth culture of the sixties and seventies was most dramatically illustrated by events at the 1968 Democratic convention in Chicago, when Yippie leader Jerry Rubin exhorted thousands of youth to wreak havoc on the city, aiming especially at the Chicago police, in the name of establishing a new culture based on "freedom." Consequently the young people engaged in numerous confrontations leading to the further polarization of the Yippies and the police. Psorakis' cartoon suggests that the rift was so great that the police would have arrested the mythological love-god Cupid for shooting one of his love-darts.

Fig. 258. *Orson Welles*. David Levine. 1970s. Ink on paper. 14 × 11 in. Courtesy Forum Gallery, New York City. © by NYREV, Inc.

As David Levine's cartoon implies, Orson Welles is a giant of American dramatic arts. He first gained national attention in 1938 through his realistic radio adaptation of H. G. Wells' *War of the Worlds*, which many people accepted in horror as the report of a Martian invasion of Earth. He has continued to stun the American public with his brilliant theatrical productions and films such as *Citizen Kane, MacBeth* and *Compulsion*. These Hollywood films are not just movies, they are art. His talent, like his physique, is enormous as an actor, director, writer and producer. And he functions in any of these roles separately or in various combinations.

Fig. 259. *Expressways and Byways*. Edward B. Koren. Aug. 12, 1972, in *The New Yorker*. Watercolor on paper. 26 7/8 × 21 3/8 in. Courtesy The Swann Collection of Caricature and Cartoon. © The New Yorker Magazine.

One of the major domestic issues of the 1970s is air pollution, primarily by factories and automobiles. The air over Hammond, East Chicago, and Gary, Indiana, was so polluted with sulphur-dioxide in 1970—ten times the legal limit—that when it rained the mixture resulted in something akin to sulphuric acid that turned lawns brown, pitted leaves with ulerous holes, and de-feathered birds. Several ecologists have predicted that freak weather combined with air pollution will begin causing waves of mass deaths in urban areas.

Fig. 260. *"On This Site Will Be Erected a 32-Story Luxury Apartment Building After the Demise of the Old Lady."* Charles Addams. 1970s, in *The New Yorker*. Ink, ink wash, and collage on paper. 27 3/4 × 19 3/4 in. (sight). Courtesy Collection of Mrs. Edgar Tobin.

By 1970 eighty-five percent of the American population lived in urban centers. The consequent need for business and housing space rose dramatically as real estate agents and developers speculated on land acquisition. The skyscraper, the most efficient means of utilizing limited space, became the symbol of the twentieth century, and cities became the scene of constant construction, demolition, and reconstruction. Critics—perhaps Addams' mischievous little old lady among them—complained that "engineering mentality" had taken over, bulldozing historic and aesthetic considerations in its path of "progress."

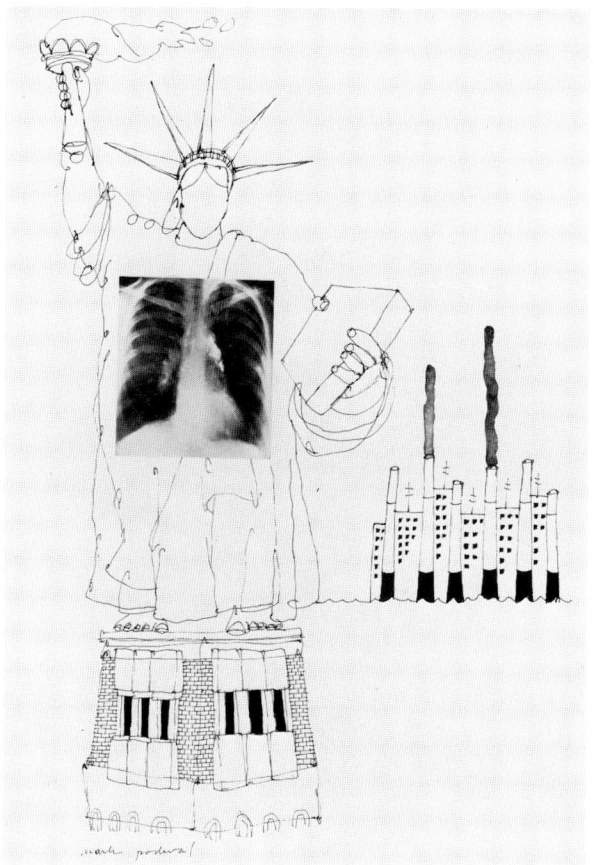

Fig. 261. *"Fun City."* Mark Podwall. 1970. Ink and collage on paper. 16 7/8 × 12 in. Courtesy The Swann Collection of Caricature and Cartoon.

Using the Statue of Liberty symbol, which several cartoonists have employed to represent America and its culture gone awry (see figs. 79, 192, and 262) Mark Podwall has graphically illustrated the fact that air pollution has reached critical proportions. Some doctors have estimated that breathing air on New York City streets can result in the same lung damage attributed to smoking nearly two packages of cigarettes each day.

Fig. 262. *Over 17 Billion Served*. R. O. Blechman. Mar., 1974 in *Architecture Plus*. Ink on paper. 14 3/4 × 11 in. Courtesy The Swann Collection of Caricature and Cartoon.

It is often surmised that Manhattanites will endure almost any urban inconvenience, but in 1974, when popular fast-food chains began to locate hamburger stores in some of New York's nicest neighborhoods, residents raised a surprising hail of protest. Blechman indicates that even a worried Statue of Liberty might not be immune from such encroachments.

Fig. 263. *The American Eagle*. John Cayea. 1974 in the New York Times. Pencil on paper. 9 × 11 in. Courtesy John Cayea.

While various devices have represented the United States in cartoon and caricature over 200 years, the American Eagle probably best captures the spirit as Americans themselves see their country. The Eagle was selected as the emblem on the Great Seal of the United States, was used to illustrate the condition of the country at the time of the Civil War, and is employed here by John Cayea to symbolize America after Watergate, after Vietnam, after the domestic turmoil of the past two decades—a proud nation, humbled by recent events yet still the same powerful country in spirit and substance that began the great experiment two centuries ago.

ARTISTS' BIOGRAPHIES

CHARLES SAMUEL ADDAMS (b. Westfield, New Jersey, 1912) studied at Colgate University, at the University of Pennsylvania, and at the Grand Central School of Art. A regular contributor to *The New Yorker* since 1935, Addams is famous for his macabre sense of humor and bizarre characters known as the "Addams Family." His work has been exhibited at major American museums, and numerous popular compilations of his cartoons have been published in book form.

ALEXANDER ANDERSON (b. New York City, 1775; d. Jersey City, New Jersey, 1870) taught himself the arts of copper and wood engraving by copying the works of British engraver Thomas Bewick and is credited with producing the first wood engravings in the United States. He gave up medical practice to pursue a career as a professional illustrator in 1798. He illustrated everything from spelling books to Shakespeare.

EMIDIO ANGELO (b. Philadelphia, 1903) studied at the Philadelphia Museum School of Industrial Art. His work has received many professional awards and has been exhibited at the Pennsylvania Academy of the Fine Arts. He has produced a nationally syndicated cartoon strip, "Emily and Mabel," several books and a film. He works as a teacher, painter and editorial cartoonist in the Philadelphia area.

ANSELL. See CHARLES WILLIAMS.

ANTONIO ARIAS BERNAL (b. Aguascalientes, Mexico, 1914; d. Mexico City, 1960) studied briefly at the Academy of San Carlos. His caricatures were first published in the magazine *México al Día*, and he became the cartoonist for the newspaper *Excelsior*. He helped to found the satirical reviews *Vea, Presente, Don Ferruco, El Serrotes*, and *El Fufurufu*, and his graphic work can be found in the magazines *Todo, Hoy, Mañana*, and *Siempre*, among others. He received the Maria Moors Cabot award from Columbia University.

PETER ARNO (b. New York City, 1904; d. Port Chester, New York, 1968) was educated at Yale University but had little professional art training. He was a musician when he sold his first cartoon to *The New Yorker* in 1925, the magazine with which he became most closely associated as cartoonist and cover artist. However, he contributed cartoons, illustrations, and articles to leading magazines in the United States, Great Britain, and Europe. His cartoons satirized with particular relish the arrogant head waiters, show girls, and snobs of New York's urbane night club society.

JAMES S. BAILLIE (n.d.) was an artist and lithographer who worked in New York between 1838 and 1855. He began as a colorist at N. Currier's lithographic establishment, but published his own prints between 1843 and 1849. Like Currier and Ives, Baillie catered to popular tastes and interests with sentimental subjects, historical scenes, and portraits as well as comic and political pieces.

PERRY BARLOW (b. McKinney, Texas, 1892) attended the Chicago Art Institute from 1912 to 1916. During World War I he served in the American Expeditionary Forces. He became a contributor to *The New Yorker* in 1926, and continued his association with the magazine until his retirement in 1970.

LEON BARRITT (b. Saugerties-on-the-Hudson, New York, 1852; d. 1938) was apprenticed to a jewelry engraver, but was primarily self-taught as an artist. In 1889 he came to New York City as a journalist, but soon opened a studio and made cartooning his career. He worked under contract to supply daily political cartoons for the New York *Daily Press* and on a freelance basis for other New York City papers, his work appearing in the *Herald, Commercial Advertiser*, and *Telegram* among others.

RALPH BARTON (b. Kansas City, Missouri, 1891; d. New York City, 1931) received his early training in his mother's studio, and in 1908 studied briefly at the Art Institute of Chicago. In 1910 he moved to New York City, and became a contributor to various magazines and journals, including *Harper's Weekly, Puck, Judge, Liberty, Vanity Fair*, and *The New Yorker*. He illustrated Anita Loos's *Gentlemen Prefer Blondes* and other books including several he himself wrote. He was best known as a satirist of the theater and its people.

SIR MAX BEERBOHM (b. London, 1872; d. Rapallo, Italy, 1956) was a renowned British essayist and caricaturist, earning a reputation while still an Oxford student for his witty writings and cartoons in *The Yellow Book*. His sleek, sophisticated caricatures broke the Victorian traditions of the genre and he developed a succinct, flowing, urbane style which is also seen in the works of Hirschfeld, Thurber, and Covarrubias. Beerbohm succeeded George Bernard Shaw as drama critic of *Saturday Review* and both verbally and pictorially served as a debonaire commentator on the social, theatrical, and literary figures of his day.

GEORGE WESLEY BELLOWS (b. Columbus, Ohio, 1882; d. New York City, 1925) graduated from Ohio State University in 1903 and went to New York City the next year to study under Robert Henri. He won a prize for a landscape at the National Academy of Design in 1908, and the next year became the youngest member ever elected to the National Academy. In 1916 he began to experiment in lithography, a medium which absorbed more and more of his time and energy. He sometimes made lithographic replicas of his paintings and often drew original scenes. He was one of the major American artists of the pre-World War II period, and examples of his paintings, drawings and lithographs are in the collections of almost every major museum in this country.

CLIFFORD KENNEDY BERRYMAN (b. Versailles, Kentucky, 1869; d. Washington, D.C., 1949) was a self-taught artist and began his career as a draftsman in the U.S. Post Office in 1886. He joined the Washington *Post* in 1896. In 1907 he joined the Washington *Evening Star* where he remained until his death. He created Theodore Roosevelt's "Teddy Bear" image and published a book caricaturing every member of the Fifty-eighth Congress (1903–1905). In 1943 he was awarded a Pulitzer Prize for his long career as cartoonist of the Washington political scene. He was succeeded on the *Star* by his equally talented and acclaimed son, Jim Berryman.

JAMES T. BERRYMAN (b. Washington, D.C., 1902) studied at George Washington University and the Corcoran Art School before joining the art department of the Washington *Star*, where his father, Clifford Berryman, was chief editorial cartoonist. In 1935 his father collapsed before finishing the cartoon intended for that day's issue, and Jim was summoned to complete it. Thereafter father and son alternated drawing the daily *Star* cartoon until the elder Berryman's death in 1949. Jim then continued as editorial cartoonist. His work is characterized by highly developed skill as a draftsman, keen ability for portraiture, and usually reflects a conservative political philosophy. He received the Pulitzer Prize in 1950 among many other professional awards for his work.

R. O. BLECHMAN (b. Brooklyn, New York, 1930) graduated from Oberlin College in 1952 and began free-lancing as a cartoonist in New York City two years later. His cartoons and illustrations have appeared in the New York *Times* and many popular magazines, but he is best known for his advertising illustrations and his animated television commercials. He has been an instructor in humorous art at the School of Visual Arts in New York City since 1960, and has written and illustrated several books.

CARINGTON BOWLES (n.d.) was one of the foremost publishers and sellers of prints in eighteenth century London. His shop was located near St. Paul's Churchyard. His hand-colored mezzotint caricatures of British types and manners were extremely popular.

LUTHER DANIELS BRADLEY (b. New Haven, Connecticut, 1853; d. Wilmette, Illinois, 1917) studied for a while at Yale University, but left to join the family business at Evanston, Illinois. After seven years he quit due to his poor health and sailed from Nova Scotia to London in 1882, and from there to Australia. Because he missed the boat home he was stranded in Melbourne and began to cartoon to earn money. He remained in Australia for eleven years, drawing for Australian *Tidbits*, *Life*, and Melbourne *Punch*. He returned to Evanston in 1892, where he did a little artwork and wrote two children's books. He joined the staff of the Chicago *Daily News* in 1899, cartooning there until his death. When war fever began to seize the country prior to our entry into World War I, Bradley alone, of the major American daily newspaper cartoonists, remained firmly opposed to American military involvement. He died before our entry into the conflict.

JACOB BURCK (b. Poland, 1904) came to America with his family in 1914. He studied in New York City at the Art Students League under Albert Sterner and Boardman Robinson and turned to cartooning during the Depression as a way of earning a living. He joined the staff of the St. Louis *Post-Dispatch* in 1937 and the Chicago *Sun-Times* in 1938, with whom he remained until his retirement. He won the Pulitzer Prize in 1941.

JOHN CAMERON (b. Scotland, c. 1828; d. ?) worked in New York between 1848 and 1862 for N. Currier, later Currier and Ives, producing many turf subjects and comic prints. He made several attempts to set up his own lithographic firms independently and with partners but apparently without commercial success.

MILES B. CARPENTER (b. Lititz, Pennsylvania, 1889) moved with his family to Waverly, Virginia, in 1901, where he joined his father's lumber business in 1912. In 1940 he adopted wood carving as a hobby when his interest in the business began to wane. Upon retirement in 1957 he turned his full energies to this avocation and began to create subjects of both topical interest, like the *Watergate* sculpture, and traditional naive concerns, such as religion and fantasy.

GEORGE CATLIN (b. Wilkes-Barre, Pennsylvania, 1796; d. Jersey City, New Jersey, 1872) was trained as a lawyer but pursued a successful career as a portraitist in the 1820s. In 1830 he made his first of many trips West. He devoted his life to, as he wrote, "rescuing from oblivion the looks and customs of the vanishing races of native men in America." He painted hundreds of Indian portraits and scenes of their tribal ceremonies, customs and way of life. These were enthusiastically viewed in the United States and Europe, and many books and articles on the American West and its peoples.

JOHN WILLIAM CAYEA (b. Queens, New York, 1948) studied at Brooklyn's Pratt Institute, graduating in 1970 with a degree in advertising design and communications. He has made drawings for Doubleday and Company, *National Lampoon*, American Airlines, Harper and Row, the New York *Times*, and the Washington *Post*, among others. His *American Eagle* is a New York *Times* candidate for the Pulitzer Prize.

CHAM. See NOÉ, COMTE DE.

KENNETH RUSSELL CHAMBERLAIN (b. Des Moines, Iowa, 1891) studied drawing under Julius Golz, a disciple of Robert Henri, at the Columbus Art School from 1911 to 1913. At age 21 he moved to New York City, took evening classes from Henri himself at the Ferrer School, and began to contribute cartoons to *The Masses*. Having early discarded the conventional academic styles, he read the radical German *Simplicissimus* and admired its artists Forain and Steinlen. Since the *Masses* artists received no pay, Chamberlain supported himself by drawing for conservative newspapers including the New York *Evening Sun*, the Philadelphia *Evening Telegraph* and *Public Ledger*, and the Cleveland *Press*. In 1920 he moved to California where he drew for the Los Angeles *Record* until 1927. He worked for Hearst's King Features during World War II, and has freelanced throughout his career.

WILLIAM CHARLES (b. Edinburgh, Scotland [?], 1776; d. Philadelphia, 1820) began publishing caricatures in his London shop in 1803–04, but fled to New York City in 1806 to avoid the consequences of prosecution for his caricatures of city officials. He did around two to three dozen caricatures in America, including a series on the War of 1812, and illustrated *The American Magazine of Wit* before moving to Philadelphia in 1814. Until his death there he ran a print and book shop, and published caricatures, chap-books, engravings, and aquatint illustrations for other writers' works.

NGUYEN HAI CHI "CHOÉ" (b. Mekong Delta, South Vietnam, 1944) started to draw at a very early age. With neither formal education (he left school after the third grade) nor art training, he published his first cartoon in 1969 for a Saigon weekly newspaper. In 1971 his cartoons published in the Bao Den *Daily* brought him recognition as an outspoken political cartoonist. He has been imprisoned in Saigon for his drawings.

JOHN SCOTT CLUBB (b. Hall's Corners, New York City, 1875; d. Rochester, New York, 1934) began caricaturing in early childhood. He studied for several years at the Cincinnati Art Academy and the Art Students League of New York. In 1900 he began drawing for the Rochester *Herald*, and when the *Herald* folded in 1926 he moved to the Rochester *Times-Union*, where he remained until his death. He created the crackerbarrel philosopher, Joel Baggs ("He sez, sez he").

PAUL FRANCIS CONRAD (b. Cedar Rapids, Iowa, 1924) received his degree in art from the University of Iowa in 1950, shortly before joining the staff of the Denver *Post*. He was the winner of the 1964 and 1971 Pulitzer Prizes for cartooning, and received the National Sigma Delta Chi award for editorial cartooning in 1963, 1969, and 1971. He is currently cartoonist for the Los Angeles *Times*.

MIGUEL COVARRUBIAS (b. Mexico City, 1904; d. Mexico City, 1957) began his career by cartooning for Mexican newspapers. In 1923 he went to New York where his rise as illustrator and cartoonist was sponsored by Frank Crowninshield, the editor of *Vanity Fair*. He also drew for *The New Yorker*, and soon became one of the city's most admired caricaturists. His interest in various art forms led to an enthusiasm for ethnology and archaeology, and he wrote and illustrated studies on Bali, the Isthmus of Tehuántepec, and pre-Conquest Mexico, and illustrated numerous other books. He was also famous as a muralist. In 1950 he became head of the Department of Dance of the National Institution of Fine Arts in Mexico City and served as a member of the Board of Art Advisers to the United Nations.

NATHANIEL CURRIER (b. Roxbury, Massachusetts, 1813; d. New York City, 1888) served his apprenticeship under William and John Pendleton, one of the first lithographic firms in the United States. Currier began his own business in 1834 in New York City. In 1852 he took his bookkeeper, James Merritt Ives, as his partner. Caricature was rarely employed in their political cartoons, but was used in other types of comic prints to depict national or racial stereotypes and stock comic characters, such as drunkards, old maids, and the like. The firm closed in 1907, when James Logan, son of the former business manager, sold out.

OTHO CUSHING (b. Fort McHenry, Maryland, 1871; d. New Rochelle, New York, 1942) studied at the Boston School of Fine Arts and Julian Academy in Paris. After serving as professor of drawing at Massachusetts Institute of Technology and art editor for the European edition of the New York *Herald*, he began his twenty-five year association with *Life* magazine. His famous *Life* series, *The Teddyssey*, followed the career of Theodore Roosevelt by parodying Homer's *Odyssey*; it was later published in book form. He served in World War I and in later life devoted himself mainly to watercolor painting.

LOUIS DALRYMPLE (b. 1865; d. 1905) joined the staff of *Puck* in the late 1880s. A keen observer from his childhood, Dalrymple is remembered for his spirited attacks on Tammany boss Richard Croker during the 1900 New York State Democratic Convention.

JAY NORWOOD "DING" DARLING (b. Near Charlevoix, Michigan, 1876; d. 1962) worked for the Sioux City *Journal* from 1900 until 1906, when he went west to the Des Moines *Register and Leader* to draw its daily cartoon until his retirement in 1949. The New York *Herald-Tribune* began to syndicate Ding's cartoons in 1916. He received the Pulitzer Prize in 1923 and again in 1943. Ding was one of the best-known and most influential cartoonists of his day.

HONORÉ DAUMIER (b. Marseilles, France, 1808; d. Valmondois, 1879) studied under the academician Alexandre Lemoir. A student at the Paris Academy in 1828, he began to draw for popular magazines. Two years later he did his first political lithographs. He drew briefly for the politically satirical weekly, *Silhouette*, before joining the staff of *Caricature* from 1831 until its demise in 1835. When Louis Philippe abdicated in 1848 Daumier returned to stronger political satire. He also began to paint that year, working for a while with the Barbizon group. Much to his disappointment the public never recognized this aspect of his career, probably due to the excellence of the more than four thousand lithographs he had executed.

HOMER CALVIN DAVENPORT (b. Silverton, Oregon, 1867; d. 1912) drew for the Portland *Oregonian* before joining the staff of the San Francisco *Examiner* in 1892. In 1895 William Randolph Hearst brought him to New York City for the 1896 campaign. His cartoons for the New York *Evening Journal* made his reputation and established him as the highest paid political cartoonist in the country. His work was responsible for an attempt to pass an anti-cartoon bill in the New York legislature. He also created the famous image of Mark Hanna in the dollar-marked suit. He was a champion of civil reform and is said to have done for San Francisco what Thomas Nast did for New York City in clearing out the Tweed Ring.

AMOS DOOLITTLE (b. Cheshire, Connecticut, 1754; d. New Haven, Connecticut, 1832) was apprenticed to a silversmith, but taught himself the techniques of copper engraving. He was one of the earliest practitioners of this art in America, engraving portraits, maps, money, diplomas, whatever was needed or desired. He was an enthusiastic supporter of the Revolution and is best known for his engravings of the Battles of Lexington and Concord, but he continued to do satirical prints long after the Revolution was over.

WILLIAM ELMES (n.d.) was an untrained British caricaturist, possibly a sailor. His *Adventures of Johnny Newcome*, published in 1812, satirized a naive British colonist, newly arrived in the West Indies. These engravings, which display a stylistic debt to Rowlandson, were executed in a series of panels, heralding the comic strip.

S. EHRHART (n.d.), along with Syd B. Griffin, was a regular contributor to *Puck*, in which The Fool Pied Piper appeared in 1909. According to Murrell, he was "equally well known for his delicately drawn pretty women and his robust travesties of immigrant Irish and the light-fingered negro."

ENDICOTT and SWETT was one of a number of printing establishments operated by George and William Endicott in New York City during the nineteenth century. This partnership with Moses Swett produced lithographic prints for popular and commercial purposes between 1830 and 1834.

MARISOL ESCOBAR (b. Paris, France, 1930) studied at the Art Students League with Yasuo Kuniyoshi, at the Hans Hofmann School, the Academie des Beaux-Arts in Paris, and at the New School for Social Research. Classified with both the assemblagists and the Pop artists, Marisol was included in a number of important exhibitions throughout the sixties, and her work is represented in many major museum and private collections. She has been a contributor to such publications as Doubleday's *The Art of Assemblage*, Praeger's *Pop Art*, Collier's *The New American Arts*, and others.

WALLY "TROG" FAWKES (b. Vancouver, British Columbia, 1924) moved to England in 1931. He attended Sidcup Art School in Kent and served during World War II in a camouflage unit. In 1949 he created the daily comic strip "Flook," a sort of British Pogo; in 1959 he began to cartoon for the *Spectator*, followed by the *Observer*, the *Daily Mail*, and *Punch*. A jazz buff, he plays clarinet in his own group, the Troglodites.

JAMES MONTGOMERY FLAGG (b. Pelham Manor, New York, 1877; d. New York City, 1960) studied at the Art Students League and with Victor Marec in Paris. He contributed illustrations to *Liberty*, *Cosmopolitan*, *College Humor*, and other magazines. He published several books of humor and satire as well as a collection of his drawings. He was appointed military artist for the state of New York during World War I and did forty-six posters for the federal government, including the one which brought him lasting fame, the "I Want You" recruiting poster. The figure of Uncle Sam is a self-portrait.

DANIEL ROBERT FITZPATRICK (b. Superior, Wisconsin 1891; d. 1969) studied at the Chicago Art Institute. In 1911 he took a job drawing for the Chicago *Daily News*. Two year later he began his career with the St. Louis *Post-Dispatch* which lasted until his retirement in 1958—forty-five years. During this time he won numerous awards, including two Pulitzer Prizes in 1926 and in 1955. He contributed cartoons to *Collier's* from 1926 to 1949. He is credited with being one of the first cartoonists to recognize the threat of Nazism to world peace and to use the swastika as a sinister symbol.

ANDRÉ FRANÇOIS (b. Timisoara, Romania, 1915) is a painter and sculptor who has lived in France since 1934. He worked with Cassandre. Since 1962 he has contributed frequent covers for *The New Yorker*. He has had one-man shows at the Stedlijk Museum in Amsterdam, the Musee des Arts Decoratifs in Paris, and the Art Institute in Chicago, among others.

BENJAMIN FRANKLIN (b. Boston, 1706; d. Philadelphia, 1790) is credited as America's first political cartoonist. In 1747 he illustrated a pamphlet, *Plain Truth*, with a woodcut showing a man trying to pray a cart and a team out of a ditch with part of a Latin motto implying, "God helps those who help themselves." Better known is his disjointed snake, *Join, or Die*, which appeared in his *Pennsylvania Gazette* in 1754 and was "syndicated" in other newspapers throughout the colonies. So effective was his image that it was used again in 1765 during the Stamp Act crisis and became an early symbol of the Revolution.

BERNHARD GILLAM (b. Banbury, Oxfordshire, England, 1856;

d. Canajoharie, New York, 1896) came to America with his parents in 1866, settling in New York. He was self-educated and began to study law, but soon turned to engraving and selling his humble drawings in 1876. An early supporter of his portrait-painting efforts, Henry Ward Beecher, found him a few patrons. After some early caricatures appeared in *Leslie's Weekly* and *The New York Graphic*, he found his true calling and remained a political cartoonist until his death from typhoid fever. In 1880 he worked with Nast on *Harper's Weekly* and the following year left to join the staff of *Puck*. In 1886 he became part owner of the reorganized *Judge*, for whom he did some of his famous and influential cartoons. *Judge* became a powerful molder of public opinion under his direction and with the help of his pen.

JAMES GILLRAY (b. Chelsea, England, 1757; d. London, 1815) born of obscure, possibly Irish parentage, began his career as a letter engraver, but eventually applied himself to serious study of design at the Royal Academy. He was famed for his scathing social and political cartoons, of which he produced over 1,200. He attacked the Regency government and society at home, and the French Revolution and Napoleon abroad with a grotesque and bitter humor in engravings crowded with details executed with masterful skill. Gillray died insane and debilitated by alcholism.

REUBEN LUCIUS "RUBE" GOLDBERG (b. San Francisco, California, 1883; d. 1970) received a BS degree from the University of California, and though trained as an engineer, he went to work almost immediately as a sports cartoonist for the San Francisco *Chronicle*. He also drew for a while for the San Francisco *Bulletin*, until he took a job in New York City drawing sports cartoons for the *Evening Mail* in 1907. He moved from comic strips to political cartooning in 1939 when he started with the New York *Sun*. He joined the staff of the New York *Journal American* in 1949. In addition to several humorous books, Goldberg has to his credit a 1948 Pulitzer Prize cartoon, but it is for his particular brand of humor, his "crazy inventions," that he is most remembered.

PETER GREEN (b. West Bend, Wisconsin, 1945) majored in fine arts at the Layton School of Art in Milwaukee and at the Art Institute of Chicago. He took up illustration in 1965 and began specializing in charcoal and pen and ink caricature. His work has appeared in the Washington *Post*, the Washington *Monthly*, *Vista*, the Los Angeles *Times*, *Life*, *Rolling Stone*, and others. He has illustrated a number of political satire books for Ballantine Publishing, and in 1972 produced "Politicards," a deck of playing cards each with a caricature of a current political figure. He currently works and lives in Los Angeles.

WILLIAM GROPPER (b. New York City, 1897) studied at the National Academy of Design, the New York School of Fine and Applied Arts, with Robert Henri, George Bellows, and Howard Giles, and received a Guggenheim fellowship in 1937. He began work as an artist in 1919 with the New York *Tribune*, but made his reputation as a social protest artist in the 1930s with his cartoons in *New Masses* and other socialist and trade union publications. He has been described as an "expressionistic Daumier" for like his French precursor, Gropper combines a deep sense of political and social injustice with exceptional artistic ability and skill. His prints and paintings which bear many elements of caricature are owned by major American museums, and he is considered a leading exponent of American art of the 1930s.

GRANT E. HAMILTON (b. Youngstown, Ohio, n.d.) had no formal art training, but brilliantly assumed the colorful graphic style for which *Judge* was known. With the death of Bernhard Gillam in 1896, he became that magazine's leading cartoonist, and is remembered by his contemporary James Montgomery Flagg as a guiding force in *Judge's* later years. He cartooned for the great New York newspapers of the day, including the *Daily Graphic* and the *Herald*.

JOHN HELD, JR. (b. Salt Lake City, Utah, 1889; d. Belmar, New Jersey, 1958) studied drawing under the sculptor Mahonri Young and by 1905 was drawing sports cartoons for the Salt Lake City *Tribune*. He moved to New York City in 1910, working for a while as a newspaper artist and an advertising artist. His work became tremendously successful throughout the twenties and appeared in *Life*, *Judge*, *Liberty*, *Cosmopolitan*, *Vanity Fair*, *College Humor*, and *The New Yorker*. His saucy flappers and brash "college Joes" became symbols of the era of jazz, gin, and flaming youth and still retain their freshness and popular appeal.

LEO HERSHFIELD (n.d.) illustrated several books on baseball for the author Ira L. Smith. These included *Low and Inside* and *Three Men on Third*.

RICHARD HESS (b. Royal Oak, Michigan, 1934) studied at Michigan State University. He worked for advertising agencies from 1955 until he formed his own company in 1965, where he expanded his design interests to include such clients as Vista, IBM, Random House, *Playboy*, *Esquire*, *Newsweek*, *New York Magazine*, CBS, Columbia Records, Xerox, and others. His work has been shown at major museums in the United States, Europe and Asia. He currently lives in Connecticut.

DON HESSE (b. Belleville, Illinois, 1918) studied at the St. Louis School of Fine Arts at Washington University before breaking into newspaper work as a photographer. He first worked as a cartoonist for the Belleville *Daily News-Democrat* from 1935 to 1940. He joined the St. Louis *Globe-Democrat* in 1946 and is also syndicated by the Los Angeles Times Syndicate. He has won the national Headliners' Award, among many other professional honors.

DRAPER HILL (b. Boston, 1935) is a publishing historian of the arts of caricature and cartoon, as well as a working cartoonist. After receiving his B.A. from Harvard University in

1957, he attended the Slade School of Fine Arts, University College, London, from 1960–1963 under a Fulbright grant. He cartooned for the Quincy, Massachusetts, *Patriot Ledger* and the Worcester *Telegram* before joining *The Commercial Appeal* of Memphis, Tennessee, in 1971. In 1975 he was elected president of the Association of American Editorial Cartoonists. He authored *Mr. Gillray, the Caricaturist* and *Fashionable Contrasts*, along with several exhibition catalogues. In 1976 his work was the subject of an exhibition at the Brooks Memorial Art Gallery, Memphis.

ALBERT HIRSCHFELD (b. St. Louis, Missouri, 1903) studied at the National Academy of Design in New York, the Academie Julien, the London County Council, and the Art Students League in New York. He has been the theatre caricaturist for the New York *Times* since 1925 and has authored and illustrated numerous books. His sharp, rhythmic, linear style not only has captured and interpreted the individual personalities of Broadway celebrities, but also has reflected the glamorous, vital mood of New York's theatrical milieu. Though best known for his theatrical work, politicians, socialites, literati, or anyone in the spotlight is fair game for his pen.

BRAD HOLLAND (b. Fremont, Ohio, 1944) began submitting cartoons to magazines at age 13 and left his home in Arkansas at age 17 to work as a cartoonist. He later moved to New York City, where he wrote stories and drew pictures for the underground press. He began work for the New York *Times* in 1971. Currently, he is finishing *Eyesore*, a book of drawings and stories of a political bent, as well as other publications. His work was included in a show of art from the Op-Ed page of the *Times*, which was exhibited at the Louvre in Paris and at the Musée des Beaux-Arts in Bordeaux, and in a touring exhibition entitled "Beyond Illustration."

WILLIAM HUMPHREY[S] (b. c. 1740; d. after 1795) was the older brother of Hannah Humphrey, the London printseller who issued the prints of James Gillray. Humphrey particularly excelled at mezzotint engraving and drew portraits after the eighteenth century British masters, Reynolds and Kneller. He also produced genre subjects after Hopper and Morland. In 1765 he was awarded the prize of the Society of Artists for an engraving after Rembrandt.

LESLIE GILBERT ILLINGWORTH (b. Barry, South Wales, 1902) began studying at the Cardiff Art School at age sixteen, working part time in the lithograph department. In 1920 he won a scholarship to the Royal College of Art in London and, after he had been there six months, was offered the job of cartoonist for the London *Daily Mail* at 6 a week. In 1926 he continued his art training in Berlin and Paris, where he studied at the Academie Julien and supported himself by free-lancing for such publications as *Strand*, London *Opinion*, *Nash's*, *Good Housekeeping*, and *Passing Show*. In 1939 he rejoined the *Daily Mail* and began an association which lasted just over thirty years, spanning nine editorships. He retired from *Punch*, for which he also drew, in 1968, and from the *Daily Mail* in 1969. In 1973 he began drawing again for the Australian *Sun* and subsequently for the *News of the World*.

ANTHONY IMBERT (b. Calais, France, ?; d. New York City, 1835) taught himself to draw and paint while a prisoner of the British during the Napoleonic Wars. He emigrated to the United States in 1824 and established himself as a painter in New York City. In 1826 he was one of the first in the city to operate a lithographic press. His thirty-seven lithographs published in Cadwallader Colden's "Memoir" in celebration of the completion of the Erie Canal are credited as the first use of lithographs as book illustrations in the United States. His lithographed political cartoons are the earliest known to be produced in this medium.

REA IRVIN (b. San Francisco, 1881) studied at Mark Hopkins Art Institute in San Francisco. He illustrated several books in the 20s and 30s, including P. G. Wodehouse's *Hot Water*, but is best remembered as artist and art editor for *The New Yorker*, a position he held for thirty years. His cover design for the magazine's first issue, February 21, 1925, is reused every year on the anniversary date.

HERBERT JOHNSON (b. Sutton, Nebraska, 1878; d. 1946) studied at the State University of Nebraska and at Columbia University. He worked in the art departments of the Denver *Republican*, Kansas City *Journal*, and the Philadelphia *North American* as a cartoonist and in managerial positions. He was art editor and a cartoonist for *Saturday Evening Post* from 1912 to 1915 and continued thereafter as a contributor of cartoons to that magazine. An opponent of Roosevelt's New Deal and its deficit spending, he created the "Little Taxpayer," who was depicted as the bewildered and hapless victim of Roosevelt's bold, expensive programs.

DAVID CLAYPOOL JOHNSTON (b. Philadelphia, 1797 or 1799; d. Dorchester, Massachusetts, 1865) was apprenticed to Francis Kearney, the engraver, in Philadelphia in 1815. By 1819 he was in business for himself, but the complaints of some of the prominent Philadelphia celebrities he caricatured caused the publishers and printsellers there to refuse to deal with his work. Johnston is best known for his publication *Scraps*, a portfolio of caricatures modeled upon Cruikshank's *Sketches* (1828–1832) which appeared annually from 1830 to 1849, and which earned for Johnston the epithet "The American Cruikshank." Johnston also published and illustrated a number of books, caricatures, and other items. He often used the pseudonyms "Gebolibus Crackfardi," "Fun," and "Quiz."

EDWARD JONES (n.d.) operated lithographic firms in New York between 1844 and 1850. He worked in partnership with George W. Newman from 1846 to 1849, then operated on his own for another year. The firms produced commercial advertisements and the usual sentimental and topical prints for popular consumption. They also produced an *Illuminated Directory of New York* in 1848, which is an important pictorial document of the growing city.

EDWARD JUMP (b. France, c. 1831; d. St. Louis, early 1870s) came to San Francisco about 1860 and there got his start in graphic work making labels for whiskey bottles. He then moved to Washington, D.C., where he enjoyed great success as a portrait painter, sometimes making $500 a week. From Washington he moved to New York City, where he drew for Frank Leslie's publications and for *Wild Oats*. In the early 1870s he went west again, this time to St. Louis, where he ultimately committed suicide.

EDWARD WINDSOR KEMBLE (b. Sacramento, 1861; d. Ridgefield, Connecticut, 1933) was self-taught. In 1881 he was the cartoonist and staff artist for the New York *Daily Graphic*, then New York's only illustrated daily newspaper. He was a frequent contributor to *Life*, and popular illustrator for such classics as Mark Twain's *Huckleberry Finn* and *Pudd'nhead Wilson*, Harriet Beecher Stowe's *Uncle Tom's Cabin*, Washington Irving's *Knickerbocker History of New York*, and the Joel Chandler Harris "Uncle Remus" stories. He is significant for the empathy, understanding and geniality, uncommon in his time, with which he illustrated Negro characters.

JON BROWN KENNEDY (b. Springfield, Missouri, 1918) attended no art school but credited an excellent high school art teacher with much of his training. He drew for the Springfield *Leader-Press* for five years while taking college courses. He joined the Little Rock *Arkansas Democrat* in 1941. During the desegregation disturbances of 1957–58 he opposed Governor Faubus and mob violence and took a strong stand via his cartoons for law and order.

JOSEPH KEPPLER (b. Vienna, 1838; d. New York City, 1894) studied briefly at the Art Academy of Vienna before emigrating to the United States and settling in St. Louis. In 1869 he began there a comic German-language paper called *Die Vehme*. After its failure and that of a similar publication, which he called *Puck*, Keppler moved to New York City and drew for a publication called *Budget of Fun*. In 1876 he again published a German-language *Puck* and in 1877 began an English version. *Puck* became one of America's leading satirical magazines of the nineteenth century. It featured a large format, color work, eye-catching, colorful covers (different each week), and employed the oustanding cartoon jounalists of its day. It wielded great political clout in its exposure and ridicule of corruption, scandal and incompetency in high places. During the national elections of the 1880s and 1890s it was a force with which the candidates had to reckon. The magazine ceased publication in 1918.

JOSEPH KEPPLER JR. (b. 1872; d. 1956) headed the staff of *Puck* after his father's death in 1894. His drawing style resembled the older Keppler's, but the son typically used fewer figures in his compositions, and more greatly exaggerated facial features. His caricatures of Theodore Roosevelt in 1907 and 1908 are particularly successful. He sold *Puck* in 1914 and retired from cartooning to become an ardent advocate of the rights of American Indians.

ROLLIN KIRBY (b. Galva, Illinois, 1875; d. 1952) was a pupil of James Abbott McNeill Whistler, John Twatchman, and others. He was a cartoonist for the New York *Post*, and illustrated articles for *Scribner's, Century, Collier's, American, Liberty, Harper's*, and other popular magazines. He also authored several articles for these and other publications. He is credited with the formula that a good cartoon consists of 75 percent idea and 25 percent drawing.

EDWARD B. KOREN (b. New York City, 1935) studied at Columbia College in New York, earning his B.A. in 1957. He studied printmaking with Stanley W. Hayter at Atelier 17, and earned an M.F.A. in painting and printmaking from Pratt Institute, Brooklyn, in 1964. Since 1969 he has been an Associate Professor of Art at Brown University in Providence, Rhode Island. He has been widely exhibited in one-man and group shows, and his drawings have been published in the New York *Times, Harper's, Punch, The New Yorker, Esquire,* and *Sports Illustrated* among others. He has written and illustrated children's books and was awarded a Guggenheim Fellowship in 1970–71.

DAVID LEVINE (b. Brooklyn, New York, 1926) studied at the Tyler School of Fine Arts in Philadelphia and at the Hans Hofmann School in New York City. He was a painter and watercolorist in the realist tradition until he began doing caricatures around 1960. He is best known for his work for the *New York Review of Books*, which has used his caricatures since its inception in 1963. He has illustrated children's books and published several volumes of his caricatures.

JACK LEVINE (b. Boston, 1915) studied with Denman Ross and Harold Zimmerman. He worked for the WPA Federal Art Project in 1935 and was exhibited at the WPA show at the Museum of Modern Art in 1936. He shuns the battles and business of the art world, but his work is collected and shown at major American museums and galleries. He is recognized as an important exponent of figurative painting and social protest art in America. The grotesque, oversized heads and small, fleshy bodies of his figures clearly demonstrate the influence of caricature in his prints and paintings. Sometimes a specific individual is satirically portrayed, but generally "types" are depicted, such as gangsters, corrupt officials, and the bourgeoisie. Like Gropper and Shahn his work is satirical, but deadly serious and haunting.

TOM LITTLE (b. Williams County, Tennessee, 1898) studied art at Watkins Institute and later at Montgomery Bell Academy, both in Nashville. Beginning in 1916 he worked for Nashville's *The Tennessean*, first as a reporter, then as police reporter, then as city editor. In 1937 during an argument the publisher fired him as city editor and rehired him as cartoonist. He went on to win the Pulitzer Prize in 1957. He also drew the syndicated comic strip, "Sunflower Street," a panel that featured Negro life in Tennessee.

GEORGE LUKS (b. Williamsport, Pennsylvania, 1867; d. New York City, 1933) studied briefly at the Pennsylvania Academy of the Fine Arts and at various academies in Düsseldorf, Munich, Paris and London, but on the whole disdained academic training. In 1894 he joined the art department of the Philadelphia *Press*, and in 1895 he covered Cuba as war correspondent and artist for the Philadelphia *Evening Bulletin*. In 1896 he joined the New York *World* as a cartoonist, drawing "The Yellow Kid" and other comic strips for several years. Luks was one of "The Eight" American painters of the "Ashcan School," who sought to free American painting from stifling European and academic traditions. Luks lived as boldly as he painted. He died as the result of a barroom brawl at the age of sixty-six.

WINSOR ZENIC McCAY (b. Spring Lake, Michigan, 1872; d. New York City, 1934) was mainly self-taught and began his career by painting street signs and theatrical posters. He first cartooned for the Cincinnati *Commercial Tribune*. In 1902 he went to New York City and worked for many years for the Hearst publications. He also created the "Little Nemo" series, as well as many others, and has been credited with inventing the animated cartoon. In 1909 the first animated cartoon was shown in motion pictures featuring 10,000 individual drawings executed by McCay.

JOHN TINNEY McCUTCHEON (b. South Raub, Indiana, 1870; d. Lake Forest, Illinois, 1949) studied at Purdue University under Ernest Knaufft. He began work in 1889 with the Chicago *Record*. In 1903 he joined the Chicago *Tribune* where he remained until his retirement in 1954. His first political cartoons dealt with the 1896 McKinley-Bryan campaign. He was a traveling artist and foreign correspondent during the Spanish-American War, the Mexican Revolution of 1910, World War I, and on various special assignments. His adventures provided material for books and stories as well as cartoons. But the *Tribune* always brought him home for presidential elections. His Teddy Roosevelt cartoons were particularly popular. McCutcheon was generally a political conservative with a Midwestern tendency toward isolationism. He opposed American entry into both world wars and into the League of Nations. However, his wartime cartoons reflect spirited confidence in America's power to win quick, sure victories and set European affairs in order. He received the Pulitzer Prize in 1931 and is regarded as one of America's most outstanding and influential cartoonists.

JOHN L. MAGEE (n.d.) was trained as an apprentice to Emil Ackerman and worked for James Baillie, Nagel and Mayer, and Thomas Sinclair before opening his own lithographic firm in New York around 1844. In 1850 he moved to Philadelphia where he operated three places of business during the 1860s. Incidents of the Civil War provided him with readily marketable subject matter, as did disasters, and a new sport, which was capturing the American interest, baseball.

MARISOL. See MARISOL ESCOBAR.

REGINALD MARSH (b. Paris, 1898; d. Dorset, Vermont, 1954) studied at the Lawrenceville School and at Yale, where he was art editor of the *Yale Record* before his 1920 graduation. After college he sold cartoons to *Vanity Fair* and *Harper's Bazaar*, and drew caricatures for the New York *Daily News*. These led to commissions for theater sets. He then studied at the Art Students League with John Sloan, Kenneth Hays Miller, George Bridgman and George Luks, and he made a trip to Paris to study with Mahonri Young. Upon his return he did sketches for *The New Yorker*. He had his first one-man show in New York City galleries in 1930 and continued to show frequently after that. Marsh was associated with the social protest artists of the thirties, but unlike Gropper and others, remained aloof from politics. His drawings and prints portray the despair and dreariness, but also the raw energy and brashness of the times.

JAN MATULKA (b. Prague, Czechoslovakia, 1890; d. New York City, 1972) studied at the National Academy of Design with G. W. Maynard and in Paris where he was exposed to the post-World War I revolutionary trends in the arts. His first one-man show was held in 1927 at the Modern Gallery in New York. He became one of the early exponents of Abstract Expressionism in America and expounded his style and theories as a teacher at the Art Students League during the thirties. His artwork is represented in important American public and private collections.

WILLIAM HENRY "BILL" MAULDIN (b. Mountain Park, New Mexico, 1921) attended the Chicago Academy of Fine Arts in 1939–40, before going overseas with the 45th Division in World War II. He soon became the outstanding cartoonist of the war as millions of stateside fans followed the antics of his bedraggled G.I.s, Willie and Joe, through the war zones by way of Mauldin's five wartime books, including the best seller *Up Front*. He received the Pulitzer Prize in 1944 for one of his Willie and Joe cartoons. After the war, Mauldin spent a period of restlessness, not wishing to capitalize upon a war-bred success. He became the cartoonist for the St. Louis *Post-Dispatch* in April, 1958, and won a second Pulitzer Prize in 1959. In 1962 he joined the staff of the Chicago *Sun-Times*. Just as he had been *the* cartoonist of the war period, he again became *the* cartoonist of the 1960s when the issue was Civil Rights.

LOUIS MAURER (b. Biebrich-on-the-Rhine, Germany, 1832; d. New York City, 1932) studied art at Mayence. He emigrated to America with his family in 1851 and became an artist with the lithographic firm of Currier & Ives. After eight years with the firm, he moved to Major & Knapp and by 1872 was successful enough to found his own firm, Maurer & Heppenheimer. He retired in 1884 to devote himself to painting. Maurer was one of the most reliable sources of information on the renowned Currier & Ives establishment and lived long enough to talk to several scholars.

ROBERT MINOR (b. San Antonio, Texas, 1884; d. 1952) had no formal art training, but by 1911 had become the chief cartoonist for the St. Louis *Post-Dispatch*. Ralph Pulitzer of the New York *Evening World* paid the costs of his studying for a year in Europe and then employed Minor in 1913. Minor drew anti-war cartoons, consistent with the *Evening World's* viewpoint at that time, but when the paper shifted its thinking, Minor refused to go along and began to draw for anarchist publications such as *Mother Earth*, the *Masses*, and *Call*. He visited Russia in 1918, returning completely disillusioned with Lenin and the Bolsheviks, but a second trip in 1920 reversed his thinking. Upon his return to the United States, he became editor, cartoonist, and writer for the *Liberator*, artist and writer for the *Worker's Monthly*, and cartoonist for *Good Morning*. In 1926 he left the field of cartooning to do full-time work for the Communist party, organizing the International Labor Defense and serving as a war correspondent for the American Communist Press in the Spanish Civil War.

FRANK ARTHUR NANKIVELL (b. Maldon, Victoria, Australia, 1869; d. ?) left Australia at age twenty-one to go to Paris to study art, but only made it as far as Japan. There he ran out of money and took a job cartooning for an English-language newspaper from 1891 to 1894. He then studied art in San Francisco for two years, where he published a fortnightly comic, *Chic*, and drew for the San Francisco *Call*, *Examiner*, and *Chronicle*. In 1896 he moved to New York and joined the staff of *Puck*, where his work appeared in 1896–97 and 1899–1909. During the Depression he put to use some of his knowledge about printing as an employee of the Federal Art Project, graphic arts division.

THOMAS NAST (b. Landau, Germany, 1840; d. Guayaquil, Ecuador, 1902) came to New York with his mother in 1846. He studied with the artist Theodore Kaufman and later entered the National Academy of Design. At age fifteen he was employed as an artist for *Frank Leslie's Illustrated Newspaper*. He left *Leslie's* in 1859 to draw for the New York *Illustrated News*, which sent him abroad. He returned just before the Civil War, drawing for the *Illustrated News* and *Leslie's* until 1862 when he became staff artist for *Harper's Weekly*, where his cartoons became highly influential in shaping public opinion. Nast is credited with the downfall of the notorious Tweed Ring in New York, with creating the Republican elephant, the modern-day image of Santa Claus, and with popularizing the Democratic Donkey and Tammany Tiger. Nast resigned from *Harper's* in 1887 due to clashes with G. W. Curtis, the editor. This led to the decline in power and influence of both the magazine and Nast, who eventually became consul to Ecuador, where he succumbed to the climate.

CHARLES HENRI AMEDÉE ("CHAM"), Comte de Noé, (b. Island of Noé, 1819; d. Paris, 1879) was born a member of ancient French nobility, but eschewed his title and a military career to study art in Paris with Charlet and Paul Delaroche. In 1839 he exhibited his first album of satirical drawings under the pseudonym "Cham." They were a great success, and he proceeded to produce some 40,000 drawings and watercolors illustrating the facets and foibles of life in France and Algeria. His puppet-like caricatures and witty commentary made his work very popular during his lifetime but less enduring than the more barbed work of his contemporaries Philipon, Grandville, and Daumier. A friend summed up his career as "Forty years of spirit but never of malice."

PATRICK BRUCE OLIPHANT (b. Adelaide, Australia, 1935) came to the United States in 1964 from Australia where he had cartooned for the Adelaide *Advertiser*. He went to work for the Denver *Post* and set to the task of winning a Pulitzer Prize, which he did in 1967 by methodically studying past winners and then creating a product to please the judges. It was a whimsical gesture in defiance of the professional establishment and not at all in keeping with the style or tenor of his work. His artistic style is bold and his humor wry, and as a distinctive touch to the main drawing he adds "Punk the Penguin," a tiny character appearing in a corner of the drawing who makes a quizzical comment expanding the humor or meaning of the cartoon. He is now cartooning for the Washington *Star*.

FREDERICK BURR OPPER (b. Madison, Lake County, Ohio, 1867; d. New Rochelle, New York, 1937) had, after fifty-eight years of participation, one of the longest careers of any cartoonist. He began to draw first for the short-lived *Wild Oats* at age nineteen. By 1899 he had spent eighteen years with *Puck* when Hearst lured him to the New York *Journal*. He later drew for the New York *American*, working with newspapers thirty-two years in all before his failing eyesight forced his retirement in 1932. He invented the character "John Public" (another cartoonist later added the middle initial "Q") and the similar characters of "the little boy" (the common people) and "the big boy" (the trusts). He was also the creator of the "Alphabet of Joyous Trusts" and the "Willie and His Poppa" series which, thanks to Opper's technique of repeating the same idea every day in a different comic, had great impact.

JOSÉ CLEMENTE OROZCO (b. Zapotlán, Jalisco, Mexico, 1883; d. Mexico City, 1949) had three major influences on his art: the stiff, academic training he received in perspective and anatomy at San Carlos, the dramatic folk engravings of Posada, and classes with Dr. Atl at the Academy of Fine Arts. He began to paint in 1909, and was active in the Revolution helping Carranza when Villa and Zapata held the capital in 1915, making political cartoons for the partisan *Vanguardia*. By 1920 he was again painting in Mexico City. He produced his first frescoes at the Preparatory School between 1923 and 1927. He made a trip to New York City in 1926, where he quickly found critical acceptance, and toured Europe. Late in life he was recognized by the Mexican government for the cultural contributions he had made to his country.

CAREY CASSIUS ORR (b. Ada, Ohio, 1890; d. 1967) attended the Chicago Academy of Fine Arts, and then worked briefly for the Chicago *Examiner*. This was followed by three years with the Nashville *Tennessean*, and in 1917 he began his distinguished career with the Chicago *Tribune*. Orr won the Pulitzer Prize in 1960. He was also the pioneer in color cartoons in newspaper works, his first appearing March 5, 1932.

ROBERT OSBORN (b. Oshkosh, Wisconsin, 1904) studied at Yale University; the British Academy, Rome; the Academy Scandinav, Paris, and with Friesz, Varoquier, and Despiau. He founded and headed the art department of Hotchkiss School in Lakeville, Connecticut from 1929–1935, and headed the School of Art and Architecture at Yale University from 1960–1965. He has work in numerous major museum collections and has been represented in many exhibitions. He has written and illustrated a number of books.

JACK PATTON (b. Shreveport, Louisiana, 1900; d. Dallas, Texas, 1968) moved to Texas with his family at age five. He attended the Chicago Academy of Fine Arts, through which he obtained a job with the art department of the Dallas *Journal*. In 1920 he became the daily cartoonist, a position he retained when the newspaper became the *Dispatch-Journal*. He later joined the Dallas *Morning News*. In the early 1920s, he initiated a comic strip, "The Restless Age," which in 1939 was syndicated under the title "Spence Easley" by the Des Moines *Register and Tribune*.

LUTE PEASE (b. Winnemucca, Nevada, 1869; d. 1963) joined the Newark *Evening News* in 1914 and remained there for the length of his career. His cartoons of John L. Lewis are outstanding and in 1949 while still working for the *Evening News* he won a Pulitzer Prize for one of them, his creativity and skill undiminished at age eighty.

MIKE PETERS (b. St. Louis, Missouri, 1943) is one of the fastest rising young cartoonists in the country. Schooled in art at Washington University in St. Louis, he later came under the influence of Bill Mauldin who found him a job doing art at the Chicago *Daily News*. Mauldin later recommended Peters for the job at the Dayton *Daily News*, where he now produces stimulating cartoons that are widely published in sources such as *Time* magazine.

MARK PODWALL (b. Brooklyn, New York, 1945) has published drawings for such publications as the New York *Times*, *Oui*, *Rolling Stone*, and *Hadassah Magazine*. He has authored several books and is illustrating a collection of songs for Paul Simon's *New York City*. Dr. Podwall is also a physician at the New York University Skin and Cancer Unit.

THOMAS E. POWERS (b. Milwaukee, 1870; d. Long Beach, New York, 1939) apprenticed as a boy to a Kansas City lithographer and studied art independently until he was hired by the Chicago *Daily News*. He soon began to specialize in political subjects, and in 1894 was hired by the New York *World*. Two years later he moved to the New York *Herald*, beginning a forty-year career with the Hearst newspapers.

GARRETT PRICE (b. Bucyrus, Kansas, 1896) attended the University of Wyoming and the Art Institute of Chicago. His earliest art job was with the Chicago *Tribune*, where he illustrated news stories beginning in 1916. Later he illustrated for *Scribner's*, *College Humor*, *Collier's*, and other major publications. But he is best known for his original and incisive covers for *The New Yorker*. He has exhibited at major American museums.

ROBERT PRYOR (b. Denver, Colorado, 1939) studied at California State University, and has taught at the California State branches at North Ridge, Fullerton, and at Prahnan College of Technology, Melbourne, Australia. His illustrations have appeared in *Time*, *Harper's*, *Newsweek*, the New York *Times*, and *Saturday Review*, among others. He has exhibited widely since 1962 and has received numerous awards for his drawings.

PAUL PSORAKIS (b. Ghana, 1941) went to England at age fifteen, where he still lives. He studied painting at the York School of Art and later at the Royal Academy in London, graduating in 1965. He now teaches illustration at the Watford College of Art. His work has appeared in *Twen*, *Pardon*, *Rapport*, *Lui*, *Lords*, *Viva*, *Nova*, *Harper's* (United Kingdom), *The Observer*, *Queen*, *Flair* and the New York *Times*.

JOHN S. PUGHE (b. 1871; d. 1909) cartooned for Keppler at *Puck*. Like most of the magazine's artists, he lampooned without compunction any person or action which he disapproved. Thus, both the trusts and Theodore Roosevelt became his targets in the early 1900s.

G. QUERNER (n.d.) was publisher of political cartoons in Washington, D.C., during the Civil War. He was a passionate abolitionist and quite vituperative toward Jefferson Davis and the secessionists. Peters wrote, in *America on Stone*, that "Querner seems to have had a very strange sense of humor, if it can be called that."

LOUIS RAEMAEKERS (b. Roermond, Netherlands, 1869; d. Scheveningen, Netherlands, 1956) studied in Amsterdam, Brussels and Paris. He was a relatively obscure Dutch cartoonist and illustrator for Amsterdam's *Die Telegraaf* until World War I, when he became one of the foremost instruments of Allied propaganda. So powerful were his haunting, bitterly ironic drawings deploring German aggression that the Germans put a bounty on his head and the Dutch prosecuted him for endangering their neutrality. His work was widely exhibited and published in the press of France and England, in which country he sought asylum in 1916. Lloyd George persuaded him to travel to the United States to use his art to enlist U.S. participation in the war. His work was syndicated with great effect in Hearst's publications throughout the country for the duration of the conflict.

ALBERT TURNER REID (b. Concordia, Kansas, 1873; d. New York City, 1958) made his start in cartooning, after several Kansas City newspapers had rejected his work, by entering a Topeka *Mail and Breeze* competition for the best political cartoon by a Kansas artist. His winning of the first prize ($15) brought him to the attention of *Mail and Breeze* publisher Arthur Capper, who contracted him to produce a cartoon a week. In 1897 he became staff artist for the Kansas City *Star*. He went to Chicago and worked on the *Record* in 1899 before moving to New York City in 1900 and joining the staff of the New York *Herald*. At this time he was also contributing to *Judge*, *McClure's*, and the *Saturday Evening Post*, as well as continuing to draw for the *Mail and Breeze* and the Kansas City *Journal*. He remained an active cartoonist until the mid-thirties, when he began to teach and paint seriously.

PAUL REVERE (b. Boston, 1735; d. Boston, 1818) supplemented his trade as silversmith with copper engraving, producing illustrations, documents, money, music, business cards and the like. He also used his skill to foment revolutionary sentiments by engraving political cartoons and propagandistic pictures; approximately twenty designs are known. These were sold as separate sheets, produced as illustrations for broadsides and newssheets, or appeared in the *Royal American Magazine*, for which Revere regularly supplied the plates. Revere did not create his own designs. He copied English engravings sympathetic to the American cause, sometimes altering them for his purposes. What he lacked in creativity and technical skills, he compensated with his enthusiasm for his subject. Revere also adapted patriotic designs for journalistic mastheads, official documents and specie.

BOARDMAN ROBINSON (b. Somerset, Nova Scotia, 1876; d. 1952) attended the Massachusetts Normal Art School, the Académie Colarossi, and the Ecole des Beaux Arts in Paris. He started his career as an illustrator for the *Morning Telegraph* in New York from 1907 to 1910, and then drew for the New York *Tribune* from 1910 to 1914. he threw off this well-paying job with the conservative paper to go to Russia with John Reed for *Metropolitan Magazine*. From 1915 until 1922 he drew for the liberal publications, *The Masses* and *Liberator*, as well as for *Harper's Weekly*. After this and a two-year stint with the London *Outlook*, he gave up newspaper and magazine illustration to draw book illustration.

HENRY R. ROBINSON (n.d.) was a publisher and designer of lithographs in New York City between 1831 and 1849. Between 1836 and 1843 he advertised in the city directory as a caricaturist, and political cartoons were a major part of his business. Though often lengthy in text, cluttered with details and allusions which are today difficult to understand, they are spirited and show appreciable wit. Robinson was a vigorous opponent of Andrew Jackson and the Tammany Hall politicos. He also added to the popular genre of disaster and crime prints, among them a series on the sensational Ellen Jewett murder of 1836. He was a pioneer in the use of color and large folio sheets.

JAMES NAUMBERG ROSENBERG (b. Allegheny City, Pennsylvania, 1874; d. 1971) began his artistic career in 1919, when his pastel sketches of a World War I victory parade were exhibited at Anderson Galleries in New York City. Through George Bellows he met the printer George Miller, thereby forming the association through which his powerful series of lithographs depicting the 1929 stock market crash emerged. From 1930 through the late 1950s he returned to his professional law practice. In 1959 and 1960 he travelled to southern France, producing a group of landscape sketches which were later lithographed. His work is included in many public and private collections throughout the United States.

CHARLES MARION RUSSELL (b. Oak Hill, Missouri, 1864; d. Great Falls, Montana, 1926) had, according to humorist Irwin Cobb, "a gorgeous wit which tickled but never stung." Charlie Russell began his artistic career by making humorous sketches and wax models to amuse his cowboy friends. Even after his enormous success as a Western artist he continued to illustrate his correspondence with cartoons of himself and his friends, and many of his paintings and illustrations are imbued with his rollicking sense of humor. He could convey the action and humor of a situation in any medium—paint, ink, bronze, the spoken or written word—and always enjoyed the fun as much as his audience.

RONALD SEARLE (b. Cambridge, England, 1920) was educated at the Cambridge School of Art. After harrowing experiences as a Japanese prisoner during World War II, he returned to England in 1945 to pursue a successful career as a cartoonist and serious artist. He worked for the London *Tribune*, *Sunday Express*, and *News Chronicle* successively from 1949 to 1954. He became theatre artist for *Punch* in 1949 and joined the staff in 1956. He has contributed special feature material for United States magazines such as *Life*, *Holiday* and *Fortune*, and has become one of the most popular and influential cartoonists of his generation. He has also worked with animated film, illustrated and written a number of books, designed for the stage, exhibited and been awarded for his work internationally.

FREDERICK OTTO "FRED" SEIBEL (b. Duranville, New York, 1886; d. Richmond, Virginia, 1968) studied at the Art Students League in New York City. In 1911 he began selling cartoons to New York papers and in 1916 joined the staff of the *Knickerbocker Press*. In 1926 he began cartooning for the Richmond *Times-Dispatch* where he worked for the rest of his career. Seibel laconically said of his cartoons, "I hope they speak for themselves. If not I've wasted a great deal of time." His trademark, included in all his work, was a small black crow wearing spectacles, a caricature of himself and a tribute to a childhood pet and drawing model.

SERRELL and PERKINS (n.d.) was the lithographic firm operated by Henry R. Serrell and S. Lee Perkins in New York City between 1849 and 1852. Serrell operated on his own for another year thereafter. Notable are their satirical prints on New York's "Tenderloin District" and on California and the Gold Rush.

BEN SHAHN (b. Kovno, Lithuania, 1898; d. New York City, 1969) moved to Brooklyn with his family in 1906. He studied at the National Academy of Design in 1922. He was apprenticed to a lithography shop at age fifteen, and continued his production in the graphic arts his entire life. He was a renowned painter and muralist committed to themes of social protest, beginning in 1931 with the exhibition of twenty-three gouaches dealing with the Sacco-Vanzetti trial. He illustrated a number of books and executed many posters and commercial assignments. His flat, simplified forms and colors are evocative of the twentieth century style of caricature, for like cartoons his works were designed to communicate terse but forceful pictorial messages.

JOHN SLOAN (b. Lock Haven, Pennsylvania, 1871; d. Hanover, New Hampshire, 1951) studied at the Pennsylvania Academy of the Fine Arts under Thomas Anshutz. Like William Glackens, George Luks, and Everett Shinn he began his career as a newspaper artist for the Philadelphia *Inquirer* and the Philadelphia *Press*. In 1904 he moved to New York City where he free-lanced for various magazines and did book illustration for the next twelve years. He became associated with Robert Henri and "The Eight" and is noted for his paintings and prints of New York City street and genre scenes. He drew for *McClure's* and *Collier's*, and as art editor the *The Masses* from 1912 to 1916 instituted a number of graphic innovations. His work is in most major collections of American art in the United States.

DORMAN HENRY SMITH (b. Steubenville, Ohio, 1892) worked in a steel mill before becoming a commercial artist in Columbus, Ohio in 1917. In 1919 he began work as a cartoonist for the Des Moines *News* and then in 1921 joined the Newspaper Enterprise Association in Cleveland. In 1927 he went to the New York *American* and from there to the San Francisco *Examiner* in 1929. Since 1935 he has worked for the Chicago *Herald Examiner*.

EDWARD SOREL (b. New York City, 1929) attended Cooper Union and the Workshop School in New York, and in 1953 founded Push Pin Studios with two Cooper Union classmates. His illustrations, political satire, and caricatures have appeared in numerous publications, including *Esquire, New York Magazine, The Realist,* and *Rolling Stone*. He has also illustrated children's books, worked for a number of commercial firms in advertising, and has done numerous book and record album covers. He recently had a one-man show at New York's New School for Social Research, and is presently the cartoonist for the *Village Voice*.

RALPH STEADMAN (b. London, England, 1936) was educated in North Wales. He held a variety of jobs until the Hungarian Revolt turned his interest to political cartooning in 1956. He has since become one of Britain's outstanding cartoonists. His dense cross-hatching and use of detail have been described as a revolt against the simplification of the twentieth century style of caricature and a return to eighteenth century drafting techniques. Steadman's work appears frequently in Britain's leading satirical magazines and press and he is art editor of *Linus*, a serious magazine devoted to cartooning.

WILLIAM STEIG (b. New York City, 1907) studied at the College of the City of New York and the National Academy of Design. Since 1930 his popular cartoons have appeared in leading American magazines, *The New Yorker, Vanity Fair, Collier's* and many others. Numerous collections of his cartoons have been published. The situational humor of his cartoons is based on his bland characters, who are ironically profound in their stupidity or vice versa.

SAUL STEINBERG (b. Romanic-Sarat, Romania, 1914) studied psychology and sociology at the University of Bucharest before taking a degree in architecture at the Polytechnico in Milan, Italy. He was a cartoonist in Italy from 1936 to 1939 and practiced architecture there between 1939 and 1940. He emigrated to the United States in 1942. Here he has worked free-lance and for *The New Yorker* where his stark, linear style and pictorial puns have been featured since 1941. His work has been exhibited and collected by major American museums, and his style has influenced the younger generation of cartoonists.

HASSAN STRAIGHTSHANKS was the pseudonym concealing the identity of an artist who designed several spirited political cartoons for the lithographers Endicott and Swett between 1833 and 1834. It is believed that Moses Swett may indeed have been the whimsical Straightshanks.

DAVID HUNTER STROTHER (b. Martinsburg, West Virginia, 1812; d. Charleston, West Virginia, 1888) studied art in Philadelphia and in Italy and France. He began work in the United States in 1844 as an illustrator of books and magazines. In 1853 he began contributing illustrated articles to *Harper's Weekly* including a series on Southern life under the pseudonym, "Porte Crayon." He received highly paid commissions to travel, write and draw for the magazine thereafter. During the Civil War he served in the Union army and rose to the rank of brevetted brigadier general. After the war he continued to contribute to *Harper's* until 1875, though his popularity waned. He served as United States consul general in Mexico City from 1879 to 1885. He died while preparing a book on his experiences there.

JEAN-CLAUDE SUARÈS (b. Alexandria, Egypt, 1942) was educated in Egypt and Italy. Before joining the New York *Times* in 1970 as art director of its Op-Ed page and New York *Times Book Review*, he was art editor for Scanlan's *Magazine* and co-publisher of the New York *Free Press*. His articles and drawings have appeared in numerous popular and professional magazines in the United States and Europe. Liberal and iconoclastic in spirit, his artwork is reminiscent of the style and techniques of nineteenth century wood engravings and have a haunting surrealistic quality. He has been an eloquent spokesman and supporter of the young cartoonists of the sixties and seventies as well as an outstanding member of their ranks.

PAUL SZEP (b. Canada, 1942) studied at the Ontario College of Art in Toronto, graduating in 1964. As a free-lance artist he has been a book and fashion illustrator, a graphic designer, and worked for Canada's largest newspapers. In 1966 he joined the Boston *Globe*, for which he draws five cartoons a week. He has published three books of cartoons, and has won the Sigma Delta Chi (1973) and Pulitzer Prize (1974) awards for editorial cartooning.

JAMES GROVER THURBER (b. Columbus, Ohio, 1894; d. 1961) was artistically untrained, and therein lies the charm and secret of the free, fluid style of his cartoons. Thurber was educated at the University of Ohio and as a journalist rose in his profession to managing editor of *The New Yorker* in 1927. His first cartoons appeared there around 1930. Absurdity and fantasies intrude into prosaic settings as his amoeba-shaped characters struggle through the morass of the daily human condition. His creations have a peculiar appeal, profundity and wit which rank Thurber as one of the twentieth century's outstanding humorists. He authored and illustrated numerous books, plays, children's stories, and many compilations of his cartoons have been published.

ELKANAH TISDALE (b. Lebanon, Connecticut, 1771; d. 1834) worked in New York in 1794 as an engraver and miniature painter. He moved to Hartford around 1798 and worked for the Graphic Company, an association of engravers. He remained there until 1825. Nine of his plates illustrate the 1795 edition of Trumbull's popular satirical epic *McFingal*. While Tisdale's plates are only mediocre examples of eighteenth century engraving, they are significant as perhaps the earliest humorous prints produced by an American-born artist.

TOMI UNGERER (b. Strasbourg, France, 1931) had no formal art training. He spent his early adult life wandering around Europe, taking odd jobs. In 1956 he arrived in New York City and began painting and drawing, and his work attracted immediate attention. He drew cartoons and illustrations for *Life*, *Esquire*, *Holiday*, *McCall's* and numerous advertising commissions, including notable campaigns for the New York *Times*. His theatrical and advertising posters are outstanding. While his advertising and poster art are characterized by bright, bold colors and childlike absurdity, many of his satirical drawings of American society portray a brutal, grotesque reality in which absurdity becomes asperity.

ADALBERT JOHN VOLCK (b. Augsburg, Germany, 1828; d. 1912) studied in Nürnberg and Munich before fleeing Germany due to his involvement there in the revolutionary agitations of 1848. In America he settled in Baltimore and became a prominent dentist. During the Civil War he was the only graphic propagandist for the South whose influence approached that of the Northerner Thomas Nast. His satirizations sharply pointed out the differences between Northern rhetoric and practice; his cartoons of General Butler (by whom he had been imprisoned at Fort McHenry in 1861) are cited as a factor in the general's defeat in the Massachusetts gubernatorial race after the war. Some of Volck's best work was published under the anagram V. Blada in *Confederate War Etchings* and *Sketches from the Civil War in North America*.

MAKOTO WADA (b. Osaka, Japan, 1936) became involved in the art of caricature after discovering the work of Shimizu. Study at the Tama College of Art in Tokyo exposed him to the work of Ben Shahn, Saul Steinberg, André François, and other Western cartoonists and illustrators. In 1957 he received the Japan Art Directors Club Prize and was commissioned to do a film for the Toshiba Electric Company. The following year he won a second Art Directors Club award, and joined the staff of Light Publicity Company. He has published many books and in 1965 he founded the magazine *Hanashi No Tokushu*, a satirical political review, and became its first art director.

VICTOR "VICKY" WEISZ (b. Berlin, 1913; d. 1966) studied art as a youth in Berlin. In 1929 his anti-Nazi sentiments led him to political cartooning, and during the 1930s he moved to England. There he was befriended by Sir David Low, the acknowledged leader of British political cartoonists. Weisz soon established his own reputation with his popular wartime cartoons for the London *News Chronicle*. An excellent caricaturist, "Vicky" subsequently worked for the *Mirror* and the *Evening Standard* in addition to his long connection with the *New Statesman*.

CHARLES WILLIAMS (b. ?; d. after 1830) was a prolific London caricaturist whose engravings were published by Thomas Tegg and S. W. Fores. After Gillray's death in 1815, he continued that artist's virulent pictorial campaign against Napoleon. Williams' early prints were signed "Ansell."

TOM WOLFE (b. Richmond, Virginia, 1931) received his only formal art instruction at the WPA school he attended as a child in Richmond. After graduating from Washington and Lee University he took his doctorate at Yale and became a journalist. His first published drawing illustrated his coverage of a murder trial for the Springfield (Massachusetts) *Union* in 1958. After that he began doing caricatures to accompany his articles, working successively for the Washington *Post*, the New York *Herald Tribune*, and *New York Magazine*. Wolfe's frenetic artwork graphically reinforces the energetic narrative style of his writing in books and magazines.

MICHAEL ANGELO WOOLF (b. London, 1837; d 1899) came to the United States as an infant. He studied painting in Munich and Paris, but did not develop his strong, Cruikshank-like compositional style until his later years. He is best known for his humorous, yet sympathetic depictions of the antics of slum children which appeared in *Life* during the decade 1886 to 1896. An actor in his youth, Woolf often captioned his works with quotes attributed to Shakespeare.

THOMAS WORTH (b. New York City, 1834; d. 1917) spent his life in New York City where he studied drawing in the school of Mr. Wells. He illustrated books and contributed regularly to *Judge* and other comic weeklies of the time, but his most popular works were lithographs he did for Currier and Ives. These prints, which satirized local life and politics, were displayed in shop windows, saloons, and barbershops throughout the city, particularly during the 1880s.

RICHARD QUINCY YARDLEY (b. Baltimore, 1902) attended the Friends School and Maryland Institute before taking a job with the Baltimore *Sun* at age twenty-one. After developing his technique in the advertising department there, he became the *Sun's* editorial cartoonist in 1949. Whether parodying local or international figures, Yardley's flat, broadly decorative style, reminiscent of folk art, reflects a simple, straightforward approach to current themes. Under the pseudonym "Quincy" Yardley began in 1961 to syndicate the cartoon strip "Our Ancestors."

CARICATURE & CARTOON COLLECTIONS

THIS SOURCE list for caricatures and cartoons was gleaned from the more than 2,000 questionnaires the Amon Carter Museum mailed to libraries, museums, and individuals, and the personal visits by members of the Museum staff and researchers. It is not intended to be complete, but rather is simply a way of sharing the information accumulated during the more than three years of research on this project. Comic strips have been excluded because they are a field unto themselves.

Alabama
Department of Archives and History, Montgomery. Collection of drawings by Frank Spangler which appeared in the *Montgomery Advertiser* during the 1920s and 1930s. Collection of Reconstruction cartoons that appeared in the *Tuscaloosa Monitor*.

Arizona
Navajo Tribal Museum, Window Rock. Small collection of cartoons.
Tucson Public Library. Collection of 131 original cartoons dated 1942–1946. Fifty-seven cartoonists represented, including Bill Baker, Leon Harold, Will Johnson and others.
University of Arizona Museum of Art, Tucson. Small collection including William Gropper, *The Speaker*; Jack Levine, *Dramatis Personae*. Reginald Marsh, *Monday Night at the Metropolitan*.

Arkansas
Arkansas State University Museum, State University. Collection of cartoons relating to the Spanish-American War.
Southeast Arkansas Arts & Science Center, Pine Bluff. Small collection of work by Ray Walters.

California
Bancroft Library, University of California, Berkeley. Collection of Rube Goldberg original drawings for comic strips and editorial cartoons.
California Historical Society, San Francisco. Collection of prints, primarily related to 19th century American history.
Downey Museum of Art, Downey. A few cartoons and caricatures, including three Tony Suth cartoons done for the *Philadelphia Inquirer*.
Grunwald Center for the Graphic Arts, University of California, Los Angeles. Collection of prints and drawings related to the graphic history of America.
Hoover Institution on War, Revolution, and Peace, Stanford University, Palo Alto. Large collection of cartoons related to the history of the United States.
Huntington Library, San Marino. Large collection of American cartoons, especially strong from 1830 to 1870 and 1890 to 1940.
Los Angeles County Museum of Art. Collection of cartoons, including *Puck* cartoons from the German edition, Gale of the *Los Angeles Times* during the 1930s, and satirical lithographs by Peggy Bacon, Daphne Dunbar, William Gropper, etc.
Jerry Muller, Costa Mesa. Collection of over 200 works representing work of more than 150 American cartoonists and comic strips such as Milton Caniff, Al Capp, Chester Gould, George McManus, Frederick Opper, Charles Schultz, Chic Young and R. F. Outcault.
Murray A. Harris Collection of Graphic Art. North Hollywood. Excellent collection of prints and drawings, 19th and 20th century history.
Pacific Center for Western Historical Studies, Stockton. More than 300 drawings by Robert Bastian, illustrator for the *San Francisco Chronicle*.
Pioneer Museum & Haggin Galleries, Stockton. Collection of J. C. Leyendecker paintings, 1908 to 1950; collection of Orson Lowell and Ralph Yardley drawings pertaining to local history.
San Francisco Museum of Art. Prints by Reginald Marsh, William Gropper, Esther Bruton, Thomas Hart Benton, José Clemente Orozco, Adolf Dehn, and Peggy Bacon.
San Jose Historical Museum, San Jose. Collection of cartoons, including many self-portraits by cartoonists.
University of California Art Museum, Berkeley. Collection of color lithographs, drawings, and sculpture relating to the Middle Period and Civil War, and Post-World War II.
Will Rogers State Historic Park, Pacific Palisades. Collection of caricatures relating to the 1930s.

Canada
Glenbow-Alberta Institute, Calgary. Small number of prints relating to Canadian-American relations.

Colorado
Buffalo Bill Memorial Museum, Golden. Collection of cartoons relating to William F. ("Buffalo Bill") Cody.
Denver Public Library. Collection of cartoons and caricatures relating to the Progressive era and World War I.
Pioneers' Museum, Colorado Springs. Collection of caricatures

by McDonald relating to the 1920s; several by Douglas Brown. One by Thomas Nast, entitled *Misnaming of Colorado Springs*.

University of Colorado, Boulder. Large collection of Pat Oliphant's work from 1965 to 1968, published in the *Denver Post*.

Connecticut

Arts of the Book Collection, Yale University, New Haven. Large collection of prints and graphic material related to the history of the United States.

Bradley Air Museum of the Connecticut Aeronautical Historical Association, Hebron. Collection of lithographs relating to the latter part of the 19th century, including an 1890s caricature of early jet flight.

Museum of Art, Science & Industry, Bridgeport. Collection of cartoons covering the Revolutionary era.

New Britain Museum of American Art. Collection of cartoons and comic strips, including the Sanford Low Memorial Collection of American Illustration (more than 100 original magazine illustrations) relating to the 1920s.

University of Hartford Library. Collection of prints, drawings, and sculpture related to the history of the United States.

Wadsworth Atheneum, Hartford. Excellent caricature of Mark Twain by Beerbohm.

The William Benton Museum of Art, University of Connecticut, Storrs. Large collection of drawings by Reginald Marsh done for the New York *Daily News*. Caricature reviews of Vaudeville.

Yale University Art Gallery, New Haven. Collection of cartoons and caricatures relating to the Revolutionary era and the Civil War era.

District of Columbia

Columbia Historical Society, Washington. Clifford K. Berryman caricatures of members of the Columbia Historical Society of the 1920s and 1930s.

Corcoran Gallery of Art, Washington. Collection of between 3,000 and 4,000 drawings and prints, some by Amos Doolittle, Emanuel Leutze, Clifford K. Berryman, Rockwell Kent, George Biddle, and others.

Georgetown University, Washington. Cartoons from the 1930s and post-World War II eras.

National Archives and Records Service, Washington. Collection of prints and drawings scattered through the holdings.

National Gallery of Art, Washington. Small collection of cartoons, including drawings by Herbert Block ("Herblock") of the Eisenhower years and prints by Reginald Marsh, John Sloan, and George Bellows.

National Museum of History and Technology, Smithsonian Institution, Washington. Large collection of cartoon prints, including the Harry T. Peters "America on Stone" Lithography Collection.

National Portrait Gallery, Smithsonian Institution, Washington. Large collection of caricatures relating to American history.

Prints and Photographs Division, The Library of Congress, Washington. Probably the largest collection of prints and drawings relating to American culture and history.

The White House, Washington. Small collection of cartoons relating to the Presidency, including one by Thomas Nast, one by Cruikshank.

Woodrow Wilson House, Washington. Collection of cartoons relating to President Wilson.

England

The British Museum, Department of Prints and Drawings, London. Large collection of English prints that relate to the American Revolution.

Fitzwilliam Museum, Cambridge. Some early Gillrays from the American Revolutionary era.

Florida

Pensacola Historical Museum, Pensacola. Collection of work by the members of the Art Cover Exchange Club.

Georgia

Department of Archives and History, Atlanta. Small collection of cartoons relating to history of Georgia.

Georgia Historical Society, Savannah. Collection of prints and drawings related to the history of the United States.

The High Museum of Art, Atlanta. Works by John Sloan, George Luks, Jerome Myers, and Kate Edwards.

Idaho

Idaho State Historical Society, Boise. Large number of cartoons by C. K. Berryman, featuring a collection on Senator Borah.

Illinois

The Art Institute of Chicago. Collection of prints and drawings, including a number of original drawings by Thomas Nast.

The Chicago Historical Society. Large collection of prints and drawings relating to Chicago and American history from the Revolutionary era to the present.

Chicago Public Library. Some drawings by Frederick Stuart Church and an incomplete set of Dr. Adalbert Volck's engravings of the Civil War era. Three playing card size caricatures of Jefferson Davis.

Evansville Museum of Arts & Science. Large collection of cartoons, including work by William Gropper, José Guadalupe Posada, Mel Casson, David Low, Larry Hill, etc., relating to various eras of American history including World War II.

Illinois Historical Society Library. Collection of John T. McCutcheon cartoons.

Krannert Art Museum, Champaign. Collection of engravings, lithographs, and drawings relating to the history of the United States from the Civil War to the present.

The Newberry Library, Chicago. A large collection of prints and drawings relating to American history from the Revolutionary era to the World War II era.

Northern Illinois University, De Kalb. Collection of 81 John T. McCutcheon cartoons; collection of almost 100 prints relating to the 19th century.

Northwestern University Library, Evanston. Collection of several hundred John T. McCutcheon cartoons from 1916 to 1945.

Stephenson County Historical Society, Freeport. Collection of fifty cartoons by Karl Kae Knecket, cartoonist for the Evansville, Indiana *Courier*.

Indiana

Butler University, Indianapolis. Large collection of drawings by Kin Hubbard and Gaar Williams.

Children's Museum of Indianapolis. Varied collection ranging from an Abe Martin caricature to an "Orphant Annie" doll and a Tammany Hall mechanical bank.

Indiana University Art Museum, Bloomington. Collection of contemporary cartoons.

The Lilly Library, University of Indiana, Bloomington. Large collection of prints and drawings relating to the history of the United States from the Revolution to the present.

Purdue University Libraries, Lafayette. Collection of more than 800 cartoons by John T. McCutcheon, Purdue alumnus of 1889 and cartoonist for the *Chicago Tribune*.

University of Notre Dame Art Gallery, Notre Dame. Small collection of cartoons including work by A. W. Steele, Jim Cassell, H. E. Godwin, W. K. Starrett, etc.

Iowa

Cedar Falls Historical Society. Collection of Charles Plumb drawings that appeared in the *Chicago Tribune*, re the plight of the farmer during the 1920s.

Davenport Municipal Art Gallery. Several cartoons attributed to Federick J. Waugh; caricatures by Al Hirschfeld.

Drake University, Des Moines. Approximately 8,000 proof sheets of J. N. ("Ding") Darling cartoons.

Herbert Hoover Presidential Library, West Branch. Small collection of cartoons relating to the career of President Hoover.

State Department of History and Archives, Des Moines. Collection of 1930s and World War II cartoons.

University of Iowa Library, Iowa City. Large collection of cartoons, primarily by J. N. ("Ding") Darling.

Kansas

Dwight D. Eisenhower Presidential Library, Abilene. Collection of drawings and sculpture related to the career of President Eisenhower.

Franklin County Historical Society, Ottawa. Collection of cartoons relating to World War II and after.

Kansas State Historical Society Library, Topeka. Large collection of the cartoons of Albert T. Reid.

Special Collections, Wichita State University, Wichita. Twentieth Century Collection.

University of Kansas Museum of Art, Lawrence. Collection of cartoons relating to the Progressive era and World War I.

Kentucky

The J. B. Speed Art Museum, Louisville. Large collection of cartoons by Paul Plaschke, who worked for newspapers in Louisville and Chicago.

Jonathan Truman Dorris Museum, Richmond. Collection of political cartoons collected during World War II.

Louisville Free Public Library. Collection of approximately 1,400 cartoons by Grover Page, cartoonist for the Louisville *Courier Journal*, 1930s to 1958.

University of Kentucky Art Gallery, Lexington. Collection of caricatures, including two works by William Gropper, relating to the 1920s and 1930s.

University of Louisville Library. Limited collection of original cartoons, contemporary.

Louisiana

Historic New Orleans Collection, New Orleans. Small collection relating to Louisiana and New Orleans.

Louisiana State Museum, New Orleans. Montages by E. Jump. Small collection of cartoons relating to Louisiana and the Civil War and Reconstruction era.

Louisiana State University Library, Baton Rouge. Cartoons by John Chase dealing with the contemporary era.

Louisiana State University, New Orleans. Collection of 1,400 original cartoons by Ralph N. Vinson of the New Orleans *States-Item* (1964–1971).

New Orleans Public Library. Collection of cartoons relating to American history from the 1930s to the present, including work by John Chase.

Tulane University Library, New Orleans. Cartoons by John Chase, 1943 to the present. Morris Henry Hobbs etchings, 1930s to 1967.

Maine

Bowdoin College Museum of Art, Brunswick. Collection of drawings and lithographs relating to the 1920s.

The Theatre Museum, Boothbay. Collection of Roland Young's caricatures. Caricatures of Eugene O'Neill, Nazimova, etc.

William A. Farnsworth Library and Art Museum, Rockland. Collection of cartoons.

Maryland

Enoch Pratt Free Library, Baltimore. Collection of more than 200 cartoons by McKee Barclay which appeared in the *Baltimore Sun* during World War I.

John Work Garrett Library, Johns Hopkins University, Baltimore. A collection of political cartoons, including campaign badges, broadsides, etc.

Lester Levy, Pikesville. A collection of more than 30,000 pieces of early American music, including many comic lithographs from the 1830s to the 1870s.

Peabody Institute, Baltimore. Collection of Adalbert Volck etchings of the Civil War.

University of Maryland, College Park. Small collection of WPA paintings and mural studies, collection of prints of the 1930s.

The Walters Art Gallery, Baltimore. Collection of drawings of Baltimore by Alfred Jacob Miller.

Massachusetts

Amherst College, Amherst. Small collection of cartoons and caricatures relating to the Reconstruction period and the Post-World War II era.

Boston Public Library. Large collection of prints and drawings relating to the history of the United States.

Boston University, Boston. Collection of comic strips, including Orphan Annie, Lil Abner, Abbie & Slats, Beetle Bailey, Moon Mullins, and Dennis the Menace. Also World War I posters.

Brandeis University Library, Waltham. Collection of Daumier lithographs, some relating to America. A few Currier & Ives lithographs relating to the Civil War.

Calvin Coolidge Memorial Room, Northampton. Cartoons by W. R. McCutcheon and others about Coolidge and his times.

Fogg Art Museum, Harvard University, Cambridge. Collection of prints and drawings related to the history of the United States.

Harvard College Library, Cambridge. Collection of prints and drawings in various holdings.

Haverhill Historical Society. Collection of drawings relating to the Civil War and local history, two Currier & Ives gold rush cartoons.

Heritage Plantation of Sandwich, Sandwich. Thomas Nast oil caricatures of General Sheridan.

Lowell Historical Society, Lowell. Cartoons and caricatures relating to the Civil War, Industrialization, and the Progressive era and World War II.

Museum of Fine Arts, Boston. Large collection of American folk art, some of which might be interpreted as caricature. Large collection of prints, including Daumier. Some sculpture.

Old State House, The Bostonian Society, Boston. Collection of wood engravings, lithographs, and drawings relating to the Revolution, the Progressive era, and the 1920s.

The Society for the Preservation of New England Antiquities, Boston. Small collection of Revolutionary War political engravings.

Michigan

Clements Library, University of Michigan, Ann Arbor. Small collection of cartoons relating primarily to the Revolutionary era.

Detroit Historical Museum, Detroit. Collection of cartoons and caricatures relating to local history from the Civil War to the present.

Michigan State University Museum, East Lansing. Collections include several dozen 19th century comic valentines, several hundred World War I posters, small collection of political posters, dozens of Civil War patriotic envelopes with slogans and illustrations printed on them.

Minnesota

Hamline University Galleries, St. Paul. Small collection of cartoons relating to the 1930s, World War II, and the Post-War era.

James Ford Bell Library, University of Minnesota, Minneapolis. Collection of Dutch cartoons on the American Revolution.

Minneapolis Institute of Arts. Collection of drawings.

Minneapolis Public Library. Collection of thirty-five Charles L. Bartholomew cartoons; twenty-four cartoons by Oz Black, which appeared in the *Minneapolis Morning Tribune* from 1941 to 1952.

Minnesota Historical Society, St. Paul. Collection of twenty-five Charles L. Bartholomew cartoons.

Morrison County Historical Society, Little Falls. Small collection of cartoons relating to local area.

University of Minnesota Gallery, Minneapolis. Small collection of caricatures and cartoons. Relating to American history from Reconstruction to Post-World War II.

Walker Art Center, Minneapolis. Caricatures by Jacob Lawrence, Jack Levine, David Hockney, and Robert Israel.

Mississippi

Meridian Museum of Art, Meridian. Small collection of lithographs by Caroline Durieux, some relating to New Orleans.

Missouri

Central Missouri State Museum, Warrensburg. Collection of World War I and World War II posters.

Harry S. Truman Library, Independence. Large collection of cartoons relating to the Presidency of Mr. Truman.

The Missouri Historical Society, St. Louis. Large collection of prints and drawings, including prints of the 19th century and drawings by cartoonists such as Fitzpatrick of the *St. Louis Post-Dispatch*.

Museum of Art and Archaeology, Columbia. Collection of lithographs and color lithographs relating to the 1930s, World War II and the Post-War era.

The State Historical Society of Missouri, Columbia. Large collection of prints and drawings relating to the history of the United States from the 19th century to the present. Several thousand examples represent work of some of America's most outstanding cartoonists.

The St. Louis Art Museum, St. Louis. Large collection of prints and drawings, many satirizing American culture or life.

William Rockhill Nelson Gallery, Kansas City. Collection of contemporary cartoons by such artists as Garrett Price.

Montana

Montana Historical Society, Helena. Collection of cartoons relating to Senator B. K. Wheeler, including work by Poinier, Berryman, Orr, Baer, Parrish, and Gregg.

Nebraska

Buffalo Bill's Ranch, North Platte. Collection of caricatures of William F. ("Buffalo Bill") Cody.

Joslyn Art Museum, Omaha. Collection of prints, including some by John Sloan, Peggy Bacon, Mabel Dwight, and Currier & Ives.

Nebraska State Historical Society, Lincoln. Collection of cartoons and caricatures related to American history from the Progressive Era to World War II.

University of Nebraska Art Galleries, Lincoln. Collection of engravings and lithographs relating to 19th century American history.

Nevada

Nevada Historical Society, Reno. Collection of cartoons, including some by Lew Hymers, Robert Cole Caples, A. Lanzini, C. B. McClelland, as well as 19th century prints.

Nevada State Museum, Carson City. Small collection of cartoons relating to Senator Patrick McCarran (1933–1954), by Berryman, Orr, Maloney, and Coakley.

New Hampshire

Dartmouth College Library, Hanover. Collection of cartoons.

Hopkins Center Art Galleries, Dartmouth College, Hanover. Prints by Currier & Ives and Thomas Nast.

New England College Library, Henniker. Large collection of cartoons relating to Senator Styles Bridges and Robert Bass, President F. D. Roosevelt, President Truman, etc.

New Jersey

Chesler Collection, Library, Fairleigh Dickinson University,

Florham-Madison. Collection of cartoons and caricatures related to the history of the United States.

The Newark Museum. Small collection of cartoons, including two drawings by David Claypool Johnston.

The New Jersey Historical Society, Newark. Large collection of cartoons related to American history from the Age of Jackson to World War II.

The New Jersey State Museum, Trenton. Collection of prints and drawings.

Princeton University Art Museum, Princeton. Collection of cartoons and caricatures relating to American history from Reconstruction to the present.

Princeton University Library, Princeton. Excellent print collection, including cartoons and caricatures: the Sinclair Hamilton Collection of Early American Illustrators, the Rollins Collection of Western Americana, the Graphic Arts Collection, the Manuscript Collection, etc.

Rutgers University Art Gallery, New Brunswick. Collection of Currier & Ives prints, Posada prints, and an uncut woodblock by Thomas Nast re Grant and Colfax election in 1868.

Rutgers University Library, New Brunswick. Collection of prints and drawings.

U.S. Army Signal Corps Museum, Fort Monmouth. Cartoons relating to the Civil War, the 1930s, World War II, and the Post-War era.

New Mexico

Lovelace Foundation for Medical Education and Research, Albuquerque. Wood carvings of "Andy" Anderson.

Museum of New Mexico, Santa Fe. Some Indian caricatures of tourists.

Roswell Museum and Art Center, Roswell. Some caricatures relating to the 1930s, World War II, and Post-World War II.

University of Albuquerque. Collection of José Guadalupe Posada woodcuts.

University of New Mexico Art Museum, Albuquerque. Small collection of prints by Gropper, Sloan, Rafael Soyer, Gavarnis, and Daumier.

New York

Albright-Knox Art Gallery, The Buffalo Fine Arts Academy, Buffalo. Drawings and watercolors by Walt Disney and Gluyas Williams.

American Museum of Fire Fighting, Hudson. Collection of Currier & Ives, "The Darktown Brigade."

Brooklyn Museum, Brooklyn. Large collection of David Levine pen and ink caricatures, many of which appeared in the *New York Review of Books*. Some cartoons relating to F. D. Roosevelt administration and World War II.

Buffalo and Erie County Historical Society, Buffalo. Collection of lithographs by Currier & Ives, and A. Hoen & Company. Drawings by E. R. Barney for the *Buffalo Republic*, Ed Joseph Roche, Bruce Shanks, and others.

George H. Cole, Schenectady. Has some originals of his own work that appeared in *The Saturday Review of Literature*.

Columbia University Library, New York City. Collection of drawings relating to Tammany Hall and New York City politics.

Cooper-Hewitt Museum of Decorative Arts and Design, New York City. Collection of wood engravings, lithographs, and drawings relating to American history from the Reconstruction era to Post-World War II.

Cornell University Library, Ithaca. Collection of cartoons relating to the Age of Jackson, the Civil War, and the Post-World War II era.

Cortland County Historical Society, Cortland. Some drawings done at the turn of the century.

Franklin D. Roosevelt Presidential Library, Hyde Park. Collection of drawings and sculpture relating to the career of President Roosevelt.

Ben Goldstein, New York City. Large collection of prints and drawings related to the World War I era.

Paulette Green, Rockville Centre. Collection of cartoons related primarily to the 1930s.

Hamilton College, Clinton. Small number of Thomas Nast original drawings and prints.

Herbert F. Johnson Museum of Art, Cornell University, Ithaca. Small collection of paintings, prints, and drawings, mostly contemporary.

The Long Island Historical Society, Brooklyn. Collection of twenty Arthur Weindorf cartoons.

Long Island University, Brooklyn. Collection of lithographic cartoons relating to the Progressive era and World War I.

Marine Museum of the City of New York. Collection of cartoons and caricatures relating to American history, including engravings, lithographs, drawings, paintings, and sculpture.

The Metropolitan Museum of Art, New York City. Large collection of prints and drawings related to American history.

Munson-Williams-Proctor Institute, Utica. Collection of cartoons and caricatures including paintings and/or drawings by John Sloan, George Luks, Boardman Robinson, and Reginald Marsh.

Museum of Modern Art, New York City. Collection of prints and drawings.

National Baseball Hall of Fame and Museum, Cooperstown. Collection of caricatures and cartoons related to the history of baseball.

New-York Historical Society, New York City. Large collection of prints and drawings relating to the history of the United States.

New York Public Library, Print Department, New York City. Excellent collection of prints and drawings relating to the history of the United States.

New York State Historical Association, Cooperstown. Large collection of 19th century prints.

New York University Art Collection, New York City. Small collection, including works of Glenn O. Coleman, Everett Shinn, and Lyonel Feininger.

Old Museum Village of Smith's Clove, Monroe. Small collection of cartoons and sculptures.

Oneida Historical Society, Utica. Small collection of cartoons.

Pierpont Morgan Library, New York City. Small collection of cartoons.

Queens College Library, Flushing. Small collection of WPA

prints, including work by Luigi Gugliemi, Reginald Marsh, and Hirschfeld.

Schenectady County Historical Society, Schenectady. Collection of caricatures relating to the 1920s.

Sleepy Hollow Restorations, Tarrytown. Five caricatures regarding the Revolution.

St. Bonaventure University, St. Bonaventure. Cartoons by Boardman Robinson, George Luks, and George Cruikshank; others relating to the Civil War, the Progressive era, and World War II.

Swann Collection of Caricature and Cartoon, New York City. Large collection of caricature and cartoon related to the history of the United States, soon to be given to the Prints and Photographs Division, Library of Congress.

Syracuse University, Arents Rare Book Room, Syracuse. Large collection of cartoons.

Syracuse University, Syracuse. Major collection of prints, drawings, and paintings. Cartoons representing various eras of American history. Paul Conrad originals.

Theodore Roosevelt Birthplace National Historic Site, New York City. Collection of cartoons relating to President Theodore Roosevelt.

University of Rochester Library, Rochester. Collection of cartoons including drawings by Thomas Nast, Charles L. Bartholomew, John Clubb, Elmer R. Messner.

University of Rochester Memorial Art Gallery, Rochester. Small collection of cartoons by Charles Dana Gibson, George B. Luks, and Thomas Nast.

Whitney Museum of American Art, New York City. Large collection of material, including caricatures by Peggy Bacon, Adolf Dehn, Saul Steinberg, Joseph Hirsch, Morris Hirschfeld, and others.

North Carolina

Duke University Museum of Art, Durham. Collection of 100 Posada woodcuts published in 1947 by A. V. Arroya.

University of North Carolina Art Center, Chapel Hill. Large collection of William M. Prince paintings and drawings, largely caricatures.

University of North Carolina Weatherspoon Art Gallery, Greensboro. Small collection of prints, including work by Red Grooms, John Sloan, and Peter Saul.

North Dakota

Frontier Museum Society, Williston. Small collection of comic strips.

Ohio

Butler Institute of American Art, Youngstown. Large collection of cartoons, caricatures, and comic strips from the Civil War to the 1930s, including a complete collection of *Harper's Weekly*.

The Canton Art Institute, Canton. Collection of thirty-one drawings by Web Brown, executed in the early 1940s.

Cincinnati Art Museum. Grant Wood, *Daughters of Revolution*; James Beard, *The Long Bill*; and various prints by Thomas Nast.

Cincinnati Historical Society. Some cartoons and caricatures of a regional interest.

The Cleveland Museum of Art, Cleveland. Drawings by Steinberg, R. Taylor and Thurber; prints by Winslow Homer and George Bellows.

Lake County Historical Society, Mentor. Collection of cartoons, including originals by Frederick Burr Opper and Frank Beard, with several from *Puck* that relate to President James A. Garfield.

The Ohio Historical Society, Columbus. Collection of comic strips relating to the historical growth of Ohio by Jim Baker. Cartoons by James H. Donahey, Leo Egli, and William A. Ireland.

Ohio State University Libraries, Columbus. Collection of drawings, primarily by James Thurber.

Oklahoma

Bizzell Memorial Library, University of Oklahoma, Norman. Collection of cartoons by Sam Cobean.

Will Rogers Memorial, Claremore. Collection of cartoons relating to the first half of the 20th century that belonged to Will Rogers.

Oregon

Oregon Historical Society, Portland. Small collection of Homer Davenports.

Portland Art Museum, Portland. Several paintings by Jacob Lawrence.

University of Oregon Museum of Art, Eugene. Large collection of WPA prints, including work by Fred Becker, Augustus Peck, Glen Wessels, and many others.

Pennsylvania

The Balch Institute, Philadelphia. Collection of lithographs and watercolors relating to immigration and ethnic groups from Reconstruction to the present. Collection of World War I and World War II posters.

Drake Well Museum, Titusville. Collection of primarily John D. Rockefeller caricatures and cartoons, from the Ida Tarbell Collection.

Erie County Historical Society. Some World War II posters.

Free Library of Philadelphia. Large collection of engravings, lithographs, drawings, watercolors and temperas relating to American history from pre-Revolution to present.

Independence National Historical Park Collection, Philadelphia. Small collection of cartoons relating to the Revolutionary era.

Library Company of Philadelphia. Large collection of prints and drawings relating to American history.

Museum of Art, Carnegie Institute, Pittsburgh. Collection of cartoons relating to the Revolutionary era.

Philadelphia Museum of Art. Large collection of prints and drawings.

The Philip H. and A. S. W. Rosenbach Foundation Museum, Philadelphia. Several drawings by Cruikshank.

War Library & Museum of the Military Order of the Loyal Legion of the United States, Philadelphia. Cartoons and caricatures relating to the Civil War.

William Penn Memorial Museum, Harrisburg. Collection of cartoons and caricatures relating to the 1850s and the Progressive era.

Rhode Island

Anne S. K. Brown Military Collection, Brown University, Providence. Collection of cartoons relating to the military history of the United States.

John Carter Brown Library, Brown University, Providence. Collection of cartoons relating to the early history of the United States.

Museum of Art, Rhode Island School of Design, Providence. Collection of cartoons and caricatures relating to American history: Revolutionary era, and 20th century.

National Lawn Tennis Hall of Fame & Tennis Museum, Newport. Collection of cartoons related to tennis, mostly by Paul Loring and Frank Lanning of the *Providence Journal* and the *Providence Evening Bulletin*.

South Carolina

Citadel Archives-Museum, Charleston. Some cartoons and caricatures from the World War I, World War II, and Post-War eras.

Tennessee

Brooks Memorial Art Gallery, Memphis. Large collection of drawings, including many by J. P. Alley, relating to the 1920s and 1930s.

Gordon M. Campbell, Nashville. Large collection of lithographs and chromolithographs that appeared in 19th century and early 20th century publications such as *Puck*.

Carroll Reece Museum, Johnson City. Collection of cartoons and caricatures relating to the thirties, World War II, and the Post-War era.

Frank H. McClung Museum, Knoxville. Thirty-seven drawings for the "Major Hoople" series by William Freyes and Bill Braucher; nine drawings for "Nancy" by Ernie Bushmiller, and small related collection.

Draper Hill, Memphis. Large collection of cartoons and caricatures relating to American history and culture.

James Knox Polk Memorial Auxiliary, Columbia. Small collection of prints, especially relating to President Polk.

Joint University Libraries Collection, Nashville. Collection of cartoons, including work by Tom Little of the *Nashville Tennessean*.

Texas

Amon Carter Museum of Western Art, Fort Worth. Small collection of cartoons relating to Western history, some Currier & Ives.

Barker Texas History Library, University of Texas, Austin. Small collection of cartoons relating to Texas.

Dallas Historical Society. Collection of John Knott's original cartoons, which appeared in the Dallas *Morning News*. A few other cartoons of the 19th century relating to Texas.

Fort Worth Art Museum. Large collection of newspaper cartoons relating largely to World War II and after.

Fort Worth Museum of Science and History. Collection of comic strips from the 1930s.

Fort Worth Public Library. Large collection of cartoons relating to Fort Worth, Texas, and the national scene, primarily by cartoonists for Fort Worth newspapers—20th century.

Iconography Collection, University of Texas, Austin. Large collection of caricatures, historic and contemporary, relating to American and British literature and letters, 20th century American notables.

Lyndon B. Johnson Presidential Library, Austin. Large collection of cartoons and caricatures, relating primarily to President Johnson and his career.

The Sam Rayburn Library, Bonham. Collection of cartoons relating to the career of Sam Rayburn, who was Speaker of the U.S. House of Representatives longer than anyone else.

Star of the Republic of Texas Museum, Washington. Small collection of prints relating to the annexation of Texas.

Texas State Library, Austin. Some cartoons relating to the history of Texas.

Theater Arts Collection, University of Texas, Austin. Large collection of caricatures relating to the theater.

Utah

Brigham Young University, Fine Arts Collection, Provo. Collection of cartoons and caricatures relating to 20th century history.

Vermont

Rokeby, Ferrisburg. Large collection of drawings by Rowland E. Robinson, who drew for *Moore's Rural New Yorker*, *Street and Smith*, and *American Agriculturalist* and other 1870s and 1880s publications.

Virginia

Chrysler Museum at Norfolk. Paintings by Bellows, Marsh, etc.

The Colonial Williamsburg Foundation. Collection of Pre-Revolution and Revolution engravings, mainly British.

The Mariners Museum, Newport News. Collection of caricatures and cartoons relating to sea-going, also large collection of caricatures published in *Vanity Fair*.

University of Virginia Library, Charlottesville. Collection of cartoons by Fred O. Seibel—cartoonist for the *Richmond Times-Dispatch*.

Virginia Historical Society, Richmond. Etchings and drawings by A. J. Volck.

Woodrow Wilson Birthplace Foundation, Staunton. Cartoons relating to President Wilson.

Wales

The National Library of Wales, Aberystwyth, Dyfed. Collection of cartoons relating to the history of the United States, including work by Leslie Illingworth.

Washington

Washington State Historical Society. Cartoons relating to 20th century history.

Wisconsin

Elvehjem Art Center, University of Wisconsin, Madison. Small collection of cartoons and caricatures, including Otto Dix, *Wild West Show* (1922 drypoint).

Madison Art Center, Inc. Prints by Ivan LeLorraine Albright, Thomas Hart Benton, Grant Wood, Red Grooms, José Chavez-Morada, Gonzalo de la Paz Pérez, and Warrington Colescott.

Milwaukee Art Center. Small collection of 1930 cartoons, mostly related to international events. Published in Milwaukee newspapers.

State Historical Society of Wisconsin, Madison. H. T. Webster collection contains cartoons from the Progressive era through the early 1950s. Also have work by William Donahey, Dan Dowling, Gluyas Williams, Fontain Fox, Frank O. King, Richard Q. Yardley, Karl Hubenthal, Kim Ivey, and others.

BIBLIOGRAPHY

BOOKS

Adams, James Truslow, ed. *Dictionary of American History*. 5 vols. New York: Charles Scribner's Sons, 1968.

Adams, John. *Works*. 10 vols. Edited by Charles Francis Adams. Boston: Little, Brown and Company, 1850–1856.

Adler, Mortimer J., ed. *The Annals of America*. 18 vols. Chicago: Encyclopedia Britannica, Inc., 1968.

———. Ed. *The Annals of America: Great Issues in American Life; A Conspectus*. 2 vols. Chicago: Encyclopedia Britannica, Inc., 1968.

Agar, Herbert. *The Price of Power: America Since 1945*. Chicago: University of Chicago Press, 1957.

American Federation of Arts. *Who's Who in American Art*. New York: R. R. Bowker Company, 1962, 1970, 1973.

The American War of Independence, 1775–1783. London: British Museum Publications Ltd., 1975.

Amstutz, Walter, ed. *Who's Who In Graphic Art*. Zurich: Amstutz and Herdeg Graphis Press, 1962.

Andrews, Wayne. *Concise Dictionary of American History*. New York: Charles Scribner's Sons, 1962.

Andrist, Ralph K., ed. *The American Heritage History of the Making of the Nation*. New York: American Heritage Publishing Company, Inc., 1968.

———. Ed. *The American Heritage History of the 20's and 30's*. New York: American Heritage Publishing Co., Inc., 1970.

Arms, John Taylor. *Handbook of Print Making and Print Makers*. New York: The Macmillan Company, 1934.

Art Essays. Boston: American Art Company, Publishers, 1895.

Bailey, D. W. "British Public Opinion on the American War in Prints." *English Reaction to the American War, Series No. 1*. London: *The Connoisseur* in association with The British Museum, 1974.

Bailey, Thomas A. *The American Pageant*. Boston: D. C. Heath & Company, 1966.

———. *A Diplomatic History of the American People*. New York: Appleton-Century-Crofts, 1964, Seventh Edition.

Baur, John I. H. *Revolution and Tradition in Modern American Art*. Cambridge, Mass.: Harvard University Press, 1958.

Bénézit, Emmanuel. *Dictionnaire Critique Et Documentaire Des Peintres, Sculpteurs, Dessinateurs Et Graveurs*. 8 vols. Paris: Librairie Gründ, 1948.

Billington, Monroe Lee. *The American South*. New York: Charles Scribner's Sons, 1971.

Biographical Directory of the American Congress 1774–1961. Washington, D.C.: United States Government Printing Office, 1961.

Biographical Sketches of American Artists, 5th ed. Lansing, Mich.: Michigan State University Library, 1924.

Blesh, Rudi. *Modern Art USA: Men, Rebellion, Conquest, 1900–1956*. New York: Alfred A. Knopf, 1956.

Blum, John Morton. *The Republican Roosevelt*. Cambridge, Mass.: Harvard University Press, 1967.

Boatner, Mark May III. *The Civil War Dictionary*. New York: David McKay Company, Inc., 1962.

———. *Encyclopedia of the American Revolution*. New York: David McKay Company, Inc., 1966.

Boorstin, Daniel J. *The Americans: The Colonial Experience*. New York: Random House, 1958.

———. *The Americans: The Democratic Experience*. New York: Random House, 1973.

———. *The Americans: The National Experience*. New York: Random House, 1965.

Boswell, Peyton, Jr. *Modern American Painting*. New York: Dodd, Mead & Co., 1940.

Bridenbaugh, Carl. *The Colonial Craftsman*. Chicago: University of Chicago Press, 1966.

Brigham, Clarence S. *Paul Revere's Engravings*. New York: Atheneum, 1969.

The Britannica Encyclopedia of American Art. Chicago: Encyclopedia Britannica Corporation, 1973.

Burnside, Wesley M. *Manard Dixon: Artist of the West*. Provo, Utah: Brigham Young University Press, 1974.

Butterfield, Roger. *The American Past: A History of the United States From Concord to Hiroshima, 1775–1945*. New York: Simon and Schuster, 1947, 1957.

Cable, Mary. *American Manners and Morals: A Pictorial History of How We Behaved and Misbehaved*. New York: American Heritage Publishing Co., Inc., 1969.

Callow, Alexander B., Jr. *American Urban History: An Interpretive Reader With Commentaries*. New York: Oxford University Press, 1969.

Cartoons by Bradley. Chicago: Chicago *Daily News*, 1917.

A Century of American Illustration. New York: The Brooklyn Museum, 1972.

Chase, John. *Today's Cartoon*. New Orleans, La.: Hauser Press, 1962.

Churchill, Winston S. *Triumph and Tragedy*. Boston: Houghton Mifflin Company, 1953.

Clement, Clara Erskine and Hutton, Laurence. *Artists of the Nineteenth Century and Their Works*. St. Louis, Mo.: North Point, Inc., 1969.

Cole, Donald B. *Handbook of American History*. New York: Harcourt, Brace & World, Inc., 1968.

College Art Association. *Catalogue of the Salon of American Humorists: A Political and Social Pageant from the Revolution To the Present Day*. Springfield: Mass.: George Walter Vincent Smith Art Museum, 1933.

———. *The Index of Twentieth Century Artists 1933–37*. New York: Arno Press, 1970.

Colonial Society of Massachusetts. *Boston Prints and Printmakers, 1670–1775*. A conference held by the Colonial Society of Massachusetts. Boston: 1973.

The Columbia Encyclopedia. New York: Columbia University Press, 1963.

Commager, Henry Steele. *Documents of American History*. New York: Appleton-Century-Crofts, 1968.

———. Ed. *Jefferson, Nationalism, and the Enlightenment*. New York: George Braziller, 1975.

Cooke, Alistair. *Alistair Cooke's America*. New York: Alfred A. Knopf, 1974.

Crouse, Russel. *Mr. Currier and Mr. Ives: A Note on Their Lives and Times*. Garden City: N.Y.: Garden City Publishing Company, Inc., 1930.

Cummings, Paul. *A Dictionary of Contemporary American Artists*. New York: St. Martin's Press, 1966.

Cunliffe, Marcus, ed. *The American Heritage History of the Presidency*. New York: American Heritage Publishing Co., Inc. 1968.

Darling, Jay N. *As Ding Saw Hoover*. Ames, Iowa: The Iowa State College Press, 1954.

Darracott, Joseph. *The First World War in Posters*. New York: Dover Publications, Inc., 1974.

Davy Crockett's Almanack, of Wild Sports in the West, Life in the Backwoods, & Sketches of Texas. Vol. I, no. 3. Nashville, 1837.

De Conde, Alexander. *A History of American Foreign Policy*. New York: Charles Scribner's Sons, 1963.

Diccionario Porrua de Historia, Biografia y Geografia de Mexico. Mexico, D. F.: Editorial Porrua, S.A., [c1964]. Second Edition.

Dulles, Foster Rhea. *Labor in America*. New York: Thomas Y. Crowell Company, 1966. Third Edition.

Eastman, Max. *Journalism Versus Art*. New York: Alfred A. Knopf, 1916.

Elman, Robert. *Bad Men of the West: The First Complete Book of the American Outlaw*. New York: Ridge Press/Pound Book, 1974.

Exman, Eugene. *The House of Harper: One Hundred and Fifty Years of Publishing*. New York: Harper & Row, 1967.

The Encyclopedia Americana. 30 vols. New York: Americana Corporation, 1957.

The Encyclopedia Britannica. 24 vols. Chicago: William Benton, Publisher, 1958.

Fairbanks, Jonathan Leo, ed. *Frontier America: The Far West*. Boston: Museum of Fine Arts, 1975.

———. Ed. *Paul Revere's Boston: 1735–1818*. Boston: Museum of Fine Arts, 1975.

Fielding, Mantle. *Dictionary of American Painters, Sculptors and Engravers*. New York: James F. Carr, 1965.

Fitzgerald, Richard. *Art and Politics: Cartoonists of the Masses and Liberator*. Westport: Conn.: Greenwood Press, 1973.

Flexner, James Thomas. *Washington, the Indispensable Man*. Boston: Little, Brown and Company, 1974.

Fogel, Robert William, and Engerman, Stanley L. 2 vols. *Time on the Cross: The Economics of American Negro Slavery*. Boston: Little, Brown and Company, 1974.

Forbis, William H. *The Cowboys*. New York: Time-Life Books, 1973.

Freidel, Frank. *America in the Twentieth Century*. New York: Alfred A. Knopf, 1965. Second Edition.

———. *The New Deal and the American People*. Englewood Cliffs, N.J.: Prentice-Hall, Inc., a Spectrum book, 1965.

Garraty, John A. *The American Nation: A History of the United States*. New York: Harper & Row and American Heritage Publishing Company, Inc. 1966.

———. 2 vols. *The American Nation: A History of the United States*. New York: Harper & Row, 1975.

Geipel, John. *The Cartoon: A Short History of Graphic Comedy and Satire*. New York and South Brunswick: A. S. Barnes and Company, 1972.

Getlein, Frank and Geitlein, Dorothy. *The Bite of the Print: Satire and Irony in Woodcuts, Engravings, Etchings, Lithographs, and Serigraphs*. New York: C. N. Potter, 1963.

Gill, Brendan. *Here at the New Yorker*. New York: Random House, 1975.

Goodrich, Lloyd. *Five Paintings from Thomas Nast's Grand Caricaturama*. New York: The Swann Collection of Caricature and Cartoon, 1970.

———, and Baur, John I. H. *American Art of Our Century*. New York: Frederick A. Praeger, 1961.

Groce, George C. and Wallace, David H. *The New York Historical Society's Dictionary of Artists In America 1564–1860*. New Haven, Conn.: Yale University Press, 1957.

Halle, Louis J. *The Cold War as History*. New York: Harper & Row, Publishers, 1967.

Hamilton, Sinclair. 2 vols. *Early American Book Illustrators and Wood Engravers 1670–1870*. Princeton, N.J.: Princeton University Press, 1968.

Handlin, Oscar. *The Americans: A New History of the People of the United States*. Boston: Atlantic Monthly Press, Little Brown and Company, 1963.

———. *The History of United States*. 2 vols. New York: Holt, Rinehart and Winston, 1967.

———. *The Uprooted*. New York: Grosset & Dunlap, 1951.

Hart-Davis, Rupert. *A Catalogue of the Caricatures of Max Beerbohm*. Cambridge, Mass.: Harvard University Press, 1972.

Hays, Samuel P. *The Response To Industrialism, 1885–1914*. Chicago: University of Chicago Press, 1957.

The Herbert Waide Hemphill, Jr. Collection of 18th, 19th, and 20th Century American Folk Art. Sandwich, Mass., and Columbus, Ga.: Heritage Plantation of Sandwich and Columbus Museum of Arts and Crafts, 1974.

Hess, Stephen and Kaplan, Milton. *The Ungentlemanly Art: A History of American Political Cartoons*. New York: The Macmillan Company, 1968.

Hill, Draper. *Illingworth on Target*. Boston: Boston Public Library, 1970.

Hiller, Bevis. *Cartoons and Caricatures*. London: Studio Vista. New York: E. P. Dutton & Co., Inc., 1970.

Hind, Arthur M. *A History of Engraving and Etching from the 15th Century to the Year 1914*. New York: Dover Publications, Inc. 1963 (1923).

Hofstadter, Richard; Miller, William; and Aaron, Daniel. 2 vols. *The American Republic*. Englewood Cliffs, N.J.: Prentice-Hall, Inc., 1959.

Holbrook, Stewart H. *The Age of the Moguls*. Garden City, N.Y.: Doubleday & Co., Inc., 1953.

James, Edward T. *Notable American Women 1607–1950: A Biographical Dictionary*. Cambridge, Mass.: The Belknap Press of Harvard University Press, 1971.

Johannsen, Robert W., ed. *The Lincoln-Douglas Debates*. New York: Oxford University Press, 1965.

Johnson, Allen, ed. *Dictionary of American Biography*. 12 vols. New York: Charles Scribner's Sons, 1964.

Jones, Maldwyn Allen. *American Immigration*. Chicago: University of Chicago Press, 1960.

Keller, Morton. *The Art and Politics of Thomas Nast*. New York: Oxford University Press, 1968.

Kennedy, Robert F. *Thirteen Days: A Memoir of the Cuban Missile Crisis*. New York: W. W. Norton & Company, 1969.

Ketchum, Richard M. *The American Heritage Book of the Revolution*. New York: American Heritage Publishing Co., Inc., 1958.

Khrushchev Remembers. Translated and edited by Strobe Talbott. Boston: Little, Brown and Company, 1970.

Koch, Adrienne, ed. *The American Enlightenment*. New York: George Braziller, 1965.

———. *Jefferson & Madison; Great Collaboration*. New York: Oxford University Press, 1964.

Kunzle, David. *The Early Comic Strip: Narrative Strips and Picture Stories in the European Broadsheet from c. 1450 to 1825*. Berkeley: University of California Press, [1973].

Leech, Margaret. *In the Days of McKinley*. New York: Harper & Brothers Publishers, 1959.

———. *Reveille in Washington, 1860–1865*. New York: Harper & Brothers Publishers, 1941.

Leish, Kenneth W., ed. *The American Heritage Pictorial History of the Presidents of the United States*. 2 vols. New York: American Heritage Publishing Co., Inc., 1968.

Leuchtenburg, William E. *The Perils of Prosperity, 1914–1932*. Chicago: University of Chicago Press, 1958.

Lincoln Library of Essential Information. 2 vols. Buffalo, N.Y.: The Frontier Press Company, 1966.

The Lincoln Library of the Arts. 2 vols. Columbus, Ohio: The Frontier Press Company, 1973.

Link, Arthur S. *Wilson: The Road to the White House*. Princeton, N.J.: Princeton University Press, 1947.

McKinzie, Richard D. *The New Deal for Artists*. Princeton, N.J.: Princeton University Press, 1973.

Malone, Dumas. *Jefferson, the Virginian*. Vol. I of *Jefferson and His Time*. 5 vols. Boston: Little, Brown and Company, 1948–1974.

Marzio, Peter C. *Do It the Hard Way: Rube Goldberg and Modern Times*. Washington, D.C.: National Museum of History and Technology, n.d.

———. *Rube Goldberg: His Life and Work*. New York: Harper & Row, 1973.

Maurice, Arthur Bartlett, and Cooper, Frederic Taber. *History of the Nineteenth Century in Caricature*. New York: Dodd, Mead, 1904.

Mayor, A. Hyatt. *Popular Prints of the Americas*. New York: Crown Publishers, Inc., 1973.

Miller, Lillian B. *In the Minds and Hearts of the People: Prologue to the American Revolution: 1760–1774*. Greenwich, Conn.: New York Graphic Society, 1974.

Morse, John D., ed. *Prints In and Of American to 1850*. Charlottesville, Va.: University of Virginia Press, 1970.

Morison, Samuel Eliot, and Commager, Henry Steele. *The Growth of the American Republic*. New York: Oxford University Press, 1962.

Morris, Richard B., ed. *Encyclopedia of American History*. New York: Harper & Brothers, Publishers, 1953.

———. *Time-Life History of the United States*. 12 vols. New York: Time, Inc., 1963.

———, and Commager, Henry Steele, eds. *Encyclopedia of American History*. New York: Harper & Row, Publishers, revised edition, 1965.

Mugridge, Donald H., and McCrum, Blanche P. *A Guide to the History of the United States of America: Representative Books Reflecting the Development of American Life and Thought*. Washington, D.C.: The Library of Congress, 1960.

Murrell, William. *A History of American Graphic Humor*. 2 vols. New York: Cooper Square Publishers, Inc. 1967.

O'Sullivan, Judith. *The Art of the Comic Strip*. College Park, Md.: University of Maryland Art Gallery, 1971.

Parkes, Henry Bamford. *The American Experience*. New York: Vintage Books, 1959.

Pagano, Grace. *Contemporary American Painting*. New York: Duell, Sloan and Pearce. 1945.

Perkins, Dexter. *The Evolution of American Foreign Policy*. New York: Oxford University Press, 1966.

Pessen, Edward. *Jacksonian America: Society, Personality, and Politics*. Homewood, Ill.: Dorsey Press, 1969.

Peters, Harry T. *America on Stone: The Other Printmakers to the American People*. Garden City, N.Y.: Doubleday, Doran and Company, Inc., 1931.

———. *Currier and Ives; Printmakers to the American People*. Garden City, N.Y.: Doubleday, Doran and Company, 1942.

Raemaekers, Louis. *America in the War*. New York: The Century Co., 1938.

———. *Kultur in Cartoons*. New York: The Century Co., 1917.

Randel, William Peirce. *The American Revolution: Mirror of a People*. New York: Rutledge Books, 1973.

Reed, Walt, ed. *The Illustrator in America 1900–1960s*. New York: Reinhold Publishing Corporation, 1966.

Remini, Robert V. *Andrew Jackson and the Bank War*. New York: W. W. Norton & Company, Inc., 1967.

Ringel, Fred J., ed. *America as Americans See It*. New York: The Literary Guild, 1932.

Russell, Don. *The Wild West, or a History of the Wild West Shows*. Fort Worth, Texas: Amon Carter Museum of Western Art, 1970.

St. Hill, Thomas Nast. *Thomas Nast Cartoons and Illustrations*. New York: Dover, 1974.

Sann, Paul. *The Lawless Decade: A Pictorial History of a Great American Transition From the World War I Armistice and Prohibition to Repeal and the New Deal*. New York: Crown Publishers, Inc., 1962.

Saveth, Edward N. *Understanding the American Past*. Boston: Little, Brown and Company, 1965.

Schlesinger, Arthur M. *The Birth of the Nation*. New York: Alfred A. Knopf, 1969.

———. *The Rise of the City*. New York: The Macmillan Company, 1933.

Schlesinger, Arthur M., Jr. *The Coming of the New Deal*. Boston: Houghton Mifflin Company, 1958.

———. *The Crisis of the Old Order, 1919–1933*. Boston: Houghton Mifflin Company, 1957.

———. *The Imperial Presidency*. Boston: Houghton Mifflin Company, 1973.

———. *The Politics of Upheaval, 1935–1936*. Boston: Houghton Mifflin Company, 1960.

Serio, Anne Marie. *Political Cartoons in the 1848 Election Campaign*. Smithsonian Studies in History and Technology, No. 14. Washington, D.C.: Smithsonian Institution Press, 1972.

Shadwell, Wendy J. *American Printmaking: The First 150 Years*. New York: The Museum of Graphic Art, 1969.

Shannon, David A. *The Great Depression*. Englewood Cliffs, N.J.: Prentice-Hall, Inc., a Spectrum book, 1960.

Sheridan, Martin. *Comics and Their Creators: Life, Stories of American Cartoonists*. Hale, Cushman & Flint, 1942.

Shikes, Ralph E. *The Indignant Eye: The Artist as Social Critic in Prints and Drawings from the Fifteenth Century to Picasso*. Boston: Beacon Press, 1969.

Stampp, Kenneth M., ed. *The Causes of the Civil War*. Englewood Cliffs, N.J.: Prentice-Hall, Inc., Spectrum Books, 1959.

Stauffer, David McNeely. *American Engravers Upon Copper and Steel*. 3 vols. New York: Burt Franklin, 1907.

Stewart, Virginia. *45 Contemporary Mexican Artists: A 20th Century Renaissance*. Stanford, Calif.: Stanford University Press, 1951.

Suarès, Jean-Claude, ed. *Art of The Times*. New York: Avon Books, 1973.

Syrett, Harold C., ed. *American Historical Documents*. New York: Barnes & Noble, Inc., 1960.

Time-Life Books. *This Fabulous Century: Sixty Years of American Life*. 7 vols. New York: Time-Life Books, 1970.

Tocqueville, Alexis de. *Democracy in America*. Edited by J. P. Mayer and Max Lerner, translated by George Lawrence. New York: Harper & Row, 1966.

U.S. National Museum of History and Technology. *Do It The Hard Way: Rube Goldberg and Modern Times*. Washington, D.C.: National Museum of History and Technology, 1970.

U.S. National Portrait Gallery. *'If Elected . . .': Unsuccessful Candidates for the Presidency 1796–1968*. Washington, D.C.: Smithsonian Institution Press, 1972.

Washburn, Wilcombe. *The Indian In America*. New York: Harper & Row, Publishers, 1975.

Weitenkampf, Frank. *American Graphic Art*. New York: The Macmillan Company, 1924.

———. *Political Caricature in the United States in Separately Published Cartoons*. New York: The New York Public Library, 1953.

Welch, Peter C. *Henry R. Robinson, Printmaker to the Whig Party*. New York: reprint from New York History, 1972.

Who's Who. London: Adam & Charles Black. New York: St. Martin's Press, 1962.

Who's Who In America. Chicago: The A. N. Marquis Company, 1932, 1936, 1966, 1970.

Williams, T. Harry. *Huey Long*. New York: Alfred A. Knopf, 1970.

Williamson, George, ed. *Bryan's Dictionary of Painters and Engravers*. Port Washington, N.Y.: Kennidat Press, 1964.

Wilson, James Grant, ed. *Appleton's Cyclopedia of American Biography*. 6 vols. New York: D. Appleton and Company, 1888.

Wish, Harvey. *Society and Thought In America*. 2 vols. New York: David McKay Company, Inc. 1950.

Young, William, ed. *a Dictionary of American Artists, Sculptors, and Engravers From the Beginnings Through the Turn of the Twentieth Century*. Cambridge, Mass.: William Young and Company, 1968.

ARTICLES

Appel, John and Appel, Selma. "The Grand Old Sport of Hating Catholics: American Anti-Catholic Caricature Prints." *The Critic*, XXX (November-December, 1971), pp. 50–58.

———. "From Shanties to Lace Curtains: The Irish Image in *Puck*, 1876–1910." *Comparative Studies in Society and History*, XII (October, 1971), pp. 365–375.

Fleming, E. McClung. "The American Image as Indian Princess, 1765–1783." *Winterthur Portfolio*, II (1965).

———. "From Indian Princess to Greek Goddess: The American Image, 1783–1815." *Winterthur Portfolio*, III (1967).

Freidel, Frank. "The New Deal in Historical Perspective," in Barton J. Bernstein and Allen J. Matusow (eds.), *Twentieth Century America: Recent Interpretations*. New York: Harcourt, Brace & World, Inc., 1969.

Richardson, E. P. "Stamp Act Cartoons in the Colonies." *The Pennsylvania Magazine of History and Biography*, XCVI (July, 1972), pp. 275–297.

Sullivan, John. "Jackson Caricatured: Two Historical Errors." *Tennessee Historical Quarterly*, XXI (Spring, 1972), pp. 39–44.

Twain, Mark. "The Temperance Crusade and Women's Rights." *The Complete Essays of Mark Twain*. Edited by Charles Neider. Garden City, N.Y.: Doubleday, 1963.

Winningham, Mrs. David. "Sam Houston and Slavery," *Texana*, III (Summer, 1965).

INDEX

The Able Doctor, or America Swallowing the Bitter Draught: 2, 5, 47
Abolition: 14, 15, 73, 79, 81
Acheson, Dean: 141
Actionnaires Californiens: 71
Adams, John: 4, 5, 7, 8, 57
Adams, John Quincy: 10, 62, 63
Addams, Charles: 190
Aesop's fables: 87
The Age of Brass. Or the Triumphs of Woman's Rights: 86
Agnew, Spiro: 39, 174, 184
Agricultural Adjustment Administration: 29, 141
Agriculture: 13, 14, 15, 19, 29, 100, 141, 162, 185
Ah-jon-jon: 72
Alabama: 177
Alamo: 10, 67
Albany Convention, 1754: 43
Albert Einstein, Citizen of the New World: 143
Alexander I: 61
Alexander, Ken: 166
Alice in Wonderland: 3, 134
Aliens Land Act: 27
Allies: 31, 33, 111, 145, 146, 148
Alligator: 11, 63
Almost Thru the Dark Alley: 117
"Alphabet agencies": 29, 30, 130, 132, 141, 154
Amédée, Charles-Henri, Comte de Noé, ("Cham"): 77
America: 18, 88
"American Cruikshank": 9
The American Eagle: 3, 40, 192
American Federation of Labor: 27, 29, 130, 132
American Protective Association: 91
The American Rattle Snake: 6, 50
The American River Ganges. The Priests and the Children: 90
"American Scarecrow": 24, 100
The American Scene, No. 1: 139
Amos 'n' Andy: 30, 159
Anarchism: 27, 103, 151
Anderson, Alexander: 58

[*Andrew Johnson caricature with a donkey*]: 87
Angelo, Emidio: 125
Another of Those Feasts of Love: 129
Ansell: 57
Anti-Mason Party: 62
Anti-Saloon League: 21, 26, 125
Anti-Semitism: 27, 93, 121, 143
Anti-Trust Legislation: 20, 23, 24, 39, 98, 101, 111
Anti-war movements. See: Isolationism, pacifism
Arabian Knights: 184
Archibold, John, D.: 106
Arias Bernal, Antonio: 142
Arkansas: 154
Arms race: 38, 149, 150, 152, 155, 156
Armstrong, Louis: 40, 165
Army Medical Examiner: "At Last a Perfect Soldier": 109
Army, U.S.: 5, 17, 33, 37, 50, 102, 107, 109, 144, 186
Arno, Peter: 121
Articles of Confederation: 3, 8, 53
Arts: 21, 30, 72, 123, 137, 164, 166, 189
Assassination: 16, 24, 39, 81, 98, 133, 163, 177
"At Last a Perfect Soldier": 109
At Least One Senator Now Knows What the President Meant by Choose: 124
Atkinson, Ti-Grace: 185
Atomic Bomb: 32, 33, 34, 36-8, 40, 146–7, 148, 149, 152
Aurora: 58
Automobile: 27, 116, 164, 189
An Available Candidate: 70
Aviation: 102, 144

"Babe Ruth": 123, 138
A Bad Egg. Fuss and Feathers: 73
Baillie, James: 69
Balaam's Ass: 66
Baltimore *Sun*: 121, 162
Bank failures: 29, 66
Bank of the United States: 12, 64–5
Banks: 12, 29, 64–5, 96
Barlow, Perry: 136

"Barnburners": 69
Barnett, Ross: 177
Barritt, Leon: 88
Barron, J.: 53
Barsqualdi's Statue. Liberty Frightening the World. Bedbugs Island, N.Y. Harbor: 91
Barton, Ralph: 118
Baseball: 120, 123, 138
Batista, Fulgencio: 38
Battle Bexar—Heroism of Col. Crockett: 10, 67
Bay of Pigs Invasion: 38, 160–1
Bear: 61, 71
Beard, Charles A.: 13, 26
Beard, Mary: 13
Beatniks: 40, 158
Beatniks: 158
Beecher, Henry Ward: 14, 21, 93
Beerbohm, Max: 94
Bell, John: 76
Belmont, (Mrs.) August: 26
Benny Goodman: 158
Benny, Jack: 179
Benton, Thomas Hart: 68
Berlin Blockade: 36
Berryman, C. K.: 23, 30, 105, 107, 113, 129, 135, 141
Berryman, Jim: 150
Beveridge, Albert J.: 97
Bevin, Ernest: 35
Biddle, Nicholas: 12, 64
Bidwell, John: 83
Big apple: 140
"Big Stick": 24, 100, 102, 107
Billy Sunday: 120
Bingham, J. A.: 83
Bison: 3, 69
Black Hand: 103
Black Power/White Power: 168
"Black Thursday": 28, 126
Blechman, R. O.: 3, 191
Bled: 104
The Blind Leading the Blind: 173
Blood, James Harvey: 86
Bolshevism: 27, 28, 111, 119
Bomb shelters: 156
Bookmark: 163

219

Booth, John Wilkes: 81
Bootlegging: 117, 129
Borah, William: 25, 112
"Boss system": 105
Boston *Gazette*: 59
Boston, Massachusetts: 5, 47, 48
Boston Massacre: 5
Boston Port Bill: 5, 47
Boston Tea Party: 5
Boston *Weekly Messenger*: 55
Boutwell, George S.: 83
Bowen, Francis: 20
Bowles, Carington: 5, 48
Bradley, Luther Daniels: 24, 99, 107
Bradley, Thomas: 176
Braggers: 152
"Brain Trust": 131
Brandeis, Louis D.: 21
Breckinridge, John C.: 14, 76
Brezhnev, Leonid I.: 178
Bridgman, G.: 18, 88
"Brinkmanship": 37, 149
Britannia: 44, 47
Bromley & Company of New York: 79
Brown, Edmund: 172
Brown, John: 81
Brown vs. Board of Education Topeka: 162
Bruin Become Mediator or Negociation for Peace: 61
"Brushfire wars": 37–8
Bryan, William Jennings: 21, 24, 26, 34 96, 105, 107, 120
Buchanan, James: 14, 74
The Buffalo Hunt: 69
Bull Moose Party: 24, 108
Burck, Jacob: 136
Burgoyne, John: 50
Burnaby, Andrew: 4
Business: 4, 20, 26–8, 65–6, 88–9, 96, 98–9, 104, 106, 111, 112, 126, 127, 130–2, 152, 190–1
Businessmen: 18, 88, 96, 99, 103–4, 124, 126, 130, 132
But Isn't It Kind of Dangerous? 125
"But It Would Make Such a Nice Scoop if You'd only Tell Me, Franklin": 136
But Only God Can Make a Tree: 139
Bute, John Stuart 3rd earl of: 44, 45
Butler, Benjamin Franklin: 3, 16, 78, 79, 83
Byrnes, James: 33, 36

Caduceus: 44, 46, 49
"Caesarism": 87
Café Society: 121

Calhoun, John C.: 62, 69
California: 12–13, 20, 70–1, 83, 91, 172, 185
Cambodia: 40
Cameron, John: 83
Campaign contributions: 39, 96, 106
Campaigns. See: Elections
Canada: 9, 61, 168
"Cannibals": 9, 54
Cannon, Joe: 117
Capitalism: 18, 20, 28, 88, 162, 180
Capone, Al: 129
"Captains of Industry": 123
Caricature of George and Cornelia Wallace: 177
Caricature of Louis Armstrong: 165
Carnegie, Andrew: 19, 23, 26, 99, 101
Carpenter, Miles B.: 183
Carranza, Venustiano: 107
Caruso, Enrico: 123
Cass, Lewis: 69
Castro, Fidel: 38, 160–1
Catholics: 20, 21, 90, 93, 121, 125
Catlin, George: 72
Cattle industry: 19
Causes: 94
Cayea, John: 3, 40, 192
Celebration of Highways: 116
Central Intelligence Agency: 160
Centralized government: 3, 7, 54
A Certain Cabinet Junto: 2, 49
Cervera y Topete, Pascual: 97
"Cham": 77
Chamberlain, Kenneth: 117
Chaplin, Charlie: 133
Charles, William: 57, 59, 61
Chase, Stuart: 28
Chesapeake: 60
Chess Players: 111
Chiang Kai-Shek: 33, 141
Chicago: 129, 170, 188
Chicago *Daily News*: 99
Chicago *Times*: 136
China: 33, 36, 38, 131, 144, 150, 167
Chinese immigrants: 20, 62, 83, 91, 95
[Chinese leaflet of an American pilot]: 144
Chinese Nationalists: 33, 36, 141
"Choé": 174, 178
Chromolithography: 22
Churchill, Winston: 33, 34–5, 145, 148
Civil rights: 39, 97, 162, 163, 167, 168
Civil War, 1861–65: 3, 13–8, 21, 54, 77–81, 84, 86, 88, 96, 186, 192
Civilian Conservation Corps: 29
Clay, Henry: 11, 12, 13, 59, 62, 63, 96

Clemenceau, Georges: 111
Cleveland, Grover: 92
Clubb, John: 23, 108, 116, 123
Cobb, Henry I.: 134
Cock: 51, 73, 91, 154
Cockburn, [Sir] George: 61
Coercive Acts, 1774: 5, 49
Cold War: 34–8, 150, 155, 156, 157, 160–1
Colfax, Schuyler: 84
Colonialism: 2, 4, 5, 22, 25, 43–51, 97
The Colossus: 6, 46
Colum, Mary: 21
Columbia: 3, 6, 8, 57, 61, 134
"*Come Up and See Me Sometime*": 130
Comic strips: 103, 181
Command of the Army Act: 17
The Commercial Vampire: 88
Common Sense: 5
Communism: 27, 33–8, 111, 141, 149, 150, 160–2, 167, 178
Communist bloc: 33–7
Compromise of 1850: 13, 14
Conant, J. B.: 140
Confederacy: 15–8, 77–8, 80
Congress: 55, 101, 113, 117, 142, 153, 183
Congress: 153
Congressional Caucus candidate: 62
Congressional Pugilists: 55
Conkling, Roscoe: 20
Connally, John: 163
Conrad, Paul: 185
Conservation. See: Environmental protection
Constitution, U.S.: 8, 9, 15, 40, 53–4, 58
Constitutional amendments:
 Thirteenth amendment: 16, 78
 Fourteenth amendment: 16
 Sixteenth amendment: 26
 Seventeenth amendment: 26
 Eighteenth amendment: 26–7, 117–8
 Nineteenth amendment: 26, 117
Constitutional Union Party: 76
Consumer goods: 27, 28, 88, 164, 171, 173
Containment of communism: 35–8
Contract Labor Act: 20, 91
Coolidge, Calvin: 23, 27, 113, 124, 125
Cooper, Peter: 88
Copley, John Singleton: 2
Cornwallis, Charles, 1st marquis: 5, 50
Corruption: 28, 39, 65, 83, 84, 91, 96, 105, 118, 122, 174
Coughlin, [Father] Charles: 30

220

Counter-art: 8
"Court packing": 30, 135
Covarrubias, Miguel: 122, 127, 133, 137
Cowboy: 95, 108, 135, 161, 166, 168, 171, 176
Cowley, Malcolm: 23
Crackfardi, Gebolibus: 62
Crawford, William H.: 62
Crèvecoeur, Hector St. John de: 6
Crime: 28, 103, 118, 129, 131, 188
Crockett, Davy: 10, 67
Croker, Richard: 105
A Cry for Help: 96
Cuba: 22, 38, 96–7, 160–1
Cuban Blockade: 38, 161
Cuban Missile Crisis: 38, 161
Cuban Missile Showdown: 161
Cupid and the Cop: 188
Currier & Ives: 11, 20, 76, 86
Currier, Nathaniel: 11, 70, 73
Cushing, Otho: 23, 99
Czechoslovakia: 35–6

Dakota Territory: 19
Daley, Richard: 170
Dallas, George Mifflin: 69
Dalrymple: 25, 110
"Dame Texas": 12, 69
"Dark horse": 12
Darling, Jay Norwood ("Ding"): 102, 124, 125, 145
Darrow, Clarence: 26, 120
Darwin, Charles: 20, 119, 120
The Darwin Club: 119
Daumier, Honoré: 12, 71
Davenport, Homer: 96
Davis, Jefferson: 80, 81
Davy Crockett's Almanack: 10, 67
Dayton *Daily News*: 155
Debs, Eugene V.: 25
Declaration of Independence: 6, 13, 15, 103
Defeat: 50, 60–1, 80, 81, 145–7, 169, 172, 176
Defence of the California Bank: 71
Democratic Party: 12, 14, 16, 18, 24, 39, 55, 64, 68, 69, 70, 73, 74–6, 83, 87, 96, 104, 105, 121, 125, 129, 134, 148, 153, 170, 188
Democratic-Republican Party: 54
Department stores: 19, 88
The Deplorable State of America or Sc---h Government: 2, 5, 44
Depression, 1929: 28–30, 100, 125, 126–36, 139, 152
Des Moines *Register*: 102
Design for a Union Station: 99

Devil: 81, 86, 112, 129, 145
Dewey, Thomas: 141, 148
Dickens, Charles: 9
Didn't Know What He Uncorked: 143
Dies Irae: 126
Directory Government—France: 56–7
Disarmament: 25, 112, 187
Disarmament Talks: 187
Dispossessed: 138
Dividing the National Map: 76
Dixon, Maynard: 25
Dog: 6, 49
Donkey. See: Jackass
Doolittle, Amos: 60
Dos Passos, John: 25
Douglas, Stephen Arnold: 14, 74–6
Downing, Jack: 9, 10, 65
Draft dodgers: 110
Dred Scott Decision: 14, 76
Drucker, Peter F.: 127
Drugs: 40, 188
Dulles, John Foster: 37–8, 149
Dumas, Alexandre: 72
Duncan, Gregory: 3, 134
Duncan, Isadora: 137
Dürer, Albrecht: 2

Eagle: 3, 9, 15, 40, 54, 58, 71, 77, 100, 102, 107, 130, 132, 154, 157, 192
Eakins, Thomas: 21
Earth Quakey Times, San Francisco, Oct. 8, 1865: 85
East Indies: 31
Eastern Europe: 33–6
Economic determinism: 26
Edinburgh Review: 13
Edison, Thomas Alva: 18, 21
Education: 28, 90, 120, 154, 162, 169
Egypt: 37–8, 178
Ehrhart: 103
Einstein, Albert: 32, 37, 143, 147
Eisenhower, Dwight David: 37–8, 152–4, 160, 172, 173
Elections: 1800: 58; 1824: 62–63; 1828: 63; 1832: 64; 1844: 12, 69; 1848: 69–70; 1852: 14, 73; 1856: 74; 1860: 16, 75–6; 1866: 17; 1868: 84; 1872: 21, 84; 1876: 18, 88; 1884: 16, 92; 1900: 96; 1904: 106; 1908: 104, 106; 1912: 23, 24, 26, 102, 105, 106, 108; 1916: 108, 1920: 112; 1924: 113; 1928: 124–25; 1932: 28, 129, 134; 1936: 30, 135; 1940: 136; 1948: 35, 141, 148, 150; 1960: 159, 160, 172–73; 1964: 38, 163; 1968: 169–70, 172–73, 177, 188; 1972: 176

Elephant: 87, 113, 128, 135, 174, 178

Ellis Island: 20, 27, 91
Elmes, W.: 60
Emancipation Proclamation: 15, 78
Embargo: 9, 58
Emergency Banking Act: 29
En Amerique: 77
Enlightenment: 4
Enrico Caruso: 23
Environmental protection: 23, 24, 29, 40, 115, 189–91
"Era of Good Feelings": 3, 10, 11, 62
"Era of Wonderful Nonsense": 118
Ernest Hemingway: 137
Espionage Act: 25
Evolution: 20–1, 26, 119–20
Exclusion Act, 1882: 91
Expressways and Byways: 189
The Eyes of GM Are Upon You: 164

The Fall of Washington—or Maddy in Full Flight: 61
Farley, James: 129, 134
Farmers: 19, 29, 100, 110, 141, 162, 185
Fascism: 132, 133, 141–43
"Fast Food": 191
"Fatal number": 83
Faubus, Orval: 154
Fay, Caleb T.: 83
Fawkes, Wally ("Trog"): 178
Federal Bureau of Investigation: 37, 39
The Federal Edifice: 2, 8, 53
Federal Highway Act, 1921: 116
Federal Reserve System: 12
Federalist Party: 3, 9, 53–4, 58, 68
Fermi, Enrico: 32
Fess, Simeon Davison: 124
Fink, Mike: 10
"Fireside chats": 29
First Ladies: 61, 102, 136, 165
Fisher, Irving: 28
Fitzpatrick, Daniel Robert: 34, 40, 120, 128, 143, 147, 149
The Five Aspirants: 62
Flagg, James Montgomery: 109, 123
Flappers: 118, 121
"Flivver": 27
Florida: 11, 61, 62
The Fool Pied Piper: 103
For Whom the Bell Tolls: 146
Forcing Slavery Down the Throat of a Free Soiler: 74
Ford, Gerald: 39, 183–84
Ford, Henry: 27, 116, 130
Foreign aid and intervention: 96, 131, 141, 157, 178
Foreigners: 20, 27, 71, 91, 93, 103, 106, 110, 119

221

Formosa: 33, 36
Fort Sumter: 80
"Forty-niners": 70
The Four Dictators: 133
Fox: 87
France: 3, 8, 31, 36, 37, 38, 43, 49, 52, 54, 56–8, 60, 71, 77, 111
Franck, James: 32
François, André: 157
Franklin, Benjamin: 2, 3, 4, 5, 6, 7, 10, 40, 43
Franklin D. Roosevelt: 127
Free love: 86
Free Soil Party: 13, 69, 73–4
Free masonry: 62
"Freeport Doctrine": 14
French and Indian War: 7, 43
Frontier society: 6
Fuchs, Klaus: 36
The Fuehrer Wallace: 141
Fugitive Slave Act: 13, 14
"Fun City": 191
Fundamentalism: 21, 26, 120

Gadsden, Christopher: 7
Gallatin, Albert: 9, 54
Gallows: 44, 48, 52, 139
Gangsters: 118, 129, 130
Gates, Horatio: 5
"Gay Nineties": 21
General Jackson Slaying the Many-Headed Monster: 65
General Motors: 164
The General P--s, or Peace: 8, 52
Genet, Edmond: 54
Geneva Agreement, 1954: 38
George III: 5, 44–7
Georgia: 148
Germany: 24, 31–4, 36, 38, 107–8, 111, 133, 142, 143, 145, 147
Gerry Elbridge: 4, 55
The Gerry-Mander: 55
"Get thee behind me, (Mrs.) Satan!" 86
Ghent, Treaty of: 9, 61, 62
Gillam, Bernhard: 89
Gillray, James: 50
Gold rush: 12, 20, 70–1, 91
Gold standard: 29
Goldberg, Reuben ("Rube"): 30, 140
Gone With the Wind . . .: 142
Goodman, Benny: 40, 158
Goodnight, Charles: 19
Gorham, George C.: 83
"Gospel of Wealth": 26
"The Government." [I] Take the Responsibility: 64

Graft: 105
Graham, Martha: 137
Grand Caricaturama: 82
Une Grande, Une Immense Mayorité Silencieuse: 175
Granny Harrison Delivering the Country of the Executive Federalist: 68
Grant, Ulysses Simpson: 3, 17, 84, 87
Grapes of Wrath: 185
Gray, George: 105
Great American Desert: 10
Great Britain: 2, 4, 5, 6, 15, 31, 36, 37, 38, 43–52, 57–61, 71, 111, 142
"Great Commoner": 46
"Great Emancipator": 14
The Great Fear of the Period: That Uncle Sam May be Swallowed by Foreigners: 91
The Great G.O.P. Middle of the Road Show: 173
"Great White Fleet": 23, 100
Greece: 22, 35, 96
Greeley, Horace: 84
Green, Peter: 177
Green, William: 130, 132
Greenback Party: 16, 88
Grenville, George: 5, 45, 46
Gropper, William: 29, 127, 130–2, 141, 418, 151
Groucho Marx: 159
A Group of Vultures Waiting for the Storm to "Blow Over."—"Let Us Prey": 92
"Gilded Age": 21–2
Gulf of Tonkin Resolution: 38, 158

Haight, H. H.: 83
Halpin, Maria: 92
Hamilton, Alexander: 12, 54
Hamilton, Grant: 92
Hampton, Lionel: 158
The Hanged Man: 139
Hanna, Marcus A.: 96
Hanna: That Man Clay was an Ass. It's Better to be President than to be right! 96
Hand currency: 66
Harding, Warren G.: 25, 27, 112
Harmon, Judson: 105
Harnett, William H.: 21
Harper's Bazaar: 118
Harper's Weekly: 16, 82, 86, 90, 92, 123
Harriman, Edward H.: 99
Harrison, William Henry: 12, 60, 68, 70
Harvey, Fred: 114
Havana Act, 1940: 142
Hawthorne, Nathaniel: 7
Haywood, William D. ("Big Bill"): 116

Head of Sinclair Lewis: 122
Hearst, William Randolph: 26, 103, 130, 132, 140
Held, John, Jr.: 118
Hemingway, Ernest: 137
Henry, Patrick: 4, 7
Hershfield, Leo: 138
Hess, Richard: 173, 176, 182
Hesse, Don: 40, 149
Hic Jacet John (Hic) Barleycorn: 118
Hicks, Edward: 176
Highways: 116, 189
Hill, Draper: 40, 179, 181, 184
The Hilton Hotel: 171
Hippies: 40, 171, 188
Hiroshima: 33, 146–7
Hiroshima: 146
Hirschfeld, Albert: 137
Hiss, Alger: 36
Historical Magazine: 55
History of Man: 156
Hitler, Adolf: 3, 31, 33, 133, 141, 145
Ho Chi Minh: 169
The Hold-Up: 111
Hogarth, William: 2
Holland: 6, 49, 52
Holland, Brad: 188
Homer, Winslow: 21
Honest Abe Taking Them on the Half Shell: 76
"Honest graft": 105
Hoover, Herbert: 28, 29, 125, 128
Hopkins, Harry L.: 35
Horace Greeley: 84
Horn of Plenty: 180
The Hornet and the Peacock, or John Bull in Distress: 60
Hot Piano: 148
Houston, David: 24
Houston, Sam: 15
How Happy I Could Be with Either if They'd Let Me Run Things: 113
Howdy Arts: 166
Howdy, Brother! 102
Hughes, Charles Evans: 108, 112
Humphrey, Hubert: 170
Humphreys, William: 51–2
"Hundred days": 29, 127
Hungarian Revolt, 1956: 37
Hungary: 35, 37
Hurley, Charles F.: 140
Hutchinson, Thomas: 47
Hydra: 65
Hydrogen Bomb: 37, 38, 149

"I think I've seen enough mud": 183

I Want You for U.S. Army: 109
I Won't Workers: 116
Ickes, Harold: 134, 135
If You Differ With Me We Will Silence You: 151
"I'll be damned. Did you know this can opener fits on the end of a rifle? 144
Illingworth, Leslie: 3, 40, 150, 152, 160–1, 169
I'm Not a Member of the Legislature: 105
The Image of Nixon Isn't Entirely Clear: 160
Imbert, Anthony: 63
Immigrants: 6, 7, 18, 19, 20, 27, 90–1, 93, 103, 105, 110, 121
Impeachment: 83, 182
Imperialism: 22, 25
Impressment: 58, 59, 61
In His Steps: 26
In the Presidential Chair: 184
In the White House Attic—a Find: 107
In the Yellowstone: 113
Income tax: 26
Indian Detour: 114
Indian (symbol): 3, 6, 8, 44, 47, 50–2
Indians: 7, 11, 60–3, 72, 76, 83, 95, 114
Industrial Workers of the World: 116
Industrialization: 13, 14, 15, 18–20, 27, 88–9, 101, 115, 130, 189–91
Inflation: 39, 156–7
Inflation: 156
Integration: 154, 162, 163, 168
Interstate Commerce Act, 1887: 20
Interstate Commerce Commission: 111
Intolerable Acts: 3
Irish immigration: 90
Iron Curtain: 33–4
Irvin, Rea: 119
Isolationism: 3, 24, 25, 27, 31, 131, 142, 143
Israel: 37, 178
It failed as a moon vehicle but as sculpture it wins an award: 164
It's That Roosevelt Kid Again: 98

Jackass: 64, 66, 87, 92, 113, 150
Jackson, Andrew: 3, 9, 10, 11, 12, 18, 62–6, 70
Jacksonian Era: 11, 62–70
Jackson's Kitchen Cabinet: 11, 64
James, Henry: 21, 25
Japan: 23, 24, 27, 31, 32, 33, 38, 100, 106, 143, 145–7, 152
Jazz: 23, 114, 140, 158, 165
Jeff Davis After the Surrender of Fort Sumter, April 13, 1861. Jeff Davis, After the Fall of Fort Sumter, 1863: 80
Jefferson, Thomas: 3, 4, 6, 7, 8, 9, 13, 18, 21, 40, 54, 58
Jingoism: 22
John Brown Exhibiting his Hangman: 81
"John Barleycorn": 118
John Bull: 8, 50, 57, 60, 61, 71
John D. Rockefeller, Sr., a caricature: 124
John L. Lewis vs. Congress: 142
Johnson, Andrew: 16, 82, 83, 84, 87
Johnson, Herbert: 115
Johnson, Hiram W.: 105
Johnson, Hugh: 132
Johnson, Lady Bird: 165
Johnson, Lyndon Baines: 38, 39, 148, 165–9, 173
Johnson, Samuel: 7
Johnston, David Claypool: 9, 11, 62, 63, 80
Join or Die: 2, 3, 7, 43
Jones, E.: 73
Jones, John Paul: 5, 49
Josephson, Matthew: 128
Joyce, James; 137
Judge: 22
Jump, Edward: 83
The Junkie: 76, 188

Kaiser: 23, 24, 108
Kansas: 14, 73, 74
Kansas City *Journal*: 100
Keep Off! Munroe Doctrine: 106
Kemble, Edward: 111
[*Kennedy and exploding Cuban cigar*]: 160
Kennedy, John Fitzgerald: 38, 159, 160–1, 163, 169, 172–3
Kennedy, Jon: 121, 164
Kennedy, Robert: 38
Keppler, Joseph: 93
Keppler, Joseph, Jr.: 101, 104
Khrushchev, Nikita: 38, 152, 161–2
"King Andy": 82, 87
"King Kong": 155
King, Martin Luther: 39, 163
"King of Swing": 158
"Kingfish": 30, 133
Kings. See: Monarchical figures
Kirby, Rollin: 117, 138, 140
Kissinger, Henry: 38–9, 178, 179, 184
Kitty Hawk: 102
Kleindienst, Richard: 39
Knight, S.: 60
Know-Nothing Party: 76
Knox, Frank: 135

Korea: 36, 37, 38, 149, 150, 158
Koren, Edward B.: 189
Kovarsky, A.: 155
Kruppa, Gene: 158
Krutch, Joseph Wood: 139
Ku Klux Klan: 17, 26, 27, 121

LBJ: 40, 165
[*LBJ and Vietnam Specters*]: 169
LBJ Armwrestling Big Steel: 166
[*LBJ suit at the Chinese laundry*]: 168
La Follette, Robert M.: 113
Labor: 20, 27, 28, 30, 89, 91, 116, 130, 131, 150, 166, 185
Lafayette, Marie Joseph du Motier, Marquis de: 5, 50
Laissez Faire: 20
Landon, Alfred: 135
Landsfeld, Countess of: 72
Lardner, Ring: 123
Latin America: 22, 23, 24, 38, 62, 142
Le Duc Tho: 38–9, 178
League of Nations: 25, 31
Learn to Dance "The Big Apple" in One Easy Lesson: 140
Lenin, Nikolai: 111
Let the "Swatting" Begin: 123
"Let Us Prey": 92
Letters From an American Farmer: 6
Levine, David: 40, 173, 184, 189
Levine, Jack: 170
Lewis, Alfred Henry: 96
Lewis and Clark: 10
Lewis, John L.: 131, 142
Lewis, Sinclair: 122
Liberal Republican Party: 84
"Liberty": 44, 49, 91
Liberty Tree: 5, 44
Life: 99
Lincoln, Abraham: 3, 14, 15, 18, 22, 75–8, 81, 157, 159
Lincoln and Butler as Don Quixote and Sancho Panza: 78
[*Lincoln as a Monkey*]: 78
Lincoln. You'll excuse me Gen. Butler, but as I cant send you everywhere at once, I'll have to take you to pieces: 79
Listening to the Radio: 136
Liszt, Franz: 72
Literature: 7, 15, 21, 94, 122, 137
Lithography: 11, 63
"Little Giant": 14, 75
"Little Hickory": 12
Little, Tom: 154
The Lives of Great Men: 159
Lloyd George, David: 25, 111

Locke, John: 6
Lodge Corollary to the Monroe Doctrine: 106
Lodge, Henry Cabot: 22, 24, 106
Logan, John A.: 83
Lola Has Come: 72
London *Daily Mail*: 161, 178
London *Evening Standard*: 159
London Magazine: 2, 47
Long, Huey P.: 3, 30, 133
Long, Stephen H.: 10
Longfellow, Henry Wadsworth: 7
Loon Na Werk: 49
Los Angeles: 39, 158, 167, 176
Louis XIV: 3, 180
Louisiana Territory: 10
Louisiana: 133
Loyalists: 6, 52
Ludlow Amendment: 31
Ludwig I, Bavaria: 72
Luks, George: 96
Lusitania: 31, 107
Lynching: 139

McArthur, Douglas: 37
McCarthy, Eugene: 169
McCarthy, Joseph: 3, 36–7, 150–51
McCay, Winsor: 26, 116, 128
McCormick's reaper: 19
McCutcheon, John Tinney: 112, 119, 135
MacDonald, Blaine: 168
McGovern, George: 176
McKinley, William: 22, 23, 96, 98
Madison, Dolly: 61
Madison, James: 10, 60, 61
Magdelena Bay: 106
Magee, J. L.: 14, 81
Magic lantern: 51
Mahan, Alfred T.: 23
Malcomb, John: 5, 48
Mandate the Magician: 181
Mao Tse-Tung: 33, 141, 167
Marisol [Escobar]: 40, 165
Mark Twain: 21, 94
Marriage à la Mode: 2
Marsh, Reginald: 126, 139
Marshall, George C.: 35, 37, 141
Marshall Plan: 35–6
Martha Graham: 137
Martin Luther King: 163
Marx, Groucho: 159
Maryland: 15, 174
Massachusetts: 27, 47–8, 140
Massachusetts—There She Stands! 140
The Massacre at New Orleans: 82
The Masses: 25, 109

Matty Meeting the Texas Question: 69
Matulka, Jan: 114
Mauldin, Bill: 144, 162–3
The Mayaguez: 40
Mayor Daley's Gesture: 170
Mayor Walker, Welcome to New York: 122
Mazzei, Phillip: 58
Meir, Golda: 178
Memphis *Commercial Appeal*: 181
Men, We've got to Improve Our Image: 121
Mencken, H. L.: 125
Mercury: 44
Mexican Revolution, 1916: 102, 107
Mexican War: 12, 70
Mexico: 12, 24, 69, 70, 106–7
Michael! Where's That Air Coming From? 121
Middle East Crisis: 37–8, 178–9
Migrant workers: 185
Milhous I: 3, 180
Militarism: 25, 31, 107, 109, 142, 155, 169, 186
Minerva: 44
Minor, Robert: 25, 109
The Miscegenation Ball: 79
Miss Democracy's Valentine: 105
Missiles: 38, 152, 155, 161, 187
Missouri Compromise, 1820: 76
"Mr. Prohibition": 117
Mitchell, John: 173
Model T Ford: 27, 116
The Modern Balaam and His Ass: 12, 66
Molotov, Vyacheslav: 34
Monarchical figures: 44, 49, 68, 71, 82, 87, 152, 180
Monkey: 59, 78, 119, 120
Monkey-Glands for the N.R.A.: 132
Monopolies: 20, 99, 101, 104, 176, 184
Monroe Doctrine: 3, 23, 24, 106
Monroe, James: 8, 10
Montez, Lola: 72
Morgan, J. P.: 23, 99, 101, 130
"Mormon Kid": 118
Motorcycle: 171
Movies: 132, 155, 158, 159, 182, 189
Muckrakers: 23, 26, 28
Mumford, Lewis: 139
Murphy, Charles Francis: 105
Mussolini, Benito: 3, 31, 133
My Dad's Bigger Than Your Dad: 178
"My Day": 136
My Lai: 38
Mythological figures: 44, 65, 99, 188

Nader, Ralph: 164

Nagasaki: 33, 146
Nankivell, Frank: 23, 98
Nasser, Gamal Abdel: 178
Napoleon I: 9, 11, 58–9, 133
Napoleon III: 71
Nashville *Tennessean*: 154
Nast, Thomas: 14, 16, 79, 82, 84, 86–7, 90
Nasu: 152
Nation: 21
Nation, Carrie: 26
National Labor Relations Board: 130
National Park as the People Inherited It . . .: 115
National parks: 113, 115
National Recovery Administration: 30, 130, 132
Navy, U.S.: 23, 59–60, 100
Nebraska: 14
Negro Jazz Band: 114
Negroes: 14–8, 62, 64, 73, 74, 76, 78, 79, 81–3, 91, 97, 114, 121, 139, 162, 163, 165, 167–8, 176
Nemours, Du Pont de: 7
New Deal: 3, 29–31, 127, 134–5, 139, 142, 154
New Deal Plan for Enlarged Supreme Court: 135
A New Era in Man's Understanding of Nature's Forces: 147
"New Freedom": 24
A New Map of the United States with the Additional Territories: 63
A New Method of Macarony Making as Practiced at Boston in North America: 48
New Mexico: 13, 107
New Orleans: 16, 165
New Orleans, battle: 9, 11, 62
New Orleans riot, 1866: 16–7, 82
New York City: 27, 90, 105, 121, 155, 188, 191
New York *Herald*: 72, 86, 87
New York *Journal*: 103
N. Y. Stock Ex.: 126
New York *Times*: 157, 180, 186
New York *Tribune*: 84
New York *World*: 103
New York Yankees: 123, 138
The New Yorker: 121, 190
Newspapers: 2, 40, 43, 84, 87, 103, 121, 132, 136, 172, 180
Ngo Dinh Diem: 38
Nguyen Hai Chi ("Choé"): 174, 178
Nightclubs: 121, 137
Nihilism: 25
Nixon in a Tape Web: 182

Nixon. Nov., 1962. "You won't have me to kick around anymore." (His Last Words): 172
Nixon, Richard Milhous: 3, 38, 39, 159–60, 170, 172–8, 180–4
Nobel Prize: 23, 39, 122, 143, 163, 178
Noe, Comte. See: Amédée-Charles-Henri
Normalcy: 112
North Atlantic Treaty Organization: 36, 37
North, Frederick Lord: 5, 47
Not a Chinaman's Chance: 95
Nuclear science: 32, 37, 40, 143, 147
Nuclear war: 33, 37, 146–7, 156, 187
Nuclear weapons: 38, 152, 155, 187
Nursery rhymes and stories: 101, 103

Oath of Allegiance: 16
October Revolution, 1917: 25
Oct. 29. Dies Irae: 126
Ograbme, or, the American Snapping-Turtle: 58
Oil: 18, 19, 106, 124, 179, 184
"Old Hickory": 11, 64
Old Northwest Territory: 56, 60
The Old Woman and the Shoe: 101
Oliphant, Pat: 40, 183
Oliver, Andrew: 47
Oliver, Peter: 47
Olson, Floyd: 30
"On This Site Will Be Erected a 32-Story Luxury Apartment Building After the Demise of the Old Lady": 190
One Man's Decision in Korea: 149
The Only Thing They Fear: 119
Opera: 123
Opper, Frederick: 94
Oregon: 12
The Origin of Species: 20–1
Orozco, José Clemente: 139
Orr, Carey: 106
Orson Welles: 189
Osborn, Robert: 146, 151, 153, 156, 160
Oswald, Lee Harvey: 163
Our National Bird As It Appeared When Handed to James Buchanan. March 4, 1857. The Identical Bird As It Appeared A.D. 1861: 77
Over 17 Billion Served: 191

Pacifism: 24, 25, 107, 109, 169, 175–6, 186
Pagliacci: 123
Paine, Thomas: 5, 6, 8, 9
Palmer, A. Mitchell: 27, 119

Panama Canal: 23
Pandora's box: 44
Panic of 1837: 12
Parade for Causes: 94
Paris Peace Agreement, 1973: 39
Parliament, British: 4, 5, 11, 45, 46, 49
Patriotism: 25
Patton, Jack: 133
Peace of Paris, 1782: 50, 52
The Peaceable Kingdom: 176
Peacock: 60
Pearl Harbor: 31, 32, 34, 143, 144, 145
Pease, Lute: 142
Pennsylvania Gazette: 43
Penrose, Boies: 106
Perdicaris, Ion H.: 98
Pershing, John J.: 107
"Pet banks": 65
Peters, Mike: 155
Peyrau, Auguste: 84
Philanthropy: 19, 124
Philbrick, Herbert: 37
Philippine Islands: 97
Pierce, Franklin: 14, 73
Pinckney, Charles C.: 57
Pitt, William (the Elder), Earl of Chatham: 46, 49
Pittsburg Pirates: 123
Playing Horse with Him: 117
Please Don't Look Behind the Screen: 92
"Please understand there is no depression in this house, and we are not interested in the possibilities of defeat. They do not exist." 152
Podwall, Mark: 3, 40, 191
The Poker Game: 95
Poland: 31, 34, 35, 148
The Political Quadrille. Music by Dred Scott: 76
Police: 188
Polk, James K.: 12, 69, 70
Pollock, Jackson: 40
Pollution: 3, 189, 191
Poor Old England Endeavoring to Reclaim His Wicked American Children: 49
Poor Richard's Almanac: 7
"Popular sovereignty": 14, 75
Populist Party: 101
Post, Emily: 118
Powers, T. E.: 23, 106
Prang, Louis: 22
Prejudice: 17, 117, 121, 162
Price, Garrett: 40, 164
The Priests and the Children: 90
Privateering: 5, 58–9
Privileges and Elections Committee: 106

Proctor, Henry: 60
Progress: 22, 25, 88, 115, 190
Progressivism: 23, 24, 26, 102, 113, 131
Prohibition: 18, 21, 23, 26–7, 117–8, 120, 125, 129, 138
Property Protected, a la Francoise: 57
The Providential Detection: 58
Pryor, Robert: 182
Psorakis, Paul: 188
Puck: 22, 89, 92, 93, 100, 101, 103, 104
Pueblo: 38
Pughe, John S.: 23, 100, 101
Pulitzer, Joseph: 103
The Pump House Gang: 171
Pure food and drug legislation: 23
Pyramid of skulls: 12, 70

Quakers: 72
Querner, G.: 81
A Quieter Spot for Him: 107
Don Quixote: 3, 16, 78, 150, 157, 184

Racism: 14, 20, 62, 79, 91, 121, 139, 162, 163, 167–8
Radical Republicans: 16–7, 82–3
Radio: 29, 30, 123, 136, 158, 159, 189
Raemaekers, Louis: 24, 108
Railroads: 18, 19, 20, 27, 88, 96, 99, 111–2
Raizuli: 98
Ranger: 5
Ratification of U.S. Constitution: 53
Raynal, Abbé: 7
Reconstruction: 14, 16–7, 82–3
Reconstruction Act, 1867: 17
Reconstruction Finance Corporation: 125
The Reconstruction Policy of Congress, as Illustrated in California: 83
Recession: 152
Red Cross: 21
"Red Scare": 27, 119
Redfield, A.: 26, 103
Reform: 18, 23, 26, 27, 84, 92, 96, 176
Reid, Albert T.: 100
Religion: 21, 26, 27, 90, 93, 120
The Religious Vanity Fair: 93
The Repeal. Or the Funeral Procession of Miss Americ-Stamp: 5, 45
Republican Party: 16, 21, 23, 35, 36, 76, 82–4, 87, 96, 104, 105, 108, 134, 135, 148, 150, 153, 173
Revere, Paul: 2, 5, 26, 43, 47, 49, 103
Revolution, American: 2, 4–6, 43–52, 59
Revolution, French: 9, 54
Revisionist history: 17

Reward of Labor: 49
Rhodes, James Ford: 13
Rice, Grantland: 123
Richard III: 3, 11, 63
Richard I. I. I.: 63
Richardson, Elliot: 174
Richmond *Times-Dispatch*: 146, 154
Rickey, Mallory & Company: 76
Riots: 16–7, 20, 39, 163, 167–8
"Robber Barons": 23, 18–9, 96, 99, 103, 124, 130
Robinson, Boardman: 25, 105, 111, 112, 122
Robinson, Henry R.: 3, 12, 65, 68, 69
Robinson, Joe: 130
Rockefeller, John D.: 18, 19, 20, 23, 99, 101, 124, 130
Rockefeller, Nelson: 173
Rockingham Ministry: 5, 45
Rogers, H. H.: 20
Rogers, Will: 29
The Rolling Stone: 3, 180
Roosevelt Corollary to Monroe Doctrine: 23
Roosevelt, Eleanor: 136
Roosevelt, Franklin Delano: 3, 22, 28–32, 34, 35, 127–136, 139, 142, 145, 148, 154, 159
Roosevelt, Theodore: 22–4, 29, 98–102, 106, 107
Rose Mary's Baby: 182
Rose of England: 45
Rosenberg, James: 126
Rosenberg, Julius and Ethel: 36
Ross, Harold: 121
Rousseau, Jean Jacques: 9
Royal American Magazine: 49
Rubin, Jerry: 188
"Rum, Romanism, and Rebellion": 21
Runyon, Damon: 123
Russell, Charles Marion: 95
Russia: 23, 25, 27, 33–8, 61, 71, 111, 119
Ruth, George Herman ("Babe"): 123, 138

Sacco and Vanzetti: 27, 151
Sacco and Vanzetti: 151
Sacramento River: 71
Sagamore Hill: 23, 108
Sailors, American: 6, 59–60
St. Denis, Ruth: 137
Sale of the deserts of Scioto, by the Anglo Americans: 56
Sampson, William T.: 97
San Francisco: 20, 71, 85, 158

San Francisco *Examiner*: 103
San Simeon: 103
"Sandlot riots": 20
Santa Claus: 3, 157
Santiago Bay Pop: 97
Santa Domingo Pueblo: 114
Saratoga, battle: 5, 50, 51
Satan Tempting Booth to the Murder of the President: 81
The Savages Let Loose, or the Cruel Fate of the Loyalists: 52
Scandals: 23, 39, 87, 92, 105, 106, 174, 177, 180–83
Scarecrow: 24, 87, 100
Scarecrow of the Pacific: 100
Scioto River: 56
Scopes Monkey Trial: 26, 120
Scott, Dred: 14, 76
Scott, Howard: 128
Scott, Winfield: 70, 73
Sculpture: 75, 84, 95, 159, 165, 183
Searle, Ronald: 158
Secession: 15, 77
Segregation: 154, 162, 163, 168
Seibel, Fred O.: 146, 154
Seigel, Anita: 186
Sense of humor: 9
Serapis: 49
Serbia: 103
Serpent. See: Snake
Seward, William H.: 13, 73
Shahn, Ben: 148, 151, 163
Shakespeare: 11, 49, 57, 63
Shannon: 60
"Share-the-wealth" programs: 30
Shaw, George Bernard: 123
Shawn, Ted: 137
Shelburne, William Petty Fitzmaurice, Earl of: 52
Sheldon, Charles: 26
Sherman Antitrust Act, 1890: 20, 101
Sic Transit Gloria: 185
"Silent majority": 175
Skyscrapers: 27, 139, 190
Slap Stic Comedy: 133
The Slave Market of Today: 89
Slavery: 13–16, 22, 69, 73–9, 81, 89
Sloan, John: 114
Smaller Does Not Mean Better: 157
The Smelling Committee: 83
Smith, Alfred E.: 125
Smith, Alice Kimball: 33
Smith-Connaly Act: 142
Smith, Dorman H.: 129
Smith, P.: 73
Smith, Seba: 9, 65

Smith, Sidney: 13
Smuggling: 58
Snake: 6, 7, 43, 44, 50, 65
"So long as the dry farce lasts, a girl who sips ice-water is looked upon as 'freezing the party' ": 118
Socialism: 25, 28, 101, 116, 119, 132, 141, 154
Sola, Vazquez de: 175
"Some Folks Might Prefer the Horse & Buggy Era": 134
Sorel, Edward: 3, 180, 185
South Carolina: 15
Southern Punch: 15
Soviet Union: 25, 27, 33–8, 111, 119, 148–9, 150, 152, 161–2, 164, 178, 187
The Space Age Toy Shop: 155
Space race: 38, 164
Spain: 22, 49, 52, 71, 96–7, 103
Spanish-American War: 22, 25, 96–7, 103
Speakeasies: 117, 121
The Special Prosecuting Attorney: 120
Specie Circular, 1836: 66
Speculators: 66, 190
Spencer, Herbert: 119
Spies: 25, 36, 37, 39, 150, 177
Spiritualism: 86, 93
A Splendid Procession of Free Masons: 62
Sports: 123, 138
Sputnik: 38, 158, 164
Square Deal: 23
Stalin, Joseph: 3, 31, 34, 35, 133, 145
Stamp Act: 2, 4–5, 7, 43–6
Stamp Act Congress: 7
Standard Oil Company: 106, 124
Stanton, Edwin: 17
State Department: 131, 148
The State Department: 131
Statue of Liberty: 3, 20, 40, 91, 150, 191
Steadman, Ralph: 187
Steel industry: 19, 166
Steffens, Lincoln: 28
Steig, William: 158
Steinberg, Saul: 3, 157
Steinem, Gloria: 185
Step by Step—Where Are We Going? 149
Steuben, Friederich Wilhelm, Baron von: 10
Stevens, Thaddeus: 16, 83
Stock exchange. See: Wall Street
Stock market crash, 1929: 28, 126
Stowe, Harriet Beecher: 15, 21
Straightshanks, Hassan: 11, 64
Strategic Arms Limitations Talks: 187

Strike-breaking: 131
Strikes: 116, 131, 142, 150, 166
Strong, Josiah: 10
Strother, David H.: 15–6, 78
Suarès, Jean-Claude: 180
Suez Canal: 37–8, 178
Suffrage: 21, 26, 86, 97, 117
Sullivan, Mark: 107
Sultan o' Swat: 138
Sumner, Charles: 16
Sunday, William Ashley ("Billy"): 26, 118, 120
Supreme Court: 30, 102, 124, 130, 132, 134, 154, 162, 182
Sutter, John A.: 70
"Swing": 140, 158
Symbols of America: 3, 6, 18
Szep, Paul: 40, 169, 172

Taft-Hartley Act: 150
Taft, Robert: 35, 150
Taft, William Howard: 24, 101, 102
Talleyrand-Périgorde, Charles Maurice de: 57
Talmadge, Eugene: 148
Tammany Hall: 20, 90, 105, 125, 129
Taney, Roger B.: 76
Tar and feathers: 5, 48
Tariffs: 89, 104
Tax deductions: 39
Taxation: 44–5, 47–9
Taylor, Zachary: 12, 69, 70
Tea Act, 1773: 5, 47–8
Tea Pot Dome Scandal: 23, 28
The Tea-Tax-Tempest, or Old Time with His Magick Lanthern: 51
Teacher's oath: 140
Technocracy Devouring the City: 128
The Teddessy: 23, 99
[*Teddy Roosevelt as a pirate*]: 98
[*Teheran Conference*]: 145
Television: 37, 38–9, 151, 159, 173, 181
Temperance movement: 21, 26–7
Tennessee: 29, 30, 67, 120, 154
Tennessee Valley Authority: 29, 30, 154
Tenniel, John: 134
Tenure of Office Act: 17
Texas: 12, 15, 17, 67, 69, 73, 148, 163
. . . That Man Clay was an Ass! It's Better to be President than to be right! 96
". . . *that we here highly resolve that this nation, under God, shall have a new birth of freedom . . .*": 150
That Western Corn. The Western Farmer— "Wot'd I care about the price of coal?" 100

There's No Free Election in Poland: 148
Third term: 87, 102, 136
The Third-Term Panic: 87
Thirteen Colonies: 2, 4–5, 43–51
This is My Territory: 154
Thistle: 44, 45
Thompson, Charles: 4
Thurber, James: 29, 132
A Ticket to Normalcy: 112
Tiger: 129
The Time Machine: 169
Time Will Tell: 106
The Times; a Political Portrait: 54
Tisdale, Elkanah: 55
To the White House, March 4th 1869: 84
Tocqueville, Alexis de: 8, 10, 34
Tokio Here We Come: 145
Tortoise: 11, 58, 63
The Tory Editor and His Apes Giving Their Pitiful Advice to the American Sailors: 59
Tourism: 113, 114–5, 116, 189
Towsend, Francis: 30
Transportation: 70, 102, 111–2, 116, 189
Transportation Act, 1920: 111
Trinidad, Corky: 167
"Trog": 178
Trollope, (Mrs.) Anthony: 9
Truman Doctrine: 35–6
Truman, Harry S.: 33–7, 141, 148–50, 153
Trusts: 20, 23, 24, 39, 98, 99, 101, 103–4, 111
Tsar: 61, 71
Tucker, Josiah: 8
Turkey: 22, 35, 96
Twain, Mark: 21, 94
Tweed, William M. ("Boss"): 20, 92
Tydings, Millard: 37
Tyler, John: 12

U-boats: 24, 107
Ulysses: 137
Uncle Sam: 3, 23, 83, 88, 96, 100, 101, 103, 104, 106, 107, 109, 112, 116, 117, 119, 123, 129, 142, 157, 162
Uncle Sam and Santa Claus as Don Quixote and Sancho Panza: 157
[*Uncle Sam shooting dice with Carranza*]: 107
Uncle Sam: "They say he needs it, but he doesn't look sick to me": 104
Uncle Tom's Cabin: 15
Unemployment: 29–30, 127, 128, 152
Unemployment: 127
Unemployment Relief Act: 29

Ungerer, Tomi: 166, 168
Unions: 27, 29, 89, 116, 142, 150, 166, 185
United Mine Workers: 142
United Nations: 32, 36, 149
The U.S. Chamber of Commerce Has a Plan: 154
United States Information Agency: 37
United States Steel Company: 19, 28
U.S. Supporting Chiang Kai-Shek against China: 141
Unity: 7, 43, 141, 173
Unknown Soldier: 25
The Upturn: 132
Urbanization: 18, 19, 40, 100, 128, 139, 155, 189–91
Utopianism: 7

Vampire: 99, 178
Van Buren, Martin: 3, 11, 12, 64–5, 68–9
Van Devanter, Willis: 30
Vandenberg, Arthur H.: 35
Vanderbilt, Cornelius: 86, 101
Vente des deserts du Scioto, par des Anglo-americains: 56
The Verdict: 96
Versailles Peace Treaty: 25
The Very Professional Underground Politico: 177
Victory I: 71, 152
Victory: 50, 51, 60, 61, 69, 81, 117, 145–6
"Vicky": 159
Vietnam: 3, 37, 38–9, 168–70, 173–6, 178, 192
A View of Winchester in North America Dedicated to Mr. President Mad I Son!! 60
Villa, Pancho: 107
Vim: 88
Vinci, Leonardo da: 2
Virginia Paw-sing: 77
Volck, Adalbert: 3, 14, 16, 78
Volstead Act: 117
Voltaire, François Marie Arouet: 9
Voting: 26, 55, 86, 97, 117, 148

Wada, Makoto: 165
Wade-Davis Bill: 16
Wagner, Robert: 130
Walker, Jimmy: 122
Wall Street: 23, 27, 28–9, 99, 101, 126, 130, 132, 139, 152, 173
Wallace, Cornelia: 177
Wallace, George: 39, 177

Wallace, Henry A.: 35, 141
War of 1812: 8–9, 12, 58–61
"War is Hell isn't it?" 110
Warren Commission: 163
Washington Conference: 112
Washington, D.C., burning of: 9, 61
Washington *Evening Star*: 150
Washington, George: 4, 5, 6, 8–9, 12, 50, 54, 58, 70, 186
Wasp: 60
Watergate: 39, 174, 177, 180–3, 192
Watergate: 183
The Way They Go to California: 70
Weed, Thurlow: 83
Weems, Parson: 7
Weimar Republic: 133
Weisz, Victor ("Vicky"): 159
Welles, Orson: 189
West, American: 95, 108, 135, 161
The West is in the Saddle: 135
West, Mae: 29, 130
"Where I come from we call it 'Cultural Revolution' ": 167
When Al Capone's Attorney Finished His Address to the Jury: 129
"When Johnny Comes Marching Home": 186
Whig Party, American: 3, 11, 14, 69–70, 73, 76
Whig Party, British: 45
White and Bauer: 91
White House or Bust: 108

"White House plumbers": 39, 177
Whitman, Walt: 21
Who Gets the Ballot, Philippines or Negro? 97
Wi-Jun-Jon: 72
Wilkinson: 2
William, you dont mean to say that you are really going to do something? 108
Williams: 61
Williams, T.: 83
"Willie and Joe": 144
Wilmot Proviso: 15
Wilson, J. F.: 83
Wilson, Ted: 158
Wilson, Woodrow: 23, 24–5, 107–8, 111, 117
Winchester, William: 60
Wobblies: 116
Wolfe, Tom: 171
Woman's Christian Temperance Union: 21, 26
Woman's Rights: 21, 26, 84, 86, 117, 185
Woodhull, Canning: 86
Woodhull, Victoria Claflin: 21, 86
Woods, Rose Mary: 182
Woolf, Michael Angelo: 77
Works Progress Administration: 30
World Peace Foundation: 24
World War I: 23, 24–5, 27, 102, 107–112, 116, 125, 133, 136
World War II: 3, 31–3, 38, 40, 141–7, 148, 158

Worth, Thomas: 3, 20, 91
Wright Brothers: 102

XYZ Affair: 57

Yalta Agreement: 34
Yankee (symbol): 18, 88
The Yankey Torpedo: 60
Yardley, Richard: 162
Ye Scoldes: 101
"Yellow journalism": 22
Yippies: 188
Yorktown, battle: 5, 50
Yorty, Sam: 176
"You ain't gaining much altitude holding me down": 162
"You Know the Way Back Do You, Herbert?" 128
"You should have been here in the old days, before the budget cutbacks . . . There were cops and fire engines and planes buzzing around . . .": 155
You'll excuse me Gen. Butler, but as I cant send you everywhere at once, I'll have to take you to pieces: 79
"Your Money or Your Way of Life": 179
"You're using the wrong kind of plow, neighbor!" 162
Young, Art: 25
Young Texas in Repose: 73
Youth cult: 40, 171, 188